"Come with Cynthia in the pages of *A Lifetime to Get Here* as she explores the wonders of San Miguel de Allende, an old colonial city in the mountains of central Mexico. Walk with her each step of the way and experience her many adventures and discoveries. Learn the history and lore of this magical place. Be dazzled by the colorful pageants and spectacles. Taste the world-famous food. Admire the timeless beauty. Meet the warm and welcoming people. But be warned: In reading *A Lifetime to Get Here*, you're likely to fall in love with San Miguel as Cynthia did and pack up to move here too."

Bonnie Lee Black, author and blogger
http://www.bonnieleeblack.com

A LIFETIME TO GET HERE

SAN MIGUEL DE ALLENDE

Cynthia Claus

A LIFETIME TO GET HERE

SAN MIGUEL DE ALLENDE

Cynthia Claus

PASHMINA PRESS

Copyright © 2020 by Cynthia Claus

All rights reserved.

This book or any portion thereof may not be reproduced
or used in any manner whatsoever
without the express written permission of the publisher,
except for the use of brief quotations in a book review.

Printed in United States of America
First Printing, 2020

ISBN 978-1687562142

Pashmina Press
751 N. Taylor St.
Philadelphia, Pa. 19130, USA

www.cynthiaclaus.com

10 9 8 7 6 5 4 3 2 1

Cover and frontispiece photos by Jayne A. Halley
Interior photos: The author, with additional photos from her archives
Book and cover design by Margot Boland

Dedication

This book is dedicated to my middle sister, Julia Ruth Claus, who died on April 29, 2020, after a valiant, many-years struggle with cancer, at her home in Taos, New Mexico, a month before her 71st birthday, and to her partner of 11 years, Scott Thayer, her loving, steadfast caregiver to the end.

I love you, Julia. I admire your incredible creativity and talent in so many different artistic endeavors, and your soulful and professional healing skills as a massage therapist. I could always see and feel your love for your son, Dylan, and his partner, Angela, and there was no mistaking your head-over-heels devotion to your two grandchildren, Freya and Alder, to whom you were Mombu. I salute the courage you showed in your fight against your cancer. You gave it your all.

And I thank you, Scott, for being there for Julia…always, no matter the difficulty of the situation. My gratitude is forever.

ABOUT THIS BOOK

A Lifetime to Get Here: San Miguel de Allende, the first in a series of two, was created from the author's almost-daily blog posts about visiting San Miguel de Allende, Mexico, for increasing amounts of time and in different seasons, spanning winter 2009 to the conclusion of 2012. The culmination of those years was the sale of her house in her fourth-generation hometown of Philadelphia and her permanent settlement in Mexico. It is a unique combination of travel memoir, how-to guide for the first-time visitor, the occasional lesson in Mexican history and culture, a Spanish grammar tutorial or two, an answer to stateside friends' questions of "What do you *do* in Mexico?" as well as honest, introspective reactions to what the older American author experiences as she navigates this unknown territory on her own. Lovingly maintained vintage family photos of trips to Mexico decades ago and the author's own carefully curated photos from more recent years punctuate and add richness to the text.

PROLOGUE

In the late 1950s, when I was a teen, my father, Anton Claus, began a love affair with Mexico, Mexicans, and the Spanish language. The genesis of this romance is unknown to me, but under its influence, my father taught himself Spanish and tried to teach me, too, although that ended badly. Long before the Internet, at a time when country-to-country phone calls were a luxury, Daddy planned a weeks-long trip to Mexico for himself and my mother, Eleanor; two friends of theirs, Molly and Helen; and me. Using his newly acquired Spanish written on brittle blue aerograms, he made hotel reservations for us all in Mexico City, Acapulco, Cuernavaca, and Taxco, and planned our complicated itinerary. My two much younger sisters, Julia and Gretchen, were left at home with a caretaker.

Although it was 60 years ago, *más o menos*, and my memory comes up short on most details, I do remember this trip with great pleasure. I was treated as one of the adults. I had my own room in all the hotels we stayed in. I had adventures. Daddy, Mother, Molly, Helen, and I flew to New Orleans and spent a few days there on the way to our first Mexico stop, Acapulco. One evening after dinner in the Big Easy, all of us went to a club where a famous jazz musician was performing. I wish I could remember who it was and what instrument he played, but his name is long gone, as is the 45 rpm record I bought and had autographed. We all sat at the bar with the stage right in front of us, and between his sets, some girls did a striptease. My father probably thought that I, at almost 16, should be exposed to some of these things.

In Acapulco, I learned to water ski with a handsome Mexican instructor not much older than myself, and a slightly older and just-as-good-looking motorboat operator. We travelers would divide our beach time between the "morning beach" and the "afternoon beach" so that at no time of day would we be where the sun was the strongest. We stayed in one of the most charming tropical hotels I've ever seen, with thatched-roof cottages ringed around a pool, and lots of brilliant, noisy birds in the palm trees nearby.

One afternoon, after returning from the beach to bathe and dress for dinner, I turned on the shower in my room, and one of the faucet's handles came off in my hand! As if it wasn't hot and humid enough already, now steaming water was pouring out with no way for me to turn it off. I threw something on and ran to my parents' cottage on the other side of the pool. My father and I raced to the office (there were no phones) and explained the problem, and in very short order a workman came to reattach the handle and turn the water off. I don't think my room ever cooled off or dried out the rest of the time we were there.

I celebrated my 16th birthday in Acapulco at what I remember as a very upscale restaurant that had been written up in a travel magazine; it had live music and dancing. We were seated in an upstairs balcony, where we could look down on the dancers below. A young *Mexicano* with shiny, slicked-back hair and a shirt half-unbuttoned, showing a bare chest, asked Molly to dance. After the dance, he took her outside to cool down and asked if she was married. When she told him that she wasn't, he admitted that he would very much like to come to the U.S., but that he needed an American wife to do so. He then asked Molly to marry him! She replied in her most pleasant and polite manner that she was flattered by the invitation but that she'd have to say no. Although several other Mexican men asked my mother and Helen to dance later in the evening, there were no further marriage proposals.

I was permitted to have my very first alcoholic drink, a margarita, to celebrate—perhaps another "adult" experience Daddy thought I was ready to have. While my father dutifully and happily took turns dancing with all of "his" women, I sipped away at my tasty, sweet margarita. Soon after my dinner was placed in front of me, I hissed urgently to my mother, "Am I acting weird, because I can't cut my meat." Of course, I was tipsy.

Our second stop was Cuernavaca, from which I have only two memories. One is of a lovely restaurant we visited for lunch, where white peacocks strode around the grounds, causing Molly to say that this was what heaven must be like. Later, a parrot came to rest on her shoulder. The other memory is of Molly and me being very, very sick with what used to be called Montezuma's revenge. Because of this, we couldn't go sightseeing with the others one day, and I was left to fend for myself, dizzily and weakly running back and forth to the bathroom in my hotel room while waiting for the meds my father always carried in his little black doctor's bag to kick in. I was coached to say *"Estoy enferma"* (I am sick) to warn away the housekeeper when she arrived.

Evidently, the drugs my father dispensed got Molly and me well enough to take an afternoon bus the next day to Taxco. I remember that the captivating town had many levels and that the taxi from the bus station could barely make it through the narrow streets up to our hotel. Silver was for sale everywhere! We bought loads of silver jewelry for ourselves and as gifts to take back. Molly was smitten by a six-year-old boy selling paintings that someone in his family had created. He explained

Taxco.

that the sale of these paintings was the family's sole support, so of course Molly purchased one, and it hung in her home until the day she died.

And Mexico City? Really, I remember nothing except that we stayed in the Zona Rosa; that the famed archeological museum we'd wanted to visit was closed on Mondays, the day we had scheduled to go there; and that we had quite a lovely day at Xochimilco, the area of canals and *chinampas* (artificially created islands that became floating gardens), a vestige of the area's pre-Hispanic past. I remember we chose a *trajinera* (flat-bottomed boat) with the Mexican name of Julia in honor of my sister whom we left at home.

Trajineras at Xochimilco.

Taking a different route back to Philadelphia, we returned by way of Atlanta and stayed in an elegant B&B decorated with all shapes and sizes of exquisite women's fans. In the taxi to the airport the next day, which of course had no air conditioning, we were the hottest any of us had ever been in our lives, and Mother swore that if hell was like this, she was immediately going to mend her ways.

Two years later, Daddy planned another trip south of the border, this time including middle sister Julia, youngest sister Gretchen, and my best friend, (another) Helen. My sisters were taken out of school for the final two weeks, much to their delight. To save money, we took a bus from Philadelphia to St. Louis. Before the days of ubiquitous air conditioning, the ride in summer's heat was pretty grim. We were offered sandwiches every few hours by a hostess on the bus: ham, cheese, or ham and cheese, all on white bread.

In St. Louis, for the first time, I experienced segregated facilities and cabs. I saw a "Whites Only" sign over a water fountain and at the entrance to the bathrooms. As we were waiting at the bus station for a taxi, we could see, off to our left, a long line of cabs, but none approached. My father asked the dispatcher why he wasn't calling to one of those nearby, and his reply was, "They're colored cabs." I didn't know what that meant exactly, but my father did. "Call one of those over here right away," he angrily demanded.

I'm not sure what mode of transportation we took to Texas from St. Louis, but Gretchen, our Trivia Queen, vividly remembers a train ride, although from Pittsburgh. However we got there, we went to a city in Texas very close to the Mexican border. From there, we traveled three to four hours by bus to Saltillo, the capital and largest city of the northeast state of Coahuila, just 250 miles south of the Texas border, for a two-week home stay with the Marrufo family and a special class in Spanish for gringo beginners at the University of Saltillo. What a blast!

Helen and I had boyfriends, Efraín and Jorge, and unlike the way Daddy treated my boyfriends back home in Philadelphia, he fell all over himself inviting these young Mexican men to join us on our evenings out; they always appeared for dates dressed in ties and sports coats. He allowed Helen and me to explore the city in Jorge's jalopy or go swimming with them when we weren't studying. I very much enjoyed the Spanish classes and meeting students from all over the U.S., and I think I even learned some basics of the language.

Jorge and I at the Marrufos' front door.

From right around the table, Efraín, Jorge, Mother, Daddy, Pepe Marrufo, Julia, and I.

My father was eager to test-drive his Spanish skills with some of the locals. He brought along rolls of lemon drops to give to fruit-sellers, for example, to start a conversation. He was sorry he couldn't hire boys to give him shoeshines (and for a chance for some conversation) because his shoes were suede Hush Puppies.

It wasn't until 1980, when I was nearly 40, that I returned to Mexico, this time with my husband, a man from what was then called Bombay, and our two children, Ajay, age 14, and Suji, 10. For this trip, *I* had made all of the reservations and plans, although not in Spanish. We went at

I'm at the far left with Helen; Efraín is in the center; and Daddy is sitting to the far right. Julia and Pepe are partially hidden behind Helen and Efraín.

From left: Helen, Pepe Marrufo, his two younger siblings, and I.

Christmastime to the city of Oaxaca, the capital and largest city in the southern state of Oaxaca.

Tourism was the primary industry there, as Oaxaca boasted a large number of colonial-era structures and the Zapotec and Mixtec cultures. Using the Spanish I'd taken in college, and with heavy reliance on a dictionary, I was our tour guide and problem-solver. Besides visiting archeological sites such as Monte Alban, we went to a bullfight. Our driver took us there early and we watched the preliminaries with much anticipation. However, when the actual bullfight began, we were horrified and fled back to the car.

Some 28 years later, twice-divorced and retired, kids grown and scattered, with families of their own, I took an Elderhostel trip to Mexico's Copper Canyon. It changed the trajectory of my life. I was enchanted with Mexico, with our tour guide, and with the Spanish he spoke, and I gamely tried to revive the language I'd long abandoned. When we had our final dinner at our hotel in El Paso, where we were asked to stand and say a few words about the experience to our fellow travelers, I burst into tears and was almost unable to get out my few halting sentences. Clearly, something was going on for me.

I determined to return to Mexico to resurrect my *español*. A man I liked and admired in my congregation in Philadelphia, Alan, had gone with his wife to a place called San Miguel de Allende to study Spanish. Most unfortunately, he died there of a pre-existing heart problem, but through its mention in his obituary, the name of the city came to my attention. I learned online that it was a place of many language schools; I could take my pick. I did a lot of research and chose El Centro Bilingue because in addition to language instruction, it had cooking classes and tours around the city, which were included in the tuition. When I, a third-generation Unitarian-Universalist, learned that one of only two English-speaking UU congregations in all of Mexico was in SMA (the other is in Lake Chapala), I knew I'd found the place for me. And so, in January 2009, I went alone, not knowing a single soul, to San Miguel de Allende, in the state of Guanajuato, in *El Bajío* (heartland) of Mexico, and my life changed.

While my family's trips to Mexico sound—and appear in the extant photos—like a picture-perfect travelogue, they were a time out of time. My parents—both only children, both osteopathic physicians, each with a two-pack-a-day cigarette habit, and both of them drowning in alcohol and their hate for each other—made my early life challenging and frightening. Because I was the oldest, and someone in the family had to be the adult, my childhood was stolen from me. But in Mexico, we were a different kind of family: a happy family; a functional, rather than dysfunctional, family; a family that enjoyed each other and our experiences together. A family in which my father's crazy, intimidating behaviors seemed to melt away, ceasing to be the backdrop of our lives. My father seemed absent of his demons for a while. I will never know why my father wanted to go to Mexico or why he was a different man and father there.

My mother and I at our Acapulco hotel.

And my mother? There are very few photos of Mother, as she was the photographer who recorded the holidays, vacations, and celebrations of our family. And because she's in very few of the photos, it's as if she weren't there as we were growing up. And, in a way, this was true. I think she can best be described as an "absent presence," not only in my life, but in her own life as well. She was afraid of my father—with good reason—and communicated that fear to me. I spent my childhood being afraid. And yet fear did not play a part in the decisions I made later on:

separation and divorce, a second marriage and divorce, early retirement, and traveling alone to a destination in Mexico.

What is the real reason I returned to Mexico a lifetime after those family trips? Why did I find so much happiness, contentment, and peace in San Miguel that after four years of visits of ever-increasing length, I sold my house in Philadelphia in 2012 and moved there almost year-round? Why *there* did my heart so frequently get broken wide open? Why *there* did I have such strong feelings and cry so often? What was I searching for: that feeling of normalcy, of happiness, that my family had for a few short weeks in that alien place; a chance to live my lost childhood? Did that need, so deeply submerged in my unconscious for over a half-century, finally find a way to express itself? Did the seeds my father planted so very long ago finally blossom?

This story helps me to answer these questions.

"NO WAY I'M RETURNING TO MEXICO.
I CAN'T STAND BEING IN A PLACE MORE SURREAL
THAN MY PAINTINGS."

Salvador Dalí,
referring to Mexico's socioeconomic contrast and cultural richness

"Not all those who wander are lost."

The Fellowship of the Ring,
J.R.R. Tolkien

Chapter 1

January 2009

Arrival and First Impressions

My flights, first from Philadelphia to Houston and then to León, Guanajuato, Mexico, were on time, both departing and arriving. After I went through immigration and customs (a piece of cake), and spied my clean-cut, attractive young driver holding a sign with my name on it, all anxieties evaporated. Efraín kept up a steady, entertaining patter of information and observations about the region we were driving through and our destination, the city of San Miguel de Allende (SMA), during the hour-and-a-half drive there. He spoke fluent English, using words like "topography" with ease. A careful driver, he knew the winding road well; he told me he makes the airport run regularly, sometimes twice a day. We pulled up to my rental house on Calle Hidalgo in El Centro a little after 10 p.m., only one hour earlier than Philadelphia time.

From the outside, the houses in San Miguel don't look like much, but just open the ancient, wooden, creaking doors, with light peeking through the crevices, and you'll be shocked. I was mightily pleased with the looks of my rental, which I had found on the Internet at the last minute. It was modern with eclectic original artwork. Both the first and second floors had outside spaces, separated from the rooms by glass doors, and flowering plants—bougainvillea, geraniums, impatiens—enhanced a large rooftop terraza.

Chapter 1

I chose the smaller back bedroom with the smaller bathroom since my rental was on a very busy street with buses passing incredibly close by. After setting up my computer, logging onto the wireless Internet connection, emailing Suji, my daughter, of my safe arrival, and then taking a quick look around the house, I went to bed, and with some distance, earplugs, and several sets of glass doors between me and bustling Hidalgo, I slept soundly. I awoke at 6:30, just before the bell that rings every 15 minutes all day and night from the tower of an immense parish church—*la parroquia,* part neo-Gothic and part baroque—only two blocks away.

Upon waking, I realized it was rather cold in the house. There is no central heat (or air conditioning) as there usually is no need for either in this climate, where it generally never gets too hot or too cold. I found a space heater and got it going while I did yoga practice on the mat I'd brought, laid atop the earth-toned ceramic tiles that were the floor surface in the entire house. A few throw rugs added vibrant color here and there.

I was famished, as all I'd had to eat the day before were the two snacks provided by the airline and some energy bars I had tucked in my backpack. Swaddled in a fleece, a light jacket, a wool scarf, and gloves, I ventured out and found a bakery with a bright blue door and hot-from-the-oven goods, and bought two apricot pastries, even though I ascertained—using my Spanish—that they contained lard. (I knew going in that this was a distinct possibility.) Now under normal circumstances I wouldn't touch anything made with lard with a 10-foot pole, but I was really starving and I didn't know how soon I'd find something else. I decided that I would survive that small infusion of lard into my body but that there would be no more. They were delicious!

I walked some more and found a nice coffee shop on the *jardín,* the gardenlike park that is the central focus of life in San Miguel, and had a

The parroquia.

delicious hot chocolate made with a touch of cinnamon, and a croissant with butter and strawberry jam on the side. I could eat only half the croissant, so I put the remainder in the empty bakery bag and proceeded to walk around, taking everything in.

As I was out before most businesses opened, I got to see the town come alive. There were beer trucks picking up last night's cases of empties and refreshing the stock; sweepers cleaning up debris; vendors of roasted corn, cut-up fruits, ice cream, and other goodies muscling their carts into place; a few folks reading their newspapers on a sunny bench; and all sorts of people hurrying to work. The place is immaculate, and the Mexicans I encountered I found to be robust, seemingly happy, and the children particularly endearing.

I started peeling off layers of clothing as the morning progressed. Efraín had warned me that all San Miguel mornings in the winter are overcast, because of the collision of daytime heat and nighttime chill over several reservoirs on the outskirts of the city. When the sun becomes higher and stronger, the clouds burn off.

I walked for a very long time, looking all around and getting lost frequently, and returned to my house about 11 to meet the housekeeper, Eleonor. This may seem an incredible luxury—and of course to me it is—but in Mexico, it's just the way things are done, and her ministrations were included in my rent. When I told her that my mother's name was the same as hers, it was an immediate bond and icebreaker. She spoke not a syllable of English, but we did quite well. Eleonor spoke very slowly and distinctly, and had a good practice of slowly parroting back to me in question form what I'd said, checking to make sure that she had understood me, making corrections as needed. I tried to determine her age but had some difficulty. I guessed late 50s because her black hair was starting to turn to gray.

By this time, I already needed a rest. San Miguel is at 6,500 feet and I'd really walked a lot. I went up to the terraza with a book and immediately realized I had to change my clothes, as it was hot, hot, hot up there! I put on capris and sandals. Actually, up there, I could have worn my bathing suit and been just fine; it was that hot. What a difference several hours of sunshine make at that elevation! I slathered myself with sunblock and settled in to read.

Later, I set out to shop for food. Eleonor told me about Bonanza, a small supermarket, and a great fruit and veggie place, both nearby. It took me a very long time to find the produce place. (I have since learned that, when looking for a store here for the first time, I should walk on the opposite side of the street, because the sidewalks are so narrow that it's impossible to be far enough away from the shops to see the signs flat against the walls over the entrances.) I came home again after buying only several kinds of fruit, as I didn't think I could carry them plus purchases from Bonanza at the same time. Eleonor volunteered to disinfect the fruit, an absolute necessity in Mexico, and flew out to buy the needed drops. I'd noted when I bought the Gala apples that they were a product of the U.S., but I had her add them to the mix anyway.

After another short rest, I went to Bonanza, again taking far too long to find it. It didn't look anything like what I had expected, but it had an amazing array of products. I spent an hour and a half buying the peso equivalent of $40 USD worth of groceries. I had to read labels—in Spanish, of course—and look up many listed ingredients in my dictionary. I was positively exhausted and went back home to rest yet again. At 5 p.m., I had a glass of red wine and some tortilla chips and salsa on the terraza, which remained warm. Everything in San Miguel is made of adobe or concrete and they absorb heat all day and then radiate it out for hours afterward.

At six o'clock, I went out to El Tomato, at that time a *naturalista* (vegetarian) restaurant, which I'd spied with its front window plastered in cards, in dozens of languages, extolling the food, mentioning particularly the cooks' skill using tofu. (Was I seeking redemption from eating the lard?) At this early hour, I was the only customer. I had a small bowl of soup made with chard and chickpeas, and a spinach, cornmeal, tomato, and cheese gratin, both of which were unbelievably delicious and cheap as dirt. I decided that I'd return to eat there, as I wanted to try some of the six varieties of vegetarian *hamburguesas* they offered, including tofu (probably not for me), spinach, and eggplant.

Back home, I did some computer work and scoped out the next day's activities. I needed to find my school, which was to begin the next week; the place to buy tickets for the every-Friday-morning guided walking tour for the benefit of Patronato pro Niños (an organization that provides free medical and dental services to poor children in SMA and the surrounding countryside); the place to buy tickets for the Saturday Adventure (more on that later); and a place for lunch.

The next day, it was so much warmer in the house, I couldn't believe it—a welcome change. Again, I had slept well, hearing not a sound. So I was launched on this two-month adventure and feeling very safe, secure, and happy, and soon, I expected, I'd find my way around more easily.

I bombarded Eleonor with questions, and she proved to be a godsend. I couldn't figure out how to turn on the TV and cable to get the channels I wanted, and the instructions for turning on the gas fireplace were so intimidating that I didn't even try. Turns out the pilot light wasn't lit on the fireplace, so even if I had tried it, I wouldn't have had any success. Also, the lighter provided was out of fluid, so it was a no-go from the get-go. Eleonor called the rental agency office, which dispatched a maintenance man who spoke English. He got the heater going and taught me how to work it. He also showed me how to operate the TV so I could watch the news in English. I was psyched to hear President-elect Obama's MLK Day speech and see his inauguration.

Eleonor washes the sheets and towels and offered to do my clothes, but the instructions that came with the house cautioned against it, plus my personal preference is to do it myself. I plan to do it on the weekends, when Eleonor is not at the house. I know she would be scandalized that *la señora* is hanging her laundry on an improvised clothesline on the terraza and not using the dryer. It makes absolutely no sense to me to use a dryer when there is more than abundant sun for free.

The Whole "Maid" Thing

I don't even like the word "maid." I prefer "housekeeper" or the Spanish *ayudante* (assistant). I'm having a lot of difficulty with this, as are others from the U.S. and Canada with whom I talk. Yes, I had someone clean my house in Philadelphia—once a month—and I didn't like to be home when he was there. Eleonor will be at my rental for 15 hours a week. So far, I just cannot stand to be there while she's working. I feel guilty. We were raised to do things for ourselves. I'm having to work hard to feel more comfortable with this cultural difference.

Figuring It All Out

A word about the narrow sidewalks here: They were never meant to be walked on! That's what the street was for. Five hundred years ago, when the streets and sidewalks were put in, there were no cars, of course. There were chamber pots in use, however, and people threw their contents out of the window. They would shout "*Aguas!*" (waters) to warn anyone nearby what was coming their way. That expression is still in use today to say "Look out!" although, of course, chamber pots are not. When the chamber pot contents were thrown out, they would hit the sidewalk and splash on the lower part of the houses' walls, thus the chest-high stripe of a darker color than the rest of the house on the outer walls of most casas in SMA. Long-ago servants would stand on those little strips of sidewalk to clean them and the lower part of the wall that got splashed and in this way maintained the façade of the house. And those gullies cut into the gutters on many streets? In addition to channeling the water from heavy rains, that's where those workers swept the waste.

The sidewalks are most often only as wide as one person carrying a parcel, large handbag, backpack, etc., and that would be almost all of us, so when you encounter another person coming toward you on the same sidewalk, it is necessary to either plaster yourself against the building (tough wearing a daypack, as I always do) or step off the high curb into the street. You have to make a determination of your course of action every time, based on the person's size, what he or she is carrying, his or her age, and/or ability or disability. Most people routinely step into the street for the elderly or those walking with a cane or with difficulty, but otherwise it was tough for me to figure out the local custom as to who should give way. Some teenagers gave way to me; some didn't. However it winds up, everyone is very good-natured about it.

Of course stepping off the sidewalk into the street presents its own hazards. Since San Miguel is a 16th-century colonial town, all the streets are narrow and cobbled; cars were never meant to drive on them, and yet they do, not to mention trucks and small buses. Most streets are one-way by necessity. When you decide to step into the street, you have to check behind you, if the traffic is moving in the same direction as you, to make sure you're not stepping into the path of a moving vehicle. (I learned later that the person facing the oncoming traffic should be the one to step off, but that "rule" is not always followed.)

Because sidewalks are so narrow, there is no way trash could be put out in anticipation of the trash collector. So a worker walks through the streets ahead of the trash truck, clanging a triangle that lets everyone know to come out with the trash. It's funny to see all the doors along the street open almost simultaneously and the homeowners/housekeepers step out with trash in hand to take to the waiting truck. And every morning when I went out, I saw that the sidewalks were wet. That is because the employees in every house/business scrub their one stone step and the sidewalk in front. It really helps to keep the dust down.

School Daze

On my second day in San Miguel, I went out to find the Spanish-language school I'd be attending starting the next Monday. In my usual obsessive/compulsive manner, I had mailed my registration form and check the previous August, and never heard a word back, so I took a copy of the form and the canceled check to the front desk of El Centro Bilingue. And it's a good thing I did, since they had no record of me. They were accommodating, however, and immediately set up a file with my name on it. The copy machine wasn't working and the receptionist wanted to keep my documents until I came back for the start of my class, but since that was my only proof, I said she could copy them on Monday, and I took them back. I filled out a personal information form and indicated that I felt my Spanish ability lay somewhere between "poor" and "fair." The only other designation was "good," and I knew that wasn't it. The receptionist said, based on our conversation in Spanish, that I was definitely "fair." I just beamed!

Perhaps to compensate for not having me registered, I was invited to join a cooking class to start momentarily—gratis. It consisted of eight to 10 students who had just been dismissed from their classes. We were given aprons and asked to wash our hands, and we congregated with a chef and a teacher in a small kitchen in a building across the street from the school. I understood about one-third of what the chef said.

We prepared guacamole a different way than I'd ever seen it made, using roasted peppers and tomatillos. I chopped the cilantro for the recipe. The funny thing is, I don't like avocados and so had never tried guacamole. However, this appetizer, scooped up with tortilla chips while we made the other dishes, was superb!

Chef Felix preparing the ingredients for the comida we were to make under his instruction.

We went on to make two types of *chiles rellenos* (chiles stuffed with cheese or a meat mixture), and crepes in a sauce made from *dulce de leche* (sweetened milk heated to the consistency and flavor of caramel), thinned with milk, then reheated. The chef talked about how, for many festivals, the dishes are made from or decorated with red, green, and white food, to represent the Mexican flag. Indeed, the chiles were green, with a white pecan sauce, and decorated with maraschino cherry bits. Usually the red decoration is pomegranate seeds, but they were out of season. The children of two of the couples in the class returned from their "camp" experience and joined all of us for a lunch of these dishes, plus rice pilaf and refried beans, and cake, as it was the birthday of one of the school staff. We toasted each other with piña coladas, in which were floating tiny chunks of piña. Everything was delicious and I stuffed myself.

I stayed a long time afterward chatting with Satomi, a Japanese woman who was also in San Miguel on her own. She had traveled the world doing international development, and spoke many languages. We really hit it off and agreed that it would be fun to go on excursions and eat dinner out together. The *biblioteca*—the public library that is the center for the expat cultural scene—publishes a newspaper every Friday called *Atención*, which has a pull-out section titled *¿Que Pasa?* (What's going on?) that lists everything there is to do in San Miguel. We agreed to use that to find things we could do together.

I started my Spanish classes at El Centro Bilingue. It was a unique experience for me to be on the other side of the desk from where I have stood for close to 15 years as an English as a Second Language (ESL) teacher. When I arrived, I was handed a four-page written test to see into which level I tested. After I completed about two-thirds of the first page, we were stopped and I was put into an unnamed level with Andrew from Toronto, originally from England.

Things were somewhat loosey-goosey in this school, to put it kindly. Letty, our teacher, was lovely and had a fine command of English. As an example of how things operate there, we spent a great deal of time mentally walking through the rooms in a home while she wrote the names of all the things you'd find—and we'd dutifully copy them—instead of what I would do, which is to hand out copies of a drawing or picture of the various rooms with all the items identified. I know this sort of thing is readily available. It seemed a sad waste of time, not to mention exhausting for Letty, to do it this way, and at $18/hour, I was feeling a little ripped off. The kicker came when she needed to make copies of some pages from a workbook that only she has, and we learned that the school does not have a copy machine for the teachers (you fed individual sheets into the one in the office; it wouldn't copy from a book). At the end of class, we trailed Letty up the street about a half block to a *papeleria* (stationery store) and waited while copies were made. We students marveled at this inefficiency; I apologized to Letty for being so "American," but I told her I thought it was ridiculous!

I made a joke in Spanglish in class one day that my classmate and teacher really enjoyed. Here it is: If you go to a *panadería* to buy baked goods, to the *zapatería* to pick out shoes, to the *carnecería* to purchase meat, and to the *tortillería* for tortillas, do you go to the *ferretería* to get ferrets? Actually, a ferretería is a hardware store. I'm assuming that the "ferr" root comes from "ferrous" for iron. Anyway, ferreterías are everywhere and seem to specialize in hardware for various needs: plumbing, cars, household, etc.

On another day after Spanish class, I again attended the free cooking class. Our chef, Felix, cooks at a local restaurant. I saw in its ad that it's closed Thursdays; that's the day Felix does the cooking classes! I staggered to a mariachi concert at the Instituto Allende filled to the gills with enchiladas, another type of guacamole, flambéed plantains and peaches, and the ever-present rice and beans, all washed down with sangria. I ate no dinner that night. The mariachis were stupendous. The performers'

outfits were really spiffy, with large silver "charms" sewn onto the side of their pant legs. Each of the charms had some movement to it, which really captured your eye, as did those handsome, skilled musicians.

Sightseeing

Satomi and I set off to visit the Instituto Allende—a world-famous art school—and along the way took in an art show in Parque Juárez, a green oasis in this high-desert town. It took a long time to get there, even though it's no more than a 15-minute walk, as we stopped in a number of shops, took many, many photos, and gawked at the preparations in the jardín for the band concert coming up that night.

We looked high and low (mostly high—we kept walking up and up and up pitched streets and stairways, and I was often out of breath from the thin air) looking for El Chorro, a spring near a church where some local women still do their laundry by hand. We were very close—we were on Calle El Chorro for Pete's sake—and saw the church, but we never located the spring. By this time, we were getting hungry, so we headed for the restaurant we'd agreed on beforehand, El Mesón de Terraplen (the name of the street it's on) for—wait for it—Lebanese food! We had both spied its ad in *Atención* and were equally intrigued. What a good choice it was!

We both chose the *mezze* plate, with five Lebanese specialties that change daily. The day's selections were hummus, baba ghanouj, falafel, a grated zucchini fritter, a lentil dish, and a bit of Lebanese coleslaw (no mayo in sight)—that's six, but who's counting?—with toasted pita triangles. We finished off with baklava, of course. During our meal, two laden burros and their master walked by and we nearly broke our necks getting to the doorway to take their picture. Actually we had plenty of time, as one burro took one of the longest pisses I've ever seen; it was oceanic!

CHAPTER 1

We never did get to the Instituto Allende, and that was fine. Perhaps *mañana*. Already I was on Mexican time.

After class one day, which runs Monday to Friday, 9 to 11 a.m., I again had lunch with Satomi, and then we had another adventure: a breathtaking—and exhausting—walk (that word doesn't nearly cover it; trek or quest might be better) to the top of one of the highest hills in San Miguel, El Mirador (the overlook). Calves and thighs screaming, we walked straight up streets that make those in San Francisco look flat, until finally, depleted and out of breath, we reached the top and saw the panorama before us that made it all worthwhile. It was an overview of the entire town of San Miguel and all of the outlying areas.

ENTERTAINMENT

Actually, everything here is entertaining to me.

Early one evening soon after I arrived, I went alone to a flamenco concert at the biblioteca. Astonishing is the only term I can use to describe what I witnessed! I am so impressed with the caliber of the entertainment. There was a *cajon* (box drum) player, a guitarist, two dancers (one a man), and a singer/dancer, who performed in various combinations. I had never seen a male flamenco dancer before, except as the rather staid partner of a flamboyant female, and OH. MY. GOD! First of all, he was gorgeous, and then he danced like nothing I'd ever seen before. The energy and complexity were astounding.

From there, I walked up to the jardín, where things were getting crowded. I had supper on the patio of a restaurant overlooking the action, and had my first margarita of the trip (it had been too cool to really appreciate one earlier), which didn't disappoint. Then I joined the crowd for the very surprising Symphonic Band of the Mexican Navy (who knew?) for the celebration of the 240th birthday of Ignacio Allende, a local hero in the War for Mexican Independence, and for whom the town's name was changed from San Miguel El Grande. I was expecting patriotic music, perhaps, but instead we were treated to selections from *Carmen,* the well-known "Guadalajara," and many upbeat selections by Mexican and other Latino composers. It was a rousing evening. A nice touch was that before each selection, one of the sailors read—in Spanish, of course—a brief biography of the composer, so that in addition to being enjoyable, the evening was educational.

The bandstand was set up right below Allende's home, a fitting tribute. But the band was nearly drowned out repeatedly by bells chiming the quarter hour from at least six churches. On Allende's real birthdate, there was to be a military parade, and then the installation of a plaque to commemorate the naming of San Miguel by UNESCO as a World Heritage Site. I felt proud on the city's behalf!

On my first Sunday in town, Satomi and I appeared a little before noon at the biblioteca to participate in the House and Garden Tour. The number of houses available for the tours is staggering; two or three are visited every week. It's a gigantic and well-coordinated operation, all run by volunteers, with all proceeds benefiting the biblioteca. Our first names and hometowns were written boldly on our tickets, which we affixed to our blouses. This was to facilitate conversation, and it certainly worked! Over 200 people eventually gathered in the central patio, along with a mariachi band to entertain, and there were displays and sales of photos and jewelry, and a couple of book-signings. We were loaded onto an endless stream of small buses to be taken to the first house. At that house, we didn't go inside; the garden was the prime reason for going. The second house was really over the top. It is hard to imagine what some people spend on these places.

Meeting People

I decided to sample Conversations with Friends, a free, informal program at the biblioteca in which locals who wish to practice English and visitors who wish to polish their Spanish come together twice a week to talk for an hour and a half. Since I was a little early and spotted another expat, I struck up a conversation. Alex and I spoke in English until the time came to speak in Spanish, and we just continued our conversation. We found we had much in common, even though Alex is a doctor, born and raised in England, who recently retired from his medical practice in Alberta, Canada. We were both renting here for two months; we had each lost a parent to Alzheimer's; and our level of proficiency in Spanish seemed identical. We were soon joined by others, including a retired couple from the U.S. who travel around Mexico and South America as volunteers, helping to sterilize dogs and euthanize near-death ones (really, there is a job out there for everyone).

I attended a service at the Unitarian Universalist Fellowship of San Miguel de Allende (UUFSMA). It is an aged congregation, but an extraordinarily vibrant one. Sunday services are in Hotel de la Aldea in a large second-floor room with killer views. During high season, attendance averages 120 at a Sunday service. They couldn't have been more welcoming. As a part of the service, we were asked to stand and introduce ourselves and, if visiting from another UU congregation, to name it and its city.

The congregation is lay-led (for the uninitiated, this means there is no minister). However, they have visiting ministers about half the Sundays a year, and I was fortunate enough to catch one that day. He was a young UU minister from Tennessee, visiting with his wife and two very young children. He was an engaging guy, quite funny, and had a good message. These visitors agree to preach and perform other ministerial duties (weddings, funerals, etc.) as needed in exchange for housing in the home of one of the members. On the Sundays when no minister is available, members of the congregation or speakers from various organizations deliver the morning talk. They are varied and most often interesting and instructive.

After the service, an elderly man came over and said he had heard me announce that I was from the Unitarian Society of Germantown in Philadelphia. He asked if I knew Alan from there. Of course I did! He had come to San Miguel with his wife a year earlier to study Spanish, and, tragically, died instantly from heart failure on the street. He was a man of extraordinary intelligence and dedication to the right causes, and he is sorely missed. The older man then told me that he was Alan's uncle. It is because I read of San Miguel de Allende in Alan's obituary that I first checked it out as a possible place to go in Mexico to study Spanish.

I went to a luncheon for the benefit of Mujeres en Cambio (Women Changing), a nonprofit group giving scholarships to smart, deserving girls in the *campo* (countryside) supported by the UU congregation here (among others, of course). They have fundraisers throughout the year, but this was their annual big do. This charity raises $75,000 USD each year! Translated into pesos, that's a heck of a lot of scholarships. They also helped a group of indigenous women get set up in a hooked rug business, and samples of those rugs were for sale. They sell in the States for quite a pretty penny, and have enabled some families to farm with a tractor for the first time in their lives!

We boarded buses and were taken about a half hour or more out of town to the rancho of a former mayor of SMA and his charming, vivacious wife, who was one of the founders of Mujeres en Cambio. They have a huge spread, but their actual home is quite modest. She is an artist and her studio is there, too, as well as a guest *casita*. Tables were set up and shaded with umbrellas. A scholarship student was seated at each table. The mayor's wife gave a warm welcome and introduced two of the mujeres, who spoke briefly about how much their scholarships meant to them and their families. We were invited to stroll the grounds after lunch and go into any of the buildings.

After a satisfying meal of chicken mole and beans and rice, provided by our hostess and her staff; a selection of salads prepared by the event committee; and scrumptious donated cookies from Petit Four, a French bakery in town, we went into the home and other buildings for a peek, then reboarded the buses to go to Mayer Schacter and Susan Page's Galeria Atotonilco, home to what is arguably the world's finest collection of Mexican folk art. We didn't roll back into town until 6 p.m.

Street Food

Satomi badly wanted to try an ice cream cone from a vendor at the jardín. I told her that if the vendor put the ice cream scoop into a bowl of water after scooping hers, I would not be partaking. I was sure that the water would not be purified. Well, lo and behold, in a brilliant move, this vendor had a scoop for every flavor, and each one resided in the stainless steel container its flavor was in, so there was no need to put them into water in between scooping flavors. So I indulged, with no bad results. I'd repeatedly read warnings that, in addition to not drinking the water, one should never eat salad or seafood in Mexico, and yet here, abundant quantities and varieties of both are on menus. I have started to eat salads (again with no bad results), but there is just no ocean anywhere near here, and I can't quite make the leap to seafood.

Gringos in San Miguel

In the late afternoon of Martin Luther King Jr. Day, I went to a service at St. Paul's Episcopal Church in honor of both Dr. King's birthday and the inauguration of Barack Obama the following day. The place was packed. Early on, they ran out of orders of service, so we happily shared, and chairs were hastily put up in the aisles.

We sang some great, rousing hymns, such as "He's Got the Whole World in His Hands," "I've Got Peace Like a River," "We Shall Overcome" (sung holding hands and swaying—is there any other way to sing it?), and "Lift Every Voice and Sing." Truly, there was not a dry eye in the house. There was a prayer for the president of the United States, which we read in unison in both English and Spanish, and we heard a recording of Nina Simone's "The King of Love Is Dead," written by her bass player right after Dr. King's assassination, and performed by Simone and her band at his funeral. Then there was a most stirring recitation by Olivia Cole, with a slight British accent, of a very long poem, "Dark Testament" by Pauli Murray, basically telling the entire story of African slavery in America, up to the present-day ills we inherited from this terrible institution.

CHAPTER 1

❁ ❁ ❁

I went to see the video *Lost and Found in Mexico* by Caren Cross, which won Best Documentary at the 2006 Boston Film Festival. The filmmaker is a former high-powered psychotherapist (she had 18 therapists working for her) who, after visiting San Miguel just once, decided to chuck it all, sell her house and furnishings, buy a house here, and settle in permanently. Her husband, David—who was running the Q&A after the showing because the filmmaker was in D.C. with her son for Obama's inauguration—apparently had come along kicking and screaming on the move to San Miguel. He seemed to have made his peace with the place, however.

To create the film, Caren went around with a videographer and asked expats why they had moved here. Many of the interviews were remarkably touching, such as the woman whose husband had committed suicide, leaving her alone with a young daughter. She spoke of how it totally knocked her off her pins to know that someone she loved and thought she knew would do something like that, without any signal that she could pick up on. She said that after a year of grieving in the States, many people thought she should "get on with her life," but she just wasn't ready. She found the time and space in SMA to continue that grieving process. Another interview spotlighted a man who'd been an extremely successful lawyer. He'd had a to-die-for house in the U.S., but one day he came home and sobbed that this was not what he wanted out of life. His wife seconded the motion, and within three months they were here to stay.

I had to bid a tearful goodbye to Satomi, as her vacation was over. The farewell served to emphasize the transient nature of the town. Expats come and go according to the seasons, work responsibilities, relationships, checking on aged parents back in the States or Canada, returning to get health care paid for by their medical plans, and a myriad of other reasons. And of course some people are just passing through.

A little history of the word *gringo*. It is important to know that it is not pejorative. There are several theories of how the word came into usage, but the one I like best is that when the Mexican-American War began in 1846, several hundred recently immigrated Irish, German, and other Roman Catholic Americans were drafted into the Army and sent by the U.S. government to fight against Mexico. The Irish soldiers soon came to question why they were fighting against fellow Catholics. This, combined with their mistreatment by their Anglo-Protestant officers, led them to desert and join the "enemy," forming the San Patricio Brigade of the Mexican Army. Dozens were killed in battle and many more were captured and executed as deserters by the Americans. The Irish soldiers frequently sang "Green Grow the Rushes, O." Spanish speakers had difficulty voicing the second "r" in "green grow," and thus produced "gringo." Today, St. Patrick's Day is a huge holiday in Mexico, as they remember the Irish soldiers who refused to fight against them, "the Irish Martyrs." "Gringos" is now widely used for *estadounidenses* (U.S. citizens), and I think that Canadians get lumped into that designation, too, as we're hard to tell apart.

Music, Dancing, Swimming

At a brunch in the restaurant of the Aldea Hotel after a UU Sunday service, I sat with Karen, a woman about my age from Ottawa, who was attending a UU service for the first time in her life. We formed an attachment right away. Sue, a UU with whom I had spoken at Conversations with Friends, had invited me to join her during the coming week at Escondido, one of the local hot springs, and said I was free to invite others, so I asked Karen.

Walking home after brunch, I came upon a charming scene in the jardín: A little band (two marimba players, a guitarist, and a man on those tall, narrow Caribbean drums, along with an MC/vocalist) was playing many types of music (salsa, Cuban, Mexican, even rock 'n' roll), and all manner of folks were dancing. After just a short time, I was roasting, and had to tear myself away to go home to change into cooler clothes. But I hurried right back to lap up the ambience of the gentle scene. The dancing went on for two hours, and was to be repeated in the evening.

Dancing in the jardín.

❉ ❉ ❉

At the beginning of my second week at El Centro Bilingue, my classmate, Andrew, and I were introduced to our new teacher, Miguel. I liked Miguel's style right away. He was organized, had his handouts already copied and ready to distribute, spoke a little more slowly and distinctly than Letty (or was my ear more in tune by then?), and over the week's time let his guard down a bit. We three really bonded and had a good time while learning a lot. Miguel never gave us homework, whereas Letty always did. I'm still not sure which I liked better.

❉ ❉ ❉

I met Eleonor's niece Carla, whom Eleonor cares for after school while she works. Carla, who is about five or six, was wearing her school uniform and looking at a princess book. With prompting from Eleonor, she showed me her schoolbook in which she was learning to write her letters. I determined to find some *princesa* books on my travels around town and leave them for Carla on my last day. I hope I'll have another opportunity to speak with a child, as my sentences are about on that level and I don't feel so tongue-tied with them.

"Tomorrow Is Not Mañana"

At a lecture at the biblioteca (natch!) titled "Adios Is Not Goodbye; Tomorrow Is Not Mañana," speaker Robert de Gast opened his presentation by posing this question: "San Miguel is not near any airport; it's not near any beach; it has no casinos; so why do throngs of people from the U.S. and Canada come here?" He also mentioned that there are no earthquakes, tornadoes, hurricanes, floods, or fires. He then proceeded to answer his own question, which was rhetorical, as we all knew the answer.

And what is the answer? First and foremost, there is the temperate weather; it's eternal spring in San Miguel. Many people, nicknamed snowbirds, come to escape the harsh winters in their hometowns to the north, and I was certainly one of those. Then there are the sweatbirds, people from states like Texas and Louisiana who visit SMA in the summer to get away from triple-digit temperatures. Imagine the most spectacularly magnificent day that you can. Got it? It is like that almost every single day. The sky is impossibly blue. Then there is the light, which is like nowhere else and of course draws visual artists.

The cost of living is very low, even though we expats have forced the prices higher here than in almost any other place in Mexico. Life is slower and more relaxed. There is an emphasis on family, and a respect for age.

Additionally, I believe that the tourists from Canada, the U.S., and other places who seek out San Miguel are a self-selected group. Generally, we are open-minded, open-hearted, liberal, well-educated, well-traveled, interested in engaging with Mexican culture and the people of the town, adventurous, and, most of all, creative. Creativity is encouraged, supported, nurtured, even expected. There are innumerable outlets for creativity in all of its expressions: art in all its media, music to suit any taste, live plays, movies and documentaries, lectures, dance performances, trips. We want to be with people like this, and so we flock here and have created a unique community. Some people, it is true, are running away from something or are disillusioned with their home countries and their governments. But I like to think that I am going toward something.

There is an emphasis on care of the body, with dozens of classes for yoga, meditation, qi gong, tai chi, tennis, water aerobics, pickle ball, and the like. There are many massage therapists.

And volunteering is a way of life and takes uncountable forms: raising money for scholarships; helping to protect the environment in a dozen different ways; rescuing, healing, and adopting out street dogs and feral cats, where possible; breathing new life into donated computers to give to students; helping to care for children in day-care centers; building simple homes for the impoverished; teaching music in the schools; serving a hot weekly midday meal to the elderly poor; helming a chapter of the Audubon Society (the only one in Mexico); caring for congregation members, friends, or neighbors who are sick. I am proud to say that the list is endless.

The colors—of the houses, the clothing, the decorations for holidays and the like—and an abundance of year-round flowers bring joy. The purple spring blossoming of the jacaranda trees thrills everyone, while also giving many allergies.

And then there's all of the Mexican stuff: the food, music, celebrations, fiestas, parades, shopping, and opportunities to meet, socialize with, and learn from the locals.

As Robert de Gast explained in his talk, mañana is an indeterminate point of time somewhere in the future, and if you can't live with that, you have no business being in Mexico. While his talk was entertaining, his slides were a hoot. He prefaced them by saying that he wasn't showing them to poke fun at Mexico or San Miguel, because he loved Mexico, Mexicans, and San Miguel in particular, but his slides showed the very particularities and peculiarities that make SMA the city that it is.

A recent experience of mine bore out what he was saying. A toy museum I wanted to visit is on Nuñez, the next street parallel to the one I would live on in 2011. The address I was looking for was 40. When I began my search on Nuñez, I saw 33 and 35, then looked in vain on the opposite side of the street for 40. I ducked into a computer school to ask where the museum was, and was told it was several blocks up. When

I went back outside, I saw that immediately next to 35 was 2, and the numbers climbed from there. I easily found 40 a few blocks up. To have both odd and even numbers on the same side? And to have 2 come after 35? There are many mysteries.

And yet another confounding experience with house numbering occurred when I went to a private arts and crafts sale at a home/display area near my house, and bought a Oaxacan table runner for a song. The continuing deterioration of the peso against the dollar makes for very enticing prices. Finding the address was an adventure, though. While looking for this place, Quebrada 41, I was in the 60s on one side, and into the 100s on the other! At least there were some numbers! Often there aren't. Seemingly, the only places with numbers are those where the owners want you to find them, such as a business. And there are times that a house/business has two or even three different numbers, or that two houses in the same block have #10 on them, for example.

The streets are fairly well-marked, except for one small thing. Some years ago, SMA tried a new street identification system. Because the word for block is *manzana* (same as apple; don't ask), every street sign says Manzana and a number—very confusing to visitors, until someone explains it to you. Basically, now that that system is defunct, one is to ignore those lovely tiles and just read the name of the street below, if, in fact, there is a street name sign. Also, streets frequently change names as they meander through town.

As I left de Gast's talk, I met one of the women who had been so welcoming to me at the UU service. When I told her I was going to a hot spring, Escondido, the following day, she gave me some very good advice. One has to take a taxi there, and because it's 25 km from the center of town, there will be no taxis to bring you home. Here's what she told me to do: Agree up front with your taxi driver on a round-trip price and then tell him that you will pay him the full amount when he returns to pick you up at an agreed-upon time. I would never have known that! This is how I learn so many things here: by dumb luck, by just speaking to the right person—who always seems to present him- or herself to me at the right time—and telling them what I have been doing or am planning to do.

So the next day in Spanish class, I asked Miguel what would be a fair price to and from Escondido, and how exactly to say what my UU friend had told me. Armed with that knowledge, I met Sue and Karen and her newly arrived friend, Nancy, in the jardín, and our adventure began. (Actually, that's wrong. This whole trip to San Miguel is an adventure!) I told the women about the taxi plan and I was immediately appointed the spokesperson. Happily, the price the taxi driver offered us was what Miguel had said, and he agreed to the return-trip plan, so we were off, with me riding shotgun, not my favorite position. When in any vehicle, I prefer the back seat.

We arrived in one piece at El Balneario de Escondido Place. We were welcomed, were given maps of the place, and paid our entrance fee (about $7.50 to $8 at the current very-favorable-to-the-U.S. exchange rate). We four intelligent women were unable to figure out the aerial maps. We couldn't locate the changing rooms, so we put our suits on in shower stalls. We did eventually find the changing rooms at the very end of our stay, but we never found the lockers, so we schlepped our stuff all around with us, taking turns watching it while the others went into the various hot springs. Escondido has 10 lakes (in which you do not swim), six pools fed by natural hot mineral springs (with no odor), a small café with an even smaller menu, a tiny store that we didn't get to go into, showers, and bathrooms. The changing rooms, showers, and bathrooms were all far from each other. And presumably the lockers were in yet another place.

We had a nice little lunch and tried five of the six pools (one didn't have any water in it). One pool that was a stand-alone was lukewarm. Some of the pools were interconnected and we followed the narrow inside passages to successively hotter and hotter water. Overhead pipes poured out water at great volume, so you could position whatever part of you was hurting under that gushing hot water to help relieve your aches. The place was immaculate but lacked any safety features whatsoever, such as railings to hold on to as you stepped into or out of the water. There were just a few families there besides us, so it all felt very friendly and pleasant. One little boy commented to his father about the *viejas* (old women)—that would be us—and his father shushed him. We ended a very relaxing afternoon getting to know each other over bottles of beer (a piña colada in my case). The taxi driver actually arrived a few minutes early and I kidded him that he had arrived *en punto* (right on time)—like an estadounidense, not like a Mexicano.

On Friday, I received an unexpected—and wonderful—invitation from my classmate, Andrew. He and his wife, Janet, invited me to go with them in their car to Atotonilco to see the 260-plus-year-old church there, which was recently recognized, along with San Miguel, as a UNESCO World Heritage Site, and then to go on to La Gruta, another of the hot springs in the area. I ran home after class to get my suit and towel. We had great fish tacos at a little shack near an RV park where they keep their car, and then we were on our way. At the church, the frescoes were being totally redone, so much of the interior was covered with scaffolding and drop cloths. Because of this, it wasn't as rewarding a visit as it might have been. I was thinking this restoration might take years. I wondered if funds came with the designation as a World Heritage Site.

Then it was off to La Gruta. This time, I left my money in their

The church at Atotonilco.

Inside the church at Atotonilco.

trunk so I didn't have to worry about it. At a little window, we paid the same entrance fee as at Escondido, walked four feet, and gave our ticket to another person. Well, it provides employment. We changed and went on to a lovely pool. Again, you swim/walk through a covered passageway to the next level of hotness. We met and talked to some fascinating folks from all over the world, even one from Tasmania! The restaurant at this place is a tiny bit fancier, and you can get a drink served to you in the pool, not of any interest to me. They also have masseuses here (that's what it said on their shirts, although they were in actuality masseurs and the Spanish word is *masajista*—for a man or a woman using either *el* or *la*). I didn't see that service offered at Escondido. The scuttlebutt is that Escondido is for the locals, and La Gruta for the gringos, but we saw both at each place.

Very relaxed and happy, we headed back to SMA, and Andrew and Janet invited me in for a drink, which led to us going out to dinner together. I had a large bowl of posole (hominy, a traditional soup or stew with meat, garnished with shredded cabbage, chiles, onion, garlic, radishes, avocado, salsa, and lime—a favorite of mine, but I'd never had it made with turkey before) for about $3.25 USD. The glass of red wine I had cost almost as much!

February 2009

I'm Feeling Very Much at Home Here Now

I went to the Fiesta de Candelaria at Parque Juarez. I remember commenting to Satomi weeks ago that they were in no rush here to take down Christmas decorations, and I found out that it's because the season really extends to February 2, Candelaria, the beginning of the planting season. Candelaria is Candlemas in English, when candles were brought to the church to be blessed. On this day in Mexico, there is the blessing of the seeds, and a very complex religious ritual of taking the Jesus figure from the home crèche to the church (and I believe the man of the family carries the baby lovingly and tenderly) for a blessing, and then Jesus and the crèche are packed away for another year.

As February 2 marks the midpoint between the winter solstice and the spring equinox, it has long been thought to be a predictor of the weather to come, which is why Groundhog Day is celebrated then in parts of the U.S. In many places, it is traditionally a time to prepare the earth for spring planting, and that is never more evident than in San Miguel. Candelaria is also a follow-up to the festivities of Three Kings Day on January 6, when children receive gifts, and families and friends gather to eat *rosca de reyes*, a sweet bread with a little plastic figurine of the Baby Jesus baked inside. The person who receives the baby in his/her slice of bread is supposed to host a party on Candelaria, with tamales and *atole*, a hot, sweetened corn flour drink flavored with cinnamon, vanilla, or chocolate.

Flower pot, anyone?

At Parque Juarez, endless numbers of plant and container vendors had set up their wares. Wherever you walked, you were surrounded by beautiful plants, both for indoor and outdoor gardens. Boys zipped around with wheelbarrows to transport your purchases to your nearby home or parked car or even a taxi. I wished I could have bought some of the lovely flowering plants. I have never seen so many planters in my life—hundreds upon hundreds stacked up in every size from thimble to bathtub! And they all had to be hand-carried in, and, presumably, since there is no way they could all sell, some hand-carried back out.

This fiesta lasts for about 12 hours a day for 10 days! Each evening finds a different type of entertainment on a large, raised stage. I saw performers from various Mexican states doing traditional dances in colorful costumes. But just yards from the stage was a gazebo where a very loud mariachi-type band was performing, so the music from the two almost-adjacent places was in competition—a bit disconcerting, but very Mexican, I was learning.

One Sunday, I cried a lot. The first place was at the UU service. Instead of a sermon, since there was no minister in the "pulpit" that Sunday, four members read to the congregation, in its entirety, Obama's speech on race, which he'd delivered at the Constitution Center in Philadelphia while he was a candidate as a response to all the flap about the Rev. Jeremiah Wright. I had listened to it then and was deeply moved, but this time the feelings were even deeper.

I hung around the hotel after the brunch, since an event I was attending at 3 p.m. was in the same space as the UU service. The UU congregation supports probably eight or so local charities. The event that afternoon was a performance by the girls of Casa Hogar Santa Julia. The girls at this home, run by the Dominican Sisters of Mary, cannot live with their own families because of various dire circumstances—illness, poverty, abuse, etc. For the first six years, the organization had no sustainable support outside of taking the girls begging on the streets. Its buildings were in terrible disrepair, and the girls were underfed and underperforming in school, and totally lacked self-esteem. A group of volunteers visited the school and wrote an article in the local paper describing their plight, and miracles began to happen. They now have a safe home, a computer lab, health care, goals, and self-esteem for sure. Two members of the UU congregation, both Juilliard-trained musicians, volunteer at the school, teaching them violin and English and leading a choir, along with Spanish-speaking musicians, other teachers, and volunteers of many kinds.

The concert featured about 25 girls, ages three to mid-teens, and they sang lots of songs in both Spanish and English with hand and body movements, and some of the older ones also played the violin, which they are being taught with the Suzuki method. Every girl had a different, beautiful hairstyle, done by the nuns (they call them *madres*). They were in immaculate school uniforms with brilliant white knee socks (a tough thing to manage here in dusty San Miguel).

I wept through most of the performance. To know where these girls had been—and where they are today and the fact that they do have a future, thanks to the hard work of the nuns and the impressive generosity of a lot of expats—was overwhelming. Also, knowing all of the advantages I had growing up, all those my children had, and those my grandchildren are now enjoying, compared to these girls and millions more like them everywhere in the world, was a heavy burden for me that day.

On Monday, I reported to El Centro Bilingue for what I thought was another week of instruction with Miguel. However, even though we saw Miguel, with no explanation we got Marysol as a teacher. We were in yet another room, and the way the sun was coming in the door made reading the whiteboard nearly impossible, plus the somewhat-rowdy *niños'* (children's) class was next door. I rebelled. I said there was no way I could learn under those circumstances, so we moved to yet another room, where Andrew couldn't even fully stand up!

It's really difficult to describe the school building, which was undoubtedly someone's home at one time. You walk in a door from the street and past the office into the usual central patio, off of which all the rooms open. The students from all the levels appear around 9 a.m. and mingle happily for a few minutes while getting coffee. Then their teachers appear and herd them to their respective classrooms. If ever a fire inspector had seen this school, it would have been shut down instantly. Tons of extra furniture—bookcases, tables, chairs, etc.—are stacked everywhere, some precariously. There are frequent interruptions. Other people—teachers, aides, cleaning people, and whoever—might come into the class with deeply polite apologies for barging in. They need a book that's in a cabinet in this room, or the teacher needs to sign a paper, or someone just needs to deliver a message to the teacher.

Marysol is probably the best-trained teacher in the school, having a master's in linguistics from UNAM (National Autonomous University of Mexico), which is recognized as not only the largest in Latin America and the oldest on the continent, but also the leading university of the Spanish-speaking world. She was to leave shortly for six months in Vancouver to teach for Berlitz. She told us that the jobs for college graduates are scarce (and for others who don't go on to further study, as witnessed by the desperate migration of Mexicans north to work to try to provide for their families). Highly trained Marysol said she had to go outside of the country to get employment, otherwise she would have had to work as a housekeeper to supplement the pay she got from El Centro Bilingue. As it is, she moonlights as a bartender.

THE SEDUCTION IS COMPLETE!

If it's Sunday, it must be time for me to cry again. At the UU service, instead of a sermon, the chairpersons of two of the five organizations the congregation supports, Mujeres en Cambio and Jóvenes Adelante (Young People Moving Forward), both scholarship programs, gave brief synopses of the work and successes of their respective organizations. They then introduced two students each, three young women and a young man, who were some of the many recipients of scholarships from their organizations.

One young woman desperately wanted to study medicine, but even with the help of the scholarship from Mujeres en Cambio, she was not able to afford it (just as in the States, it's prohibitively expensive). So she decided to study law, she said, because in either profession she could help her countrymen, which was her only desire. She is taking a double load in law school so she can finish more quickly. She said that perhaps when she has become a lawyer and is making sufficient money, she can then study to become a doctor! What these *jóvenes* had to say—some in basic English, some in translated Spanish—was incredibly touching. The young man, who really wanted to study to be an opera singer, but is not, cried when he started to talk. He spoke of the congregation as his angels. All offered their heartfelt thanks, and said they had no doubt that without this help, they would not be in school.

These scholarships are given directly to the students, not to the schools. In addition to tuition, there are other expenses such as books, transportation, room and board, etc., and on the high-school level, uniforms. If any money is left over after their expenses, they are free to give it to their families for food or health care. They must all maintain at least an 8.5 grade point average out of a possible 10. Every student who spoke also works, many nearly full time, in addition to being full-time students. The programs also assign a mentor to each student, and some receive tutoring in English. All of the university students receive a reconditioned laptop.

CHAPTER 1

❀ ❀ ❀

I went on a trip called Saturday Adventure. Each week, the group is taken to a different place in or close to town that tourists would not normally get to see. For the peso equivalent of $12, you are taken on a four-hour journey to a different world, whatever the world may be that week. And it all benefits a worthy charity for handicapped children. The Mexican woman who 33 years ago started Centro de Crecimiento (Growth Center, an organization that provides all types of help for handicapped children), Lucha Maxwell—a physical therapist now 93 years old—goes on every trip, gives a little talk about the charity and its work, and invites guests to visit to see their accomplishments.

A brick-making facility was the first place on the schedule. There, we were to have been invited to take off our shoes and help to mix the brick "dough" into the right consistency (sort of like stomping grapes). The mixture is set to "ripen," poured into molds for bricks or tile roofs or whatever, dried, and baked in a gas kiln. The products are then shipped to the U.S. However, when I arrived at the tour's meeting place, the brick factory was no longer in the offing. Instead, we were given a paper listing an amber mine as one of two places we were to visit. But, alas, that, too, was canceled. I was really disappointed, as either of those things would have been of real interest to me. The trip leaders said this happens all the time. They'll get everything set up and then a frantic last-minute phone call will say something has happened that prevents the group from coming that week. Then it's scramble time.

So we were loaded onto a couple of small buses and went to a two-year-old house in a gated golf community that was for sale for $695,000 USD (how convenient—a free open house). The house was lovely, although the community lacked life, in my opinion. So far, I was feeling gypped.

Then we drove for about a half hour out of town to one of the most fantastic places I've ever seen. It was the weekend home of a New York couple who also had a place in San Miguel. They found this place about 10 years ago, almost by accident. In the 16th century, the Spanish priests set up a huge number of chapels around the area in which to convert the local indigenous people to Christianity. Almost all of these structures are now in severe disrepair; however, the one on this property is in excellent condition. It has frescoes in very good shape.

Perhaps an old station of the cross?

When they originally found the ruin, squatters were living in it and in various outbuildings around it. They bought the property and paid the squatters to move away. When they returned the following weekend, they found that the squatters were removing all of the stones of their shelters in order to rebuild elsewhere, so once again they had to pay them to cease and desist. The couple think that the whole site, including the chapel, was set up for some sort of more elaborate religious ceremony, such as the stages of the cross.

They built a house onto the existing ruin and now have a total showplace. They rent the place out when they don't need it, and offer horseback riding, meals, weddings in the chapel, and lunches for a chef-led cooking group from town. They even grow their own corn for the tortillas! (Well, of course, the couple are not out in the fields planting and harvesting corn; there are workers to do that.) Sipping cool drinks and nibbling cookies while overlooking a pastoral scene, no one wanted to leave.

My daughter, Suji, and her husband, Geoff, had arrived to spend a month with me in the house on Hidalgo, so we went on another of the house and garden tours. The first place was so extravagant that no one could believe it. It was like a pleasure palace of Kubla Khan. It was quite a way out of town, and seemingly in a development of other homes of like extremes. It also was for sale, for $3 million USD, which, considering what it was, seemed way underpriced. It was done entirely in Moroccan style. The owners had brought home more huge, magnificent light fixtures than you could ever imagine (actually, I did like them a lot), and things like opium beds.

But the second place we visited, not far from my rental in El Centro, was worth the price of admission. The homeowner was a down-to-earth younger woman, and her home had been featured in the Rizzoli book *Haciendas* in October 2008. It had undergone several reconstructions over the past 10 years. One of the more spectacular features was a hand-carved wood fireplace with a map of the world in the 1560s. An outdoor living room with comfortable seating areas, an enormous chandelier, and a fireplace overlooked the walled-in garden, a pool, and a guest casita.

Valentine's Day turned out to be huge here. All of the stores displayed Valentine's merchandise weeks before the event, and because the holiday fell on a Saturday, throngs of Mexican tourists poured into San Miguel, meaning that traffic in the already-overburdened streets was in gridlock much of the weekend. We had decided early on not to try to eat dinner out that night, so had a big, delicious meal out for lunch, and then Suji bought a rotisserie chicken and fresh-made tortillas, and we made yummy tacos. We went up to the jardín after dinner to check out the scene. The balloon and flower sellers were doing a brisk business, and competing mariachi bands were in different corners, serenading couples. It was a happy, loving, exciting place to be.

A balloon man in the jardín.

Unique Experiences

Suji, Geoff, and I were eager to experience the Tuesday Market (Tianguis or La Placita). I didn't know what to expect. It was absolutely gigantic!

CHAPTER 1

Not necessarily the way I'd want to buy a bra and panties...

What a bountiful display of produce and fruit!

Happily, there were tarps high up over all of the stands, so it wasn't hot. It would have been unbearable without them, as it was held in a huge open lot under the blazing sun on a particularly warm day. There was everything and anything for sale that you could possibly ever want or need. I bought a princesa coloring book and crayons for Eleonor's niece, to leave for her as a parting gift, and we bought a small serrated knife, since we were all frustrated with the sharpness (or lack thereof) of the knives in the rental.

Suji and Geoff got quite hungry and were tempted to eat at one of the stalls. Good sense prevailed, however, and they didn't. We were told by others afterward that that had been a wise decision. We saw vendors cooking large pieces of pig skin in vats of boiling fat. This is a favorite snack of the Mexicans, called *chicharrón*, eaten somewhat like potato chips, but with the addition of hot sauce. After about two hours of roaming and gaping, we caught a bus back to Centro and headed to a favorite restaurant of mine, a fish taco place, for a late lunch. The thought of people putting up and taking down that immense market every single week is mind-boggling.

One afternoon, I went to the Instituto Allende for a lecture about an overnight trip the following weekend to see the migrating monarch butterflies at Santuario El Rosario in the nearby state of Michoacán. The presenter, César, had an encyclopedic knowledge of just about everything Mexican and gave "the history of Mexico in one hour." He literally had me on the edge of my seat—he made it that interesting—with no visual aids, just his voice (speaking English) and vast knowledge. When I reported the trip's details to Suji and Geoff, we decided to go.

Our group of 27 had to be at the Instituto Allende at 7:45 in the morning to board the bus for the *mariposa* (butterfly) trip. Because it was a three-and-a-half-hour ride, we stopped frequently at points of interest along the way, including a museum with evidence of a spectacular civilization in the area 3,000 years ago, and in the city of Acambaro, Guanajuato, to see the Convento y Templo de San Francisco.

In the late afternoon, we arrived at our lodgings, "a four-star hotel with all the amenities of the big city in a rustic area." Don't believe everything you read! On the way to our rooms, we passed a small grassy area where there were no fewer than nine different sliding boards. We were all pretty punchy by this time, and Suji dubbed it the Sliding Board Museum. We were given time to settle in and rest until our 7:30 dinner. My toilet did not flush. I went down to the front desk to report this, as there were no phones in the rooms, and watched while the clerk dispatched a workman to my room. However, when I returned after dinner, the situation was exactly the same. Geoff to the rescue! The food in this restaurant was not good. Instead of serving us some delicious Mexican specialties, they gave us bland renditions of American food.

The next day, after a bad breakfast, we were on our way to the santuario by 8:30 a.m. It is at 10,000 feet and we were warned it could be quite cool. During the 20-minute ride, surgical masks were distributed to block our noses and mouths from dust stirred up by the high wind. When we left the bus, it was indeed cold and windy. Vendors were doing well selling knitted wool hats and gloves and renting walking sticks. I had the right clothing, but did rent a bamboo pole for the long climb up.

All bundled up to go see the mariposas.

The brochure promised a "leisurely high-altitude walk." HA! Formerly you could rent a horse to take you to the top (which of course I wouldn't dream of doing, as I'm frightened of horses), but we'd been told on the bus that just the previous week, there had been a bad accident involving the horses, and they were no longer being used. We walked through a phalanx of vendors selling more of the wool hats and gloves, all kinds of snacks and drinks, even full meals, and every item you can imagine with a butterfly motif.

Two other women my age and I had a somewhat-difficult time

dealing with the stress of the high altitude and the straight uphill climb. One woman was an absolute scream. She spoke abysmal Spanish with an even worse accent, and she had us and any people we encountered along the way laughing until our sides hurt. I begged her to cease and desist, as there was no way I could climb and laugh at the same time. We called ourselves "*las tres abuelas*" (the three grandmothers). We met up with a Mexican *abuelo*, Samuel, and his son and walked and laughed with them partially in Spanish and partially in English all the way to the top and the butterfly viewing. Samuel was a handsome guy, a retired professional, and I think he really enjoyed the attentions and the company of the abuelas. His son, who knew English well, laughed as hard as we did at *la chistosa* (the funny lady).

Las tres abuelas and Samuel making the climb.

The climb took over an hour and a half, and we were thankful that the wind subsided the higher we got in the forest. The butterflies cling in bunches that look like grapes to a special tree, the oyamel pine, at a metabolic level just slightly more vigorous than hibernation. As the sun rises and warms them, they begin to shake their wings, making the trees appear to undulate. As the sun climbs higher and warms them more, they fly from the trees, and we were told that at this sanctuary, we would see upwards of seven million monarch butterflies. I heard from another tourist earlier that the locals had been cutting down the oyamel pines for firewood, thus destroying the butterflies' habitat, but that recently the federal government had stepped in, and this practice is now strictly prohibited. "Vigilantes" (it actually said this on their shirts) were on duty to enforce the law.

When I reached the top, where the butterflies were, I immediately started to cry. I'm not sure whether it was because of my relief at finally reaching the top or because I was so overwhelmed by the sight of the monarchs; it was likely a combination of the two. At that exact moment, one of them lighted on Samuel. It transferred to his finger and he presented it to me.

Samuel's gift to me.

As it was a weekend, the viewing site was quite crowded. We spent well over an hour at the top watching the butterflies detach from their clusters on the trees and fly about and mate, and of course some dropped to the ground and died.

We returned to our hotel for a lousy lunch about 3 p.m., and then began the exhaustingly long bus trip back to SMA. Now that the thrill was over, the ride seemed unending. We were eager to get back in time to see the Oscars. We were served margaritas on the bus around 6 p.m., and that smoothed everything out. My calves ached for days when I went up or down stairs. Geoff made a great joke about the supposed four-star hotel we stayed in. He said there were two stars on Saturday and two stars on Sunday. Even by Mexican standards, this was no four-star hotel!

On this bus trip I saw some of the real poverty of Mexico. So much work is needed to help the country rise to the next level. In the higher elevations, there was abundant agricultural activity going on, as it frequently rains. Acres and acres of crops were being grown under plastic, I guess to get a head start on the planting season. What can we in the U.S. and Canada do to help our neighbors to the south enjoy some of the riches we take for granted?

Already Planning for Next Year

I've been looking at a number of properties for next year with several rental agents. I'm going to stay for three months in 2010 and that will include *Semana Santa* (Holy Week). I'm really eager to experience all of the ceremonies and street processions that go on then.

I went to a Circle *Cena* (dinner), organized by the UU congregation. They are a very popular way for folks to share a delicious cooperative meal and to really get to know each other on a different level than is possible on a Sunday morning. You sign up with a coordinator, and hosts and hostesses volunteer (OK, so it's almost always a hostess), to whom people are assigned. The hostesses contact their guests and ask them what they'd like to bring. In this way, each course of the meal is covered, and no one has too much of the work. I was assigned to Betse in an interesting apartment/casita complex, Quinta Loreto. I volunteered to bring appetizers, so I went on a search for a nice selection of cheeses, crackers, hummus, and pita bread. I was successful, and the other guests loved them. The rest of the meal was divine. We nine women had a rollicking good time. Betse's casita was charming. When I asked her how I could rent one like it in the complex, she said I'd have to wait for somebody to die. There are only a few of the casitas; they are very much in demand, and there is a long waiting list to rent them.

As place cards, the hostess had bought *cascarones* and added a bit of tape with our names. Cascarones are a charming pre-Lenten tradition in Mexico. Starting around Christmastime, people carefully break eggs by cutting off the tops, and after emptying the contents, they rinse and save the shells. Close to Ash Wednesday, the shells are filled with confetti, gold powder, or—horrors!—flour, and a small piece of tissue paper is glued over the opening. Vendors sell plastic bags of 10 of these for just a few pesos. You then catch friends or family members unawares and break the eggs over their heads, showering them with the contents. The teenagers in town have taken this formerly harmless custom to a new, unfortunate level. They crack the eggs actually on a person's head, not above it, and often with quite a knock. While they usually do it only with their friends, a number of gringos told me they had gotten egged in the jardín. We all stayed clear of it during those days. At night, we could hear teens running up and down in front of the rental, laughing and screaming, and in the morning, sparkles, confetti, and eggshells littered the streets and sidewalks until it was swept up by the beleaguered street cleaners.

I was particularly happy to have my own cascarone because Eleonor's niece Carla, with whom I have grown close, had asked her mother if she could break a cascarone on la senora's head. Her mother unequivocally said no. When Eleonor reported this, I was disappointed—I wanted Carla to do it to me if she wanted to. So when Eleonor came the next time, I excitedly told her that I had a cascarone for Carla to break over my head. Carla was thrilled and did it the proper way. My egg was filled with gold powder, and Carla wound up with much of it on her hands. She was so enamored of it that she wouldn't wash her hands. I was afraid she'd get gold dust on everything her aunt had just cleaned, but just then her mother came to collect her, and the last thing I saw as she went out the door was her showing her mom her golden hands.

Carla cracking a cascarone over my head.

VOLUNTEERING

One Wednesday morning, I went to mattress-making at St. Paul's Church. What, you might ask, is that? Well, it's a win-win-win if there ever was one. Many children who live out in the campo are very poor, and sleep directly on a dirt floor in their homes. This mattress-making program uses clean, discarded plastic bags made into balls to stuff mattresses for these kids. About 20 to 30 people show up on a Wednesday morning. The bags have been brought into a large room set up with long tables with chairs on either side.

Someone else sews colorful, heavy-duty mattress covers with handles to hang them up by day, and the plastic-bag balls are stuffed into the covers and the mattress is "quilted," that is, sewed through in various spots to keep the bags from shifting. It takes 1,200 to 1,500 plastic-bag balls to stuff one child-sized mattress! This group generally completes two mattresses per session. Solicitation is made for funds to buy a pillow, a blanket, and an additional cover that can be washed, and then the whole package is wrapped with ribbon. The woman who has been running the program for the past seven years said that during her tenure, more than 500 mattresses have been made and delivered to families in the campo. It was easy, mindless work and the conversation was good. I left feeling light as air! It felt good to do something so simple that will really make a difference to a child and to the environment.

Preparing to help stuff the thousands of donated plastic bags.

Lots of folks are now leaving for home. The snowbird season is pretty much over at the end of March. May, I was told, is not a fun time to be in SMA, as it gets pretty hot and dry right before the rainy season sets in, June through August. In the summer in SMA it rains torrentially for about an hour every day in the mid-to-late afternoon. Wherever you are when it starts to rain, you just stay there, because the cobblestones are treacherous during the downpours, and the streets run with water. Then the clouds depart, the sun comes out, the place gleams, and people resume their activities. The dust is kept down, and the countryside comes to life in a riot of blooming flowers.

March 2009

The Days Are Dwindling Down Now

One day dawned cooler than most, so Suji, Geoff, and I decided to visit the botanical garden, El Charco del Ingenio, on the edge of town. We got an early start with a taxi ride there, during which we saw some gorgeous homes and neighborhoods we hadn't known existed. Unfortunately, many houses had "For Sale" signs, a harbinger, I believe, of the money crisis. The botanical garden, established in 1991 for the conservation of nature, especially Mexican flora, comprises 220 acres and features many outstanding species of cactus and succulents. Plants and wildlife are distributed in three zones: the dry chaparral, the canyon, and the wetlands, which include artificial islands in the reservoir. The garden is also a recreational and ceremonial space for the community. We walked the grounds, snapped photos, and looked through binoculars for several happy hours. It was just beginning to get uncomfortably warm in the open fields when we called it a day around noon. El Charco has a charming gift shop and a lovely place to eat lunch, but we had leftovers awaiting us from our meal the previous night, so we had them call us a taxi to return home.

Suji and I shopped for our final fruits and veggies. As we left our favorite *tienda* (store), she asked me if I'd noticed that the prices had been coming down during our time there. A gringo behind us overheard this and told us that that is how they do business here. He said that you should pick a shop and stick with it and that as the workers see you regularly and get to know you, the prices will come down.

On our way to dinner, we came upon the dancers for the Feast of Our Lord of the Conquest just getting started in front of the parroquia. Their marathon religious celebration is carried out annually on the first Friday in March. This Thursday night part was just a warmup to the drumming and dancing the following day. It's a celebration I totally don't understand. It represents the acceptance of Catholicism by Mexico's indigenous peoples at the hands of the Spanish invaders. "Acceptance"!? How about "coercion"? I asked my conversation leader about it. She said the indigenous people simply overlaid Catholicism on top of their own beliefs and ceremonies to create a unique amalgam.

There were hundreds of dancers from all over Mexico in plumed headdresses, brilliant costumes, body paint, and makeup. No two costumes were alike. The Indian dancers burn incense and dance nearly nonstop to loud drumbeats. The faithful recite 33 prayers—one for each year in the life of Jesus. I was mesmerized. It was difficult to take photos because they were in constant motion. Some, I noticed, got into an ecstatic state. It was truly a highlight of my trip here.

Painfully early Friday morning, the whole town was awakened by the sounds of hundreds of firecrackers. All of the guidebooks about SMA warn of this phenomenon, saying they're not gunshots and the next revolution has not begun. For any holiday—civic or religious—firecrackers are set off at dawn. Later, I beat it back up to the parroquia as soon as I heard the drums start again, and spent probably three hours just watching and photographing the Indian dancers.

As is so often the way here, one celebration is not enough. On top of all of these dancers—not to mention all those who were there to see them—a bicycle race was starting at the same exact spot. I mean, really! Talk about poor planning. These dancers do their thing only once a year on the same day. And weather is certainly no problem. Couldn't they have had the bicycle race another day? (On my ride to the airport, I asked my driver about this. He told me that Lance Armstrong had been present and that it was a very prestigious national bike race that couldn't be rescheduled.)

In the early evening, Suji, Geoff, and I went to a fascinating lecture at the biblioteca on art fraud, and then to dinner at La Posadita, a restaurant near the parroquia with a rooftop terraza, from which we could see the fireworks that signified the conclusion of the festival day.

Our final night together, we had a fabulous dinner in the restaurant of the Sierra Nevada Hotel, right across the street from El Chorro, the ancient laundry place of the women of SMA that Satomi and I had tried in vain to find so many weeks before. I vowed to return to see it in the daylight.

The next morning I packed up, and in the afternoon, when it was really quite hot, I played with Carla on my computer at the PBS Kids site. I'm sure there was a way to make it be in Spanish, but I couldn't see it quickly, so we just played lots of kids' computer games. I would see what was required, show Carla, and explain as best I could, and then she ran with it, picking up the mouse action quickly. She absolutely adored it, and the time flew by.

A week earlier, I had let Carla use my camera to take some photos, and Geoff printed out two that I had taken of her (yes, they brought a printer with them, as they were continuing to run their business from afar during their vacation!), and I gave the photos to her, along with the peso coins I had left over that I didn't want to bother taking home with me. I also gave her the box of crayons and princesa coloring book that I had bought at the Tuesday Market.

A little later, I said a teary farewell to Eleonor and thanked her profusely for her work in the house on our behalf. She told me that some of the renters do not leave her a tip—which is a requirement of the lease and is repeated in the instruction book in the house—and that some do not allow her to bring Carla over after school. I was shocked and saddened to hear this. I promised to come visit her—and hopefully Carla—next year even though I'd be renting elsewhere.

In the later afternoon, when it had cooled down a little, I went to see El Chorro and to try to see the nesting herons near there that Suji and Geoff had discovered and told me about. Sure enough, right across from El Chorro were several trees filled with the giant birds and their equally giant nests.

The same airport driver picked me up punctually the next morning, and every part of my trip home was smooth. My house in Philly was in fine shape.

Epilogue

As I write this part, I have been home in Philadelphia for a week. Re-entry was not too difficult. I worked nonstop for three days to get my tax preparation materials in order for my accountant. The weather has been quite springlike, and crocuses and Lenten rose were in bloom in my backyard upon my return. The flowering cherry trees in the neighborhood were ready to pop.

After a few days at home, I had my first post-SMA Spanish lesson with Milagros, my Peruvian ESL student. She said she could detect a big change in my speaking ability.

Three comments that I either overheard or read in and about SMA come to mind as I wrap up my experience there. When we were on the Saturday Adventure, a woman asked the homeowner a question, and she answered that she had lived in Mexico on and off for her entire life, and she still didn't have any answers. She said that there are so many mysteries in Mexico, and I found this to be true. At a totally different time and venue, I heard a man say, "You don't find San Miguel; San Miguel finds you." This also is true for me.

And finally, this from Caren Cross, the maker of the video *Lost and Found in San Miguel*, as quoted from the magazine *Inside Mexico*. Her words resonated with me. "While interviewing almost 40 expats, I was struck with how many of them said, about San Miguel, 'I felt I had come home.' This was an alarming response to hear over and over and over. The photographer and I would just look at each other in amazement. I can't say that I totally understand this but here's my theory: I think that expats come here and are no longer a part of the U.S. culture. We can give up all the pressures that are put upon us (mostly unconsciously) by that culture. Furthermore, we are not a part of the Mexican culture. In this position we are now free. We can be more true to ourselves. In this sense, we are home."

Only in San Miguel...

Because of the somewhat-treacherous cobblestoned sidewalks and streets, necessitating strict attention to where you're walking, it is said that in San Miguel, one can walk, talk, or gawk, but you can't do any two at the same time.

In that same vein, SMA is called "the City of Fallen Women," not a joke to the many who have.

"Live in a new country and you find yourself making compromises. Make them, and you are rewarded many times over."

The Caliph's House,
Tahir Shah

Chapter 2

January 2010

Rinconcito Escondido

Except for a long layover in Houston, the flights were fine, and I arrived in San Miguel on January 12 precisely on time. Last year, being a complete novice at getting here, I used a private car service recommended by my real estate agent to pick me up at the airport, which was excellent, though pricey. This year, being savvy in what I could expect and also trying to save money, I booked a shared shuttle online at a mere fraction of last year's tariff.

Happily, my landlady, Heather, lives next door to my rental, so I rang her bell at 11:30 p.m. (this was pre-arranged), and she came down to let me into my place, Rinconcito Escondido. All of the rental places here have names, some often endearing. Mine translates to "little hidden corner," *rincon* meaning corner, with *cito* one of the charming diminutives Mexicans are so fond of using. And it's well named. It's the only apartment in the building. On the first floor are two galleries (we share the front door, which is open during their business hours). You go up a long flight of stone steps to the second level, and there is an attractive, decorative wrought iron "cage" at the top so that no one without a key can enter the landing where my rental is. Then there are two locks on my apartment door, which opens into a huge studio.

In the time since I saw it last March, a second bedroom and bath were added on the floor above, which was formerly all terrace area. This new area is accessed by a flight of stairs at the back of the studio space. And just outside that new room is the terrace, now quite a bit smaller because of the new construction, but still big enough for an umbrella-topped table with four chairs, a chaise longue, a glider, a gas grill, a little fridge, a sink, a cabinet with plates and glasses, and, of course, a dazzling view of the parroquia.

The new addition was beautifully done with a high-end queen sleep-sofa and a sunken tiled bathtub. The place was decorated by Toller Cranston, one of the greatest men's figure skaters of the 20th century, and also "a painter, writer, illustrator, costume designer, choreographer, coach, TV commentator, and general bon vivant," as his website attests. An interior decorator, too, evidently. For a treat, Google "Toller Cranston San Miguel de Allende" and read about him and his home here, which is "eclectic, whimsical, creative, a bit outrageous, and totally over the top." I think that correctly describes my place, too.

I knew I would not be able to carry my big suitcase up the stairs fully packed, so, anticipating this, I had brought a number of small tote bags to carry the contents up piecemeal in many trips, with which Heather helped me. That worked fine, but then I had piles of stuff all over—and I do mean all over—the apartment. I located pajamas and my toiletries and, at 12:30 a.m., collapsed into bed; I'd been up since 5 a.m. the previous day.

A good friend, Sandy, from NYC, whom I'd met last year in SMA, lives next door, in the same building as Heather. Sandy called me around 8 a.m. and invited me over for breakfast at 9. I couldn't figure out which button to push to answer the phone, but heard her voice message. When I got there, she told me I also had a lunch date at 2 p.m. and an invitation to a short-story discussion group on Friday morning, if I was interested.

I was. After a tour of her place and breakfast, I returned home to face many technological challenges, starting with getting onto the Internet (solved by an instructional chat with English-speaking Jesús at a number left by Heather). I also learned how to answer the local phone, erase the previous tenant's voicemail greeting, record my own, and access new messages (solved by reading the phone's manual).

As if that weren't enough, I had to teach myself how to use the Vonage phone, erasing and recording voicemail greetings on that one, too. (I solved it by going online—after I had Internet access—and finding the instructions and successfully following them, since the on-site instruction manual was in Spanish and my Spanish is not that good. Heck, reading an instruction manual in English is a challenge for me.) And, finally, turning the TV on and changing channels—not as easy as it sounds—required two remotes and written instructions from Heather. Anyway, success all around. I felt quite proud of myself, as I'm frequently technologically challenged.

The lunch date was for the Wednesday Comida, a weekly lunch group from my UU congregation at a different restaurant each week. This time it was at Dragon Chino, a Chinese place. Sandy and I met up with two other women from the congregation whom I remembered from last year, and we hopped in a taxi for a ride in extremely heavy traffic. We had a bounteous and delicious lunch, equaling the Chinese food in any U.S. city.

On Thursday, Carlos, my Spanish teacher, was due to arrive at 11:15 a.m. Last year, Carlos was the tutor of a Canadian friend of mine, Alex, and came highly recommended. I had made email contact with him before I left Philadelphia, and here I was, 36 hours after my arrival, having my first lesson with him. Actually, *two* men I'd never laid eyes on before had been scheduled to show up at my apartment at approximately the same time. In addition to Carlos, Diego, a locksmith, was supposed to look at a lock I was having trouble with. Happily, Diego had called me to ask if he could come earlier, and he did.

Carlos is probably in his mid-50s and has a wife and a 20-year-old son in university. Carlos is highly educated. He shared with me that he was an industrial engineer and had worked for a large Japanese firm in Querétaro, a nearby city, for years. There he had a good salary and paid vacation. The Japanese bosses were very kind to him, but they sold the business during a financial crisis and a Spanish owner came in. Some time later, Carlos developed cancer, and he was fired. For four years, he did fine art painting, but that produced a very unstable income, so he began to offer both painting and English classes.

He then worked for many years at two Spanish-language instruction schools, Academia Hispano (AHA) and Habla Español. Now he works full time teaching Spanish to *extranjeros* (foreigners) in their homes as a private tutor. He is very good at it and obviously loves the job. He came with his whiteboard and markers, and we sat on my terrace in the sun with the umbrella raised (his request). I can't imagine that he's making the same money he did as an engineer. He told me his story after he asked me what kind of work I did, and where. When I told him that I had worked as an editor, writer, and proofreader at a Lutheran seminary, but that I wasn't Lutheran, he asked me what my religion was, and when I told him Unitarian Universalist, he lit up. He said he was raised Catholic but had abandoned it, and really resonated with UU beliefs. He said he's had many UU students over the years.

Carlos told me that although the official Mexican government policy is against discrimination based on skin color, there is rampant discrimination against *morenos* (dark-skinned people) in Mexican society, and that even in his own family, he was discriminated against. He mimed his mother saying "my angels" and patting the heads of his siblings, and then, "y Carlos," because Carlos was moreno and the others weren't. He said that those working in higher positions in banks, restaurants, hotels, etc., are almost always *blancos.* He didn't seem at all bitter, just stating the facts. I told him about that same kind of discrimination in the U.S. Then I told him about my marriage to Suresh, an Indian, and about my children and grandchildren, all morenos of varying shades. I told him I much preferred morenos to blancos any day, that I found them immensely attractive. He thanked me for saying that. It was a very intense discussion and I was proud of myself that I could have it in Spanish. He pronounced my Spanish *muy fluido* (very fluent). I was ecstatic!

He cleverly teased out my political views by using a sentence to test my knowledge of direct and indirect objects about President Bush giving money (direct object) to the poor (indirect object) (NOT!), then we had a nice political discussion about the quagmire Bush had left for Obama, and how much we both loved the new president. He told me that Mexicans were overjoyed at the election of Obama. They kept saying, "See, a moreno like us has been elected the president of the United States."

On Friday morning, I attended the weekly short-story discussion group with Sandy. It was a group of 13, including two husbands. We read "Fiesta, 1980" by Junot Díaz, a Dominican. I read the story twice, thoroughly enjoying it, and we managed to discuss it for over one and a half hours! The power went off twice during the discussion, which wouldn't have been that much of a problem, except for the space heaters, which were sorely needed, as the weather in the first half of January was dreadfully cold this year. I've re-met many of the women who were in the group around town since then. That's the way it is in SMA. If you meet someone, you're bound to see him or her again soon. The town is quite small, after all, and all the gringos are doing essentially the same things and frequenting the same places.

※ ※ ※

The next day I went to the Blessing of the Poodles, an annual event at the Oratorio church. Don't ask me why it's called that, because it's open to all the other breeds of dogs, and I saw roosters, rabbits, goats, sheep, lots of caged birds, and even a turtle.

My favorite photo from the blessing. The dog's name is Princesa.

One of the actual blessings.

On Monday, January 18, Martin Luther King Day and my daughter Suji's 40th birthday, I started the day with a Spanish lesson on the terrace while a carpenter was fixing a door and drawers inside that wouldn't close properly (sometimes it's a madhouse around my place). I showed Carlos some photos of *mi familia morena* on the laptop, and he was most grateful.

CHAPTER 2

❊ ❊ ❊

All too soon, it was time to tackle my laundry. My housekeeper, Reyna, would do it for me—she washes the sheets and towels—but I prefer to do it myself. I parked my desk swivel chair in front of the washing machine with the manual in Spanish in one hand and my Spanish dictionary in the other, to try to make sense of the 14(!) possible types of cycles. Several of the words on the machine were not in my dictionary, but I decided that a key one meant "load."

While the first load was washing, I took three Spanish-language children's books that I had bought in Philadelphia to the place I rented last year, which was just around the corner. I particularly wanted to visit with my housekeeper from that rental, Eleonor, and to ask her to give the books to her now six-year-old niece, Carla, who was a frequent visitor at my rental last year. Eleonor was very pleased by my visit but seemed taken aback by my enthusiastic hug. Probably la señora doesn't usually embrace her housekeeper. Since there were no renters yet in the house, she invited me in to chat. She told me that Carla would be there at 3 p.m. the next Monday, and that I should return if I could to give her the books myself. I hoped to read them with her then, also.

Then it was on to buy more fruits and veggies. One needs to disinfect all produce before consuming it. A variety of disinfecting products are available, but I favor Sin-Bac. I'm fortunate to have purified water coming out of the taps in this rental; I did not have that last year, and most people here don't have it. In addition to the city water, which is fine for bathing, laundry, and washing the dishes, there is a five-gallon dispenser of purified water (*garrafón*) for drinking and cooking. I scrub my teeth with the purified water from the tap, but I still use the bottled water for drinking.

I successfully did two loads and then "hung" them out to dry on the wrought iron furniture and the light fixture on the terrace. Last year, that same system worked fine for me until Suji and Geoff came to visit and we ran out of furniture drying space, so we bought a clothesline and clothespins, which I brought with me this year. Unfortunately, there was no place on my terrace to attach the clothesline, so I had to revert to my earlier method. I clipped the pieces onto the chairs so they wouldn't blow away when they got dry. I was going to open the umbrella and hang the laundry from its edges, but I had been cautioned not to allow the umbrella to stay open on the terrace in my absence, as the previous week it had taken flight and ended up in a neighbor's garden. I had my lunch and did my homework on the terrace, moving the laundry-laden chairs around to keep them in the direct sun.

Laundry drying in the sun on my terrace.

A few days later, I had my first Spanish conversation class of the year with my leader from last year, Chely. She is a native Mexican, born in SMA, who married an Argentinian from Montreal, so they spend three-quarters of the year up north and then winter in San Miguel. I was her only student as the others had not yet arrived. She complimented me on my accent, and I said that it was thanks to Milagros, my private teacher at home. We had a fun lesson. Since plumbing problems of all kinds are rampant in San Miguel, Chely taught me many words I might need to describe a problem to a plumber, such as faucet, toilet bowl, blocked pipe, etc., and also some words I might need with the housekeeper, like shower curtain, sheets, blankets, bath mat, and bedspread.

After my lesson, I took a bus to Mega, as I was in search of a hygiene product that neither my local store nor my favorite pharmacy had. I was sure Mega would have it. The bus ride was slow and incredibly bumpy, since it goes over cobblestones punctuated by speed bumps. Actually, the whole town is one big speed bump. Mega did indeed have the desired product, so I bought two. Then I looked for some nonfat plain yogurt. I had earlier given up on finding my usual soy yogurt; it simply does not exist here. Mega had so many types of yogurt that I must have spent 20 minutes reading labels and checking my dictionary. I never did find exactly what I wanted but bought something close.

On my way home, a clown got on the bus! He spoke in many funny voices and had everyone laughing except me, as I caught only three words: *payaso* (clown), "Coca-Cola," and *leche* (milk). I fantasized that he was encouraging the children to not drink Coca-Cola, but to drink only

The clown on the bus.

milk. Someone told me he was advertising the circus in town. He passed the hat and I contributed.

I attended a speak-out titled "Change to Believe In: One Year Later," a discussion of Obama's first year in office. It was timed to coincide with the devastating results of the Massachusetts senatorial vote, which brought in Republican Scott Brown to fill the seat of Ted Kennedy. It was offered by the Center for Global Justice, a fine organization here that presents what it calls the Snowbird Symposium, featuring lectures, movies, and field trips for those in town escaping frigid weather in places up north.

An upcoming trip to an *ejido*, Peñon de los Baños, was described, and I signed up to go. Ejidos were born from the agrarian reform that started in 1938 and continued until the 1980s; they were the crowning achievement of the Mexican revolution. Then-President Lázaro Cárdenas began the process of land expropriation, giving that owned by the church and the hacienda owners to the peasants who had worked on it in a collective ownership model called an ejido. Each family retained its own plot to farm, but the parcels could not be sold. Ultimately in 1992, President Carlos Salinas de Gortari changed the Mexican constitution to allow the sale of ejidos as a condition for Mexico joining NAFTA. However, many remain intact.

That afternoon, I went to a tea with entertainment at Casa de la Cuesta B&B, which was a fundraiser for Casa de los Angeles, a day-care center started in 2000. Until it opened, many single mothers from the outskirts of town who worked or sold their wares in SMA locked their children in the house and went to work, leaving, for example, a five-year-old in charge of a two-year-old. Can you imagine? Now, in its 10th-anniversary year, it serves around 100 children annually, providing them with not only safe, stimulating day care but also two meals a day and total medical care to all the family members, and it has supported 13 of the mothers as they returned to school. It has built nine houses, 11 bathrooms, one apartment building, two community centers, and a clinic. Most of the expats here are involved in one way or another with supporting charities that help the families and particularly the children of SMA in the surrounding campo. The people who own the B&B also own the Mexican Mask Museum next door, but their house was a museum as well.

Peñon de los Baños

The ejido Peñon de los Baños (Rock of the Baths), in addition to running a 500-head dairy farm, grows organic tomatoes cooperatively in greenhouses nearly year-round using drip irrigation. The name Peñon de los Baños comes from the name of a displaced ejido that was originally in Mexico City where the airport is today. In the 1950s, in preparation for building the airport, the residents of this ejido were relocated to an area just north of SMA. The displaced residents soon dispersed instead of recreating their community. Other displaced peasants from the Celaya and Salvatierra areas came to occupy the new ejido. Today, their children and grandchildren live and work there.

The Center for Global Justice has been working with a group of residents of that ejido since 2006. The residents wanted to build a greenhouse to raise tomatoes to provide jobs for their children who had emigrated to the U.S. because of a lack of work; dairy farming didn't provide enough employment for the next generation. Today, nine greenhouses produce organic tomatoes for the local market. The Center has provided loans for the purchase of the greenhouses and helps to keep the cooperative spirit alive. The all-day trip was to see both the dairy and tomato operations and to meet some of the co-op members to learn about the progress they have made, to find out whether their children had returned, and to see how they are surviving the current economic crisis. In addition, we were to be served a midday comida.

In recent years, as many as 30 people at a time have taken this trip and a bus was used. On this trip, however, there were just three of us and the leader, Bob, a bilingual gringo about my age. We went in Bob's car. The trip was scheduled to leave at 9 a.m., but I was advised to arrive at 8:30 for an orientation. I had set my alarm for the first time during this trip, for 6:30. I reached the Center's office at precisely 8:30. I rang the bell. No one answered. I hung around for 15 minutes and then another participant arrived. At 9, Bob came and we went inside the Center. The last participant arrived soon thereafter. We got on the road about 9:30. I had been told that the trip took about 20 minutes. We pulled into the ejido at 10:30. So far, everything had been on Mexican time.

As we neared the ejido, as far as the eye could see on both sides of the road was newly planted acreage in neat rows. These were the fields of a huge agribusiness owned by the brother of the current Mexican president; he is also the secretary of agriculture. Because of the depressed economic situation, this conglomerate has been buying up the land of other ejidos and, I'm sad to say, hiring the former owners to work on it, mostly as stoop laborers, bringing things full circle.

We then drove around the ejido for a while, seeing lots of cows and the nine greenhouses. We got out at one of them and met Valentín. He has two sons without documentation in Houston and two grandchildren he has never seen. His sons could come home to work on the tomato operation, but they have elected to ride out the economic downturn in the U.S. Even in the slump, they felt that their standard of living in Houston was better than in Mexico. They cannot come home to visit as there is no way for them to return to Houston legally. This situation is a great weight on the hearts and minds of Valentín and his wife. Every single other co-op member had at least one child in the U.S.

Valentín, front left, with the members of our small tour group.

Valentín explained the entire tomato enterprise to us and gave us samples of unbelievably sweet tomatoes right off the vine (which I ate without any purification drops and with no ill effects). One problem with the tomatoes was that there is no market for the entire crop—it's too large for any of the outlets that currently exist—so they've had to sell individually to various buyers. They also don't have any trucks big enough to deliver the whole crop; they have only small trucks. This is a detriment to the cooperative spirit. Also, the agribusiness sells its chemically grown tomatoes for far less, so the ejido owners have had to reduce the fair price of their organics. Their bottom line has been seriously affected. Vía Orgánica, one of the organic markets in town to which they sell their tomatoes, is a place that I had already been frequenting. When it came time for picture-taking, I was surprised to see Valentín whip out his cellphone and take pictures of us, too.

We met some other members of the cooperative and then went to Valentín's house for the comida. When the larger groups came to visit, they ate in the schoolhouse. We were served by Valentín's wife and Lupe, who I think is married to Valentín's brother. Lupe has four daughters, ranging in age from 11 to 27. In a way, she is probably luckier than the others, as it's most often the sons who go to look for work in the U.S., while the daughters stay at home. One of Lupe's daughters actually completed two years of college but had to drop out because of a lack of funds. I told them about Mujeres en Cambio; this is exactly the type of person that scholarship organization helps. They had never heard of it. The youngest daughter, Estrella, who was at the comida, is a very bright young woman, and they have high hopes that she could go to college and finish.

For the comida, we had *sopes*, thick tortillas made with coarsely ground corn, what we would call Spanish rice, and a spicy mushroom dish. When we had almost eaten our fill, Lupe arrived with *huevos* (eggs) and chiles and also stupendously delicious chiles rellenos. We all said we would have eaten more lightly of the first dishes had we known so much more was coming. Valentín and another co-op member arrived for the meal, and then we sat around and talked for two hours, with Bob translating. When I told them I lived in Philadelphia, Valentín immediately said, "Rocky!" We all felt very close to these people by the end of our visit. As a parting gift, we were each given a shopping bag full of red, ripe organic tomatoes, which I shared around on my return.

I attended a lecture by an American economist titled "Mexico: So Far from God, So Close to Wall Street." This was a play on the words of the former controversial president/dictator, Porfirio Díaz, who served from 1877 to 1880 and 1884 to 1911 and said at one point, "Poor Mexico, so far from God, so close to the United States." The talk was an eye-opening explanation of the disaster that NAFTA has been for Mexico. One of the biggest problems is that the U.S. government is subsidizing the cost of growing corn there, and thus it can be sold at dirt-cheap prices across the border. This has put many thousands of corn farmers in Mexico out of work.

Casa Woes

There is a nightclub, The Mint, right across the street from my rental that—*gracias a Dios!*—operates only on the weekends. Early Saturday morning—4 o'clock to be exact—I was awakened by a persistent bass thumping. I couldn't believe that I could hear it through triple-glazed windows and two sets of noise-abating drapes, plus earplugs. Once up, I stayed awake until I arose at 6:30 to go on the field trip. When I returned and told Heather about the early-morning disturbance, she suggested that I turn on the two floor fans in the rental, pointing them away from me as they weren't needed for cooling, and use them as white noise. Voilà! It worked! I slept through the night on Saturday.

The wrought iron drapery rods in the apartment were wavy—quite lovely, but totally impractical. I came to dread the opening and closing of these humongous drapes, hanging 10 feet or more off the floor, with a decorative metal rod with a hook on the end. Because I'm so short, I could barely reach the lead ring on the drapes with the hook, and when I pulled and the other rings moved over the waves, they would get stuck or the hooks would fall off the rings, etc. It was awful, and I complained. Actually, it was the only bad thing about this rental, but it had become a really big deal for me. *¡No hay problema!* My landlady spoke to our sainted handyman, Javier, whose brother just happens to be in the metal fabricating business. Javier measured the existing drapery rods and a week or so later he came with straight rods, installed them, and even greased them up a little, and it was like night and day!

On the Sunday after the ejido visit, I caused something of a disaster. I was leaving my apartment to deliver some of the organic tomatoes to my landlady on my way to meet Sandy for the walk to the UU service. I had to unlock a total of four locks to get from my apartment out onto the street. One of the keys had a notch on it, which had to be facing up. In my haste, I put the notch down and turned the key, and that particular lock, a sliding bolt, would not fully open nor return to the locked position. I was locked inside my apartment! Nothing I did changed the situation, so I called Heather, and again, *gracias a Dios!* she was there. We determined that there was no point in her coming over with her key, because it wouldn't fit in with mine stuck in there, so she called Javier, and he said he would come in a half hour. I then remembered to call Heather back to ask her to tell Sandy—who was waiting to meet me in the courtyard—that I would not be able to accompany her.

Javier arrived in 45 minutes and pretty quickly determined that he would have to enter my apartment by going up to the roof of the apartment complex next door, hoisting himself onto my roof from there (and he has a handicap involving one of his legs), and then coming in via the door out to my terrace. He asked me to go up and unlock that door. We were having this conversation in shouted Spanish through a heavy wooden door. He came in and had to remove all of the screws that fastened the lock to the door in order to get it off and set me free. He took the lock apart and many fragments fell out. The lock was kaput. I told him that since there were so many other locks, he could wait until the next day to replace this one. He said he'd rather do it then, as he had a lot of work the following day.

I had decided it was my responsibility to pay for his service call and also a new lock, since it had totally been my fault, so I gave him 500 pesos and went to the UU fellowship. I had particularly wanted to hear the day's sermon, as it was by a visiting UU minister with whom I had chatted at length in the jardín one day. However, I arrived as he was winding up, so I simply joined the congregation for the final hymn and the brunch afterward.

Sandy asked me to stick around after the brunch to speak with a man who was in town to teach International Dances of Peace in an after-school program in the campo, and was looking for volunteers to join him. He has done this around the world. I was intrigued by his sales pitch and decided that I would join him the following Wednesday afternoon.

When I returned home, there was a new lock installed on the door along with a key on the counter to fit it. Happily, this key cannot be put in the wrong way! This debacle cost me a total of $64 USD, plus a 100-pesos tip (under $10). This included a many-hours-long Sunday service call, a brand-new lock, plus installation, and four keys.

On Monday afternoon, I appeared at my last year's rental at the agreed-upon time to visit with Eleonor and Carla, and give Carla the Spanish children's storybooks I'd brought from Philadelphia. Carla is now in the first grade and able to read the books. They turned out to be at the precisely perfect level for her. Eleonor and Carla then gave me a present, a charming little etched-glass presentation box with a pair of earrings inside. I was so moved, and felt terrible that they had used some of their very limited resources to buy me a gift. I spent about 40 minutes with the two of them, and had a wonderful time. Carla taught me some Spanish names of animals and insects from one of the books, and I taught her the English words. I hope to visit with them another time before I leave.

One evening, I attended one of the marvelous PEN lectures. PEN stands for "Poets, Essayists, and Novelists," and the SMA group is one of 140 branches in 104 countries around the world. At the weekly PEN lecture series during the high season, authors come to talk about their books and there are sales and signings afterward. The entrance fees collected for the lectures go to aid writers around the world who are being silenced, jailed, and tortured. Currently, PEN is tracking and helping

1,000 writers. That evening's talk was by David Lida, the author of *Mexico City: Capital of the 21st Century*. He was introduced by Tony Cohan, the author of *On Mexican Time*, a book about SMA that I read last year. David has lived in Mexico City for the past 20 years and told us innumerable facts, figures, anecdotes, and vignettes about this unbelievably populous city, and also verbally sketched some of the different people living there.

One person he talked a lot about was Carlos Slim Helú, the president of Tel-Mex and the richest man in the world with a net worth of $67.8 billion USD (that's with a "b"). He makes about $8 billion to $10 billion (again, with a "b") per year, putting him ahead of Bill Gates and Warren Buffet. Interestingly, he's of Lebanese descent, and the fifth of six children. And by the way, he now owns Prodigy. His company has a virtual monopoly on all landlines and cellphones in Mexico, and is involved with almost every other type of business there. David was charming and funny, and every seat in the auditorium at the Bellas Artes was filled.

Odds and Ends

Here are some stories and stray facts I've learned along the way here. One day, the carpenter came to plane down the door to the second-floor bathroom and also to fix some drawers that wouldn't close properly. I knew about the door problem, but not the drawers. So when he arrived and said something I couldn't understand except for the word *cojones* (even if we don't know any Spanish, we all know that word!), I repeated "cojones?" incredulously and let him do his work. Then I saw what he was fixing and turned to my dictionary. The word for drawers is *cajones*, very, very close, and obviously that is what he was saying.

While checking something out for my daughter on the street where their rental is to begin in mid-February, I noted that it was totally ripped up. Actually, since then, I've seen that about half of the town is ripped up, and half of the buildings in El Centro are being scraped, patched, and repainted. Turns out that when the town was designated last year as a UNESCO World Heritage Site, lots of money came with the honor. The street dig-up is to bury all electrical lines underground, and the painting project is sure to spruce things up. 2010 is the bicentennial of the War for Independence from Spain, so this fall, thousands will be coming to town and SMA wants to show its best face. On February 1, a national holiday, there is to be no electricity in certain parts of the city, as they're going to turn off the power coming through the old overhead wires and try the power coming through the new ones underground.

Scraping and repainting walls on Calle Insurgentes in El Centro.

I was having some difficulty with the reasoning behind the use of some Spanish verbs and asked Carlos to explain them. The two verbs in question were "to be married" and "to die," and both use the verb "to be" *estar*, rather than the being verb *ser*. Spanish has two different verbs "to be." Simply put, the verb "ser" is used for permanent conditions, such as "*Soy una mujer*" (I am a woman), whereas the verb "estar" is used for temporary conditions, such as "*Estoy enferma*" (I am sick). OK, I'm fine with that, but then why when you get married do you use "estar," and even more shocking, why do you use "estar" when you die? Surely there is no more permanent condition than death. Carlos' answer showed the power of the rulings of the Catholic Church on the culture and thus the language. Years ago, before there was any possibility of divorce, one used "ser" with *casarse* (to get married), but now that divorce is permitted, one uses "estar" with casarse. I told him that using the impermanent verb seemed to me to set up the marriage for failure right from the start. Now as to death. One uses "estar" with *morir* (to die) because one is only temporarily dead, until the *juicio final* (final judgment). How's that for theology influencing language? A person *está muerto hasta el día del juicio final* (is dead until the final judgment).

Wednesday afternoon, as planned, I accompanied a group of gringos and Mexicans on an interesting volunteer outing. A man from the Children's Global Peace Project, William Day, had come to the UU fellowship the previous Sunday to tell of his volunteer work, which is teaching Dances of Universal Peace to children. One of the members of the congregation, Elsmarie, runs an after-school program called Ojalá Niños at her home in Viejo San Miguel. Viejo San Miguel? (Old San Miguel?) I thought plain old San Miguel was plenty viejo, but I was wrong; there is an even older settlement that was the original San Miguel. It was moved to its present location because of a lack of water.

Elsmarie, a recent retiree to Mexico, built a little house there for herself with a large back patio, which has a straw roof to keep the sun off—but not the rain. There is also an older building across the street. The story is that she started out about five years ago handing out pencils to the kids walking by her house on their way to school. Soon a few stopped by to visit with her after school and she did some simple art projects with them. Then they brought their friends, and pretty soon there was a full-fledged after-school program going every Wednesday. She recruited some volunteer teachers from the community and divided the group into age-appropriate "classrooms" and art projects. Elsmarie has discovered some extremely talented artists among the teenage boys, and they help out with the projects, too. The group I was traveling with was going to teach the little kids the peace dances first and then use them to teach the dances to the older kids.

I met William and more people than could fit comfortably or legally into his borrowed car, and off we went to Viejo San Miguel. We stopped at two places along the way to pick up other people and cars. Even more volunteers arrived from different directions, some from as far away as Guanajuato (an hour from SMA), so there was an excellent ratio of adults to children. We met Elsmarie and saw her house and back patio set up for that afternoon's art projects: stained glass for the older kids and making simple puppets for the younger group. William taught the adults the dances, accompanied by singing and drumming, and then we got the littlest kids into a shady place to do the dances together.

The kids posed themselves against this truck.
You see that they all have name tags. Some kind gringo
came to Elsmarie's a while ago, took their photos, and made up the name tags.

When the older kids came across the street to join us, they were less enthralled with the dancing. I saw some rolling of eyes, and I wouldn't say it was a total success. Afterward, bowls of cut oranges and cookies were passed around to all. Elsmarie was to host a "raise the roof" party to put a real roof on her back patio so that it can continue to be used for the children's projects even in bad weather.

That evening I attended a State of the Union potluck dinner party at Sandy's. We ate, then tuned into Obama's speech, the Republican response, and lots of commentary. I stumbled home, exhausted, at 10:45.

The next day was the 15th anniversary party of Mujeres en Cambio, which puts on monthly fundraising events in order to fund scholarships, this time a luncheon at a gorgeous small hotel, Hacienda de las Flores, a steep walk up from the jardín. The owner of this hotel, Alicia, donates her small dining room, staff, and some of the food for these events several times a year. At each luncheon, wherever they may be held, a visiting chef from a local restaurant prepares the entree, and members of the organization bring salads and desserts. The chef this month provided the antipasto and chicken tetrazzini. Dessert was a coffee-flavored *tres leches* (three milks) cake. I have never tasted anything quite so good.

Because it was the 15th anniversary, they treated it like a *quinceañera* celebration (15th birthday party, a huge deal for Mexican girls, sort of a combination of a debutante party and a Sweet 16 party). One of the organization's members told us all about the tradition of the quinceañera, the costs involved (staggering!), the planning, the execution, etc. Three of the girls in the Mujeres en Cambio program are celebrating their 15th birthdays this year and we saw photos of them. At the conclusion of the meal, the hat was passed, and enough was raised from those in attendance to pay for one year of high school and one year of college for two girls in the program. This in addition to what was raised by ticket sales.

Sandy and I and two other people bolted at the end of the meal for the biblioteca, where we watched—breathlessly—the 1946 movie *Great*

Expectations, starring an extremely young Alec Guinness and an equally youthful Jean Simmons, who had recently died. Seeing this movie was in preparation for the next PEN lecture, by Austin Briggs, called "The Joys of Dickens: Reading *Great Expectations.*"

One night soon after I had returned to SMA, I had dinner at the Santa Ana Café at the biblioteca, and there was a bit of a misunderstanding between the waiter and me when I ordered my dinner. I had been waiting for nine months to sink my teeth into my favorite Mexican dish. I ordered *enchiladas verdes con pollo* (chicken enchiladas with green salsa), or thought I did anyhow, and when the plate came, I saw that it was *ensalada verde con pollo* (green salad with chicken). My face dropped and I told him that it was not my meal. He confirmed that it was, and I figured that I had been misunderstood and that I'd eat what was brought to me. But the waiter, sensing my deep disappointment, took the wrong meal back and replaced it with my long-awaited enchiladas.

Guanajuato

Last year, except for a weekend trip to experience the monarch butterflies, I didn't venture far from SMA, although there are a great number of fascinating places nearby suitable for day trips. I was determined to get to many of them this year. With that in mind, earlier in the week, I had signed up for an all-day trip to Guanajuato, Dolores Hidalgo, and Atotonilco to benefit Casa Hogar Santa Julia, a home for abused girls, which UUFSMA also supports. When I arrived at 9 a.m., I was the only participant. Another gringo had signed up, but there was no sign of him. I suggested that the trip be canceled, but the young Mexican guide would not hear of it. So I got into a Suburban with him and headed out of town, realizing only when we were underway that I had forgotten to tell anyone where I was going. Not a single person in the world knew.

The guide's name was Dalí Amaro. Naturally I asked him about his first name. His father was an elementary school principal who dabbled in painting and appreciated Salvador Dalí's work so much that he named his son after the artist, giving him no other names, which is highly unusual in Mexico. Dalí has at least four jobs. He leads these tours, is an artist working in clay, and makes candles. He also owns a clothing store, which is where I met him to go on the tour. He was the concierge at the Hotel Sierra Nevada for three years, and hoped soon to be its official tour guide.

Dalí at the mirador. And the view!

I can't say enough about how great the day was. First of all, Dalí drove beautifully, which is not something I can say about some other Mexican drivers. I was not afraid a single moment—thank God, since I was sitting up front with him. He is a graduate in tourism of the University of Guanajuato, and does he know his stuff! It took us about an hour to get to Guanajuato, and we spoke in Spanish the entire way! He spoke slowly and in a manner that I could understand. First we went to a mirador to overlook Guanajuato, then into the town, where he drove me through some of the famous tunnels. Afterward we parked in an indoor lot where I used the cleanest restroom you can imagine. We toured Teatro Juarez and the Diego Rivera home. Dalí had so many tidbits to share with me; for example, Rivera was a twin, and his twin died very early on. When Rivera asked his parents why his twin had died and he had not, they said it was God's will. Rivera couldn't accept that, and that was the seed of his atheism, which was the seed of his Communism.

Guanajuato is the capital city of the state of Guanajuato, and is renowned as a mining town. At one time, about half the silver in the world was mined in this city. There is a gigantic statue of El Pípila, a miner from SMA and hero of the struggle for Mexican independence whose real name was Juan José de los Reyes Martinez Amaro. The sculpture shows him holding high the torch with which he set fire to the *portal* (large, elaborate entrance) of the Alhóndiga de Granaditas (grain storehouse), thus making possible the taking of it by the insurgents.

The top floor of Diego Rivera's house has many of his early paintings and sketches in preparation for his later works that we know and recognize. You would never believe that it was Rivera who did the early work; it's nothing like his later art. We saw Dalí's university and several churches, toured the Don Quijote Museum (pretty fabulous), and walked around the streets, which had a European flavor. There is a Cervantes Festival, Cervantino, every October in Guanajuato, the largest in Latin America. The story of why there is a Don Quijote museum and Cervantes festival is so fascinating, and Dalí knew all about it. It involves Jews imprisoned in a concentration camp in France during WWII, believe it or not!

We did not see the famous mummies of local people, preserved by the peculiar mineral composition of the region's soil, which have been on display since 1870, but I bought a guidebook at the mirador that shows them. I loved the city. We went into an upscale restaurant for comida. The prices were cheaper than in SMA, which is really saying something!

I treated Dalí to lunch because I felt so bad that he was doing this whole thing and spending money on gas and parking, etc.—and giving a donation to Casa Hogar Santa Julia—with only one client. During the meal, he worked his cellphone, while I watched a street entertainer out of the window.

Then we went to Dolores Hidalgo. Since I wasn't interested in looking at or buying any of the famous Talavera pottery there (although he offered), I just had an ice cream cone after taking some photos. Dolores Hidalgo is famous for its wacko ice cream flavors. There is even a contest each year to see which vendor can come up with a new and strange flavor. They'd have to go some to beat the ones being offered that day: chicharrón (fried pigskin—probably the most "out there" flavor I saw), *cerveza* (beer), *aguacate* (avocado), tequila, and *beso de ángel* ("kiss of an angel"). I never found out what that last flavor consisted of.

The most famous church there, on the steps of which the battle for independence from Spain actually began, had a wedding going on

The very famous steps in Dolores Hidalgo, where El Grito *(the shout), the first call for independence from Spain, was made. You can see the decorations for the wedding in the doorway.*

inside. At the church in Atotonilco, where we went next, there was also a wedding, so I couldn't view it either. Last year I had gone to see that 250-plus-year-old church, but all of the good stuff to see inside was shrouded in scaffolding and drapes, as it, too, had been named a UNESCO World Heritage Site and had received money for much-needed repairs. It didn't matter, as I was exhausted by then, anyway.

February 2010

The Deluge

My day in Guanajuato was the last decent day before The Deluge. It began to rain late Sunday afternoon and continued, torrentially, often accompanied by lightning and thunder, until Friday. I would be awakened in the middle of the night by the pounding of the rain, and every morning when I opened my eyes and heard that it was still pouring, I didn't even want to get out of bed. It was difficult to keep my spirits up. Ankle-deep water ran in the streets, and it was dangerous to go out. In the neighboring state, Michoacán, 39 people died, and sewers backed up. No one died in SMA and the sewers didn't back up, but everyone's house leaked. I had a small amount of water come in around the skylight over the steps going to the second floor, but it caused me no problems; others told of water dripping right onto their beds and loss of electricity and/or water. Every house was cold and we all had a major case of cabin fever.

During the storm, the water pouring out of the *canales* (channels that drain water from the open terraces on the roofs of all the houses) would hit the road or the sidewalk directly or would hit parked cars and then spray out onto the sidewalk. Let me tell you, it was a real trick to walk during the rain, what with two people with umbrellas trying to navigate the narrow sidewalks, water pouring down from the canales, and then the addition of the horizontal spray. And rushing water when you tried to cross the streets. A true circus. I'm able to laugh now, but it was grim.

The worst part for SMA, though, was the almost total wash-out of Candelaria, held annually in Parque Juarez for the first 10 days of February. The vendors sleep right in the park in tents near their displays or in their trucks. Everyone in SMA, from hotels to restaurants to homeowners, buys all of their spring plants at this festival. Very little of it could take place. Some vendors pulled up stakes and went home. I felt so very bad for them. This rainstorm made a desperate economic situation here even worse.

Since it was raining on my regular laundry day, I was forced to use the dryer, which is stacked on top of the washer inside a cabinet. Picture this: I am standing on a stepstool in front of the stacked appliances, with a flashlight (to see the dials, which are, of course, high up, way in the back, and in the darkness of the surrounding cabinet, not to mention that they're in Spanish), the manual for the dryer, also in Spanish, and a Spanish dictionary. I had success, and I view this as an adventure, but I wonder if, over the long haul, these sorts of things would begin to get old and then finally be relegated to a pain in the butt?

The truly bizarre thing about this rainstorm is that it usually NEVER rains a single drop in SMA in the winter. When I arrived here in mid-January, I came in on the last five days of two hideous weeks of cold that included lots of wind and rain. Less than three weeks later came this latest storm. And, according to *weather.com*, starting soon there is to be rain again for many days. I didn't bring an umbrella, as usually one is not needed during the time I'm here. Happily, my landlady had one for me to use. Carlos, my Spanish tutor, said that not in his lifetime had there been rain like this. I think it can be said that Mexico's years-long drought is officially over.

CHAPTER 2

❁ ❁ ❁

I attended another of the PEN lectures. (This was easy, as the Bellas Artes is practically right across the street from my rental.) "The Joys of Dickens: Reading *Great Expectations*" was the lecture for which I had seen the movie the previous week. Austin Briggs, the lecturer, was a Joyce scholar and taught for 50 years at Hamilton College after doing postdoc work. He is a resident of SMA, and he gave a fascinating talk, then took some 30 minutes of questions.

I joined a sizable portion of the lecture's audience for dinner at Vivoli, an Italian restaurant across the street from Bellas Artes, including some of Sandy's friends who have taken me under their collective wing. Vivoli was a popular destination because of its proximity to the lecture in the pouring rain, and also because many SMA restaurants are not open on Tuesdays and Vivoli is. I had a scrumptious mushroom risotto and the delicious house merlot. Sandy didn't join us because her Korean guests, two women who had been ESL students of hers 10 years ago and with whom she's remained close, were arriving from Mexico City.

While at dinner, I was telling some of my tablemates about my friendship with Eleonor and Carla. One of the women, Viv, questioned me more closely about them, and it turns out that we shared Eleonor last year! Since this couple are in the same rental this year, they still have Eleonor as their housekeeper. What a small world! Viv also likes Eleonor very much, and also had brought a gift for Carla.

After so many days of rain, I had to get out of the house, and so I waded and hopped through deep water to get to the UU Wednesday Comida at the Parroquia restaurant. Most of the restaurant was unusable because its main dining room is a central patio open to the sky, but I could see a small covered dining room in the back, where a Mexican waitress was standing in the doorway. I asked her, in Spanish, about the group from the UU meeting there at 2 p.m. She told me it had been canceled because of the weather. I was so upset, and I trooped back home very dejectedly and ate lunch alone there. I had already read about as much as I could stand by that time, and wound up watching the last half of *Tootsie* on the TV. Later in the day, Sandy called to tell me that she'd taken her two Korean visitors to the UU lunch. When I told her of my experience, she was incredulous. She said they were all in that dining room behind the waitress. It was up a few steps, so I wasn't able to see into it while I was speaking to her. Sigh.

Wednesday night, I went out for dinner in the rain to Hecho en México (taking a cab there, something I'd ordinarily never do!), and after a chicken fajitas dinner, walked the short distance to St. Paul's for the Playreaders' staging of a hysterical comedy about later-age dating called *Looking* by Norm Foster, a prolific Canadian playwright. During the intros, the director expressed her thrill at seeing almost a full house given the weather. Are you kidding? I was thrilled to get out and be with people, particularly given my disappointing experience at the UU lunch earlier! That play and all of us laughing together riotously did raise my spirits.

I had the most delightful happy accident one night. Last year, I had been in a Spanish class with Andrew and Janet from Canada, although Janet dropped out, so it was only Andrew and I and the teacher for four weeks. We all really got on well and I visited the couple at their rental twice and we went out for dinner together a few times. I knew they were in the process of buying a place here in SMA. I had emailed them last August to see how things were progressing, but emails to both their addresses were returned, undeliverable. I figured I'd lost them forever, but I'd been keeping an eye out for them since I'd been here. Turns out they went to last year's rental agent, as they used the same one I did, and inquired of me. They remembered my last name as Kringle, which I found pretty funny—it does have a Santa connection. As you might expect, the agency had no record of me with that name.

That night, I went to La Posadita, and after about five minutes, Janet came up to my table and shrieked, "I told Andrew that was you!" It was her birthday and they invited me to join their table. We had a wonderful time catching up. We exchanged contact info and they promised to invite me out to their new place. They had just moved—in the deluge—so they were going to settle in a little first. They'd been renting here and going back and forth to Canada to sell their house, etc., since last spring.

When, sometime later, the dinner invitation to their new home arrived, I followed their careful instructions and waited for the Ruta 7 bus for 20 minutes in the rain, and finally gave up and hailed a cab. Cabs are amazingly cheap and are fixed-price, although certainly more than the 5-pesos bus fare.

Sometimes the cabbies do not know the location of your desired destination. That was the case on this trip, as it turned out. And rarely will a driver stop to ask for directions. But my driver did stop to ask at a couple of tiendas when he thought we were close. When we finally pulled up at their door, it was no wonder that my driver didn't know the address, as it was a new unpaved dead-end street only one block long, and their house was at the very end!

The asking itself was something of a miracle, as frequently taxi drivers have refused my suggestion that they ask for directions. I chalk it up to machismo. Sometimes, when they can't find the address, they get angry with me! One, after driving around hopelessly for quite a while, even asked me to get out, but I refused. We did eventually find the house, but it was not a good experience.

And often when *taxistas* do ask people on the street, they frequently haven't a clue. They have no idea what street they're walking on, let alone where another street is, and sometimes if they don't know—being Mexican, loath to disappoint, a holdover from the Conquest, I believe—they make something up and send you off on a wild-goose chase. It certainly doesn't help that many streets outside of Centro have no street signs. Occasionally, neighborhood residents take matters into their own hands and paint the name of their street on the wall of a building at the corner.

Learning the Subjunctive

I now do Spanish four mornings a week: two private lessons in my rental with Carlos, and two conversation classes with—now that they've arrived—two other folks, plus Chely, our leader. Before I left Philly, Milagros, my teacher there, had started teaching me the subjunctive, and Carlos, after doing a thorough review of common problem areas, swung into teaching me that dreaded subject matter. It required a shift in my thinking. To Mexicans, he told me, nothing is sure, and thus a simple statement that we'd make in English, such as "I'll see you tomorrow," would use the subjunctive in Spanish, as there is certainly no guarantee that I will see you tomorrow. I understand everything he taught me—in theory—and I can do the homework without a problem, but actually remembering to switch to the subjunctive in conversation is totally beyond me at this point. And that's only the present subjunctive; there are five more tenses in the subjunctive!

Later on Sunday, which finally dawned dry, I went to Candelaria. I didn't know what to expect after the deluge, but the place was jumping. I had heard that, because it had been rained out for so many days, it was going to be extended, perhaps by as much as two weeks. It was as magnificent as I had remembered from last year, and after wandering around to look at the many gorgeous flowers until I was properly exhausted, I headed to the center of the park, where a marimba band was playing for public dancing and I could sit down to watch and enjoy. Everyone was having such a fine time being outdoors after the rain.

*This is one of my favorite photos. (Turn to the back cover to see it in color!)
If only that car weren't there...*

In addition to plant vendors, others were selling things like pottery, paintings, fresh-squeezed juices, water ice, cotton candy, and, of course, kitsch. And more pots for sale! I always hope they sell a lot of them, so they don't have to schlep them back out and home again.

※ ※ ※

The next weekend, I went on yet another Saturday Adventure. First we went to Jennifer Haas' El Jaguar Museum, a private home/museum where she has a world-class collection of folk art, mostly Mexican, but other countries were represented, too. There were costumes and masks worn in ceremonial dances, pre-Columbian instruments, and a drum made from a skin stretched over a carved jaguar.

Our second stop, next door, was perhaps the most unusual place

I've ever been in my life. Someone described it as Gaudí meets Dr. Seuss. I'd add Alice in Wonderland and the old woman in the shoe. At the front gate of this private residence, built by a gringo architect for himself, was a gaggle of large, friendly but skinny dogs and several gigantic concrete reptiles whose bodies snaked back through the garden. There were other brilliantly colored reptiles, all made of concrete. The house was equally unique and colorful. As the ad for the trip said, "This is the place to wander in wonder." I could not live in that house; it was entirely too weird.

Later that day, I attended a Pro Música offering at St. Paul's Episcopal Church, this time a program of love songs in honor of Valentine's Day, which was the following day. That holiday is celebrated a little differently in Mexico. It is called El Día del Amor y la Amistad (The Day of Love and Friendship), and it celebrates not only romantic love but also a close relationship between amigos. Not every person has a partner, but everybody has friends. I really like this idea. Featured at the concert were up-and-coming tenor Rodrigo Garciarroyo and his piano accompanist, tutor, coach, and friend, Mario Alberto Hernandez. As a younger man, the tenor had been awarded the Plácido Domingo Scholarship to study in the young artist program in Mexico City, among many other awards. One of his teachers was Sherrill Milnes.

Garciarroyo has sung in operas in New York City and sang the Verdi *Requiem* as his debut at Lincoln Center, at Alice Tully Hall. The brochure describes his "Pavarotti-like style, huge stage presence, film star looks, and mesmerizing voice." That may all be true, but he did two things that further endeared him to me. First, when he sang one piece, he failed to hit a high note, and everyone winced. We applauded politely. He then declared that he would do it again, and he hit a home run. The place went wild. Then, near the end of the program, he announced that he would sing a love song to his wife, who was in about the third row. He looked directly at her the whole time he sang. Afterward, while the audience exploded in applause, they kissed each other quite passionately. I don't think there was a dry eye in the house.

Busy, Busy, Busy!

Heather, my landlady, told me that I should register with the U.S. consul in case of illness, accident, need to be evacuated, etc., so bright and early on Monday morning, I appeared at the consulate agency, quite near my rental. How could I have forgotten so quickly that Monday, February 15, was Presidents Day in the U.S., and thus the consulate was closed? So I trudged home, returning at 9 a.m. the next day, when the office ostensibly opened for the day. There must have been 20 people in line, about half Mexicans and half gringos. At 9:45, the man next to me had had it, whipped out his cellphone, called the emergency number listed on the door, and got the consul, Ed, directly. He asked him when the office would be opening, and was told that Ed would be there in 15 minutes. Yeah, right. I packed it in yet again. On Thursday morning—cold, raining—I tried again, and finally at 9:30, the secretary inside opened the door. I found out from her that I could do the whole thing online—in fact I must do the whole thing online—and she gave me the web address. I'll bet that they close the doors at 1 p.m. sharp, the official closing time, regardless of how late they open. They have pretty chintzy hours, only Monday through Thursday, and from 9 a.m. to 1 p.m., if you believe the sign on the door!

After my Spanish lesson, laundry, and lunch, I took a bus to Mega. It would have been faster to walk, although I seemed to be the only passenger who was hot under the collar about the delay. The bus was following a detour off a main street, and it took ages for every vehicle, including a very old, long trailer, which, in my opinion, had no business on the streets of SMA, to make the turn. While I was in Mega, which has a metal roof, it started to hail. The lights were flashing on and off. I thought the end times were nigh! I have never heard such a noise in my life. It lasted probably less than a minute, but I was really scared. Again, I seemed to be the only one glancing nervously at the roof.

One night, Sandy's downstairs neighbors, Dick and Lee, invited us both at 8 p.m. to meet the man with whom Dick has been trading language practice. When we walked into the apartment, we were introduced to an extraordinarily handsome man in a suit and tie, something you rarely see here. I immediately asked Guillermo what he did for a living that required this attire. Turns out he's the branch manager of Bancomer in SMA. He's been here for only a few months. His wife and two children are still at their home in Aguascalientes, where he returns on weekends. He said they were committed to this commuting lifestyle for one year. At that time, they would all move to SMA, unless he is posted elsewhere, which he said is a very good possibility. He is trying to improve his English to advance his career in the bank.

Over tea and cookies, we talked in two languages, laughed, taught each other idioms, and argued over words until I said at 10:30 that I really had to get home to bed. I think Guillermo might have wanted the session to end earlier but was too polite to be the first to leave. I was so enlivened by this exchange that I couldn't get to sleep for a long time.

※ ※ ※

My rental must be on a common route to a cemetery, because I have seen and heard many funerals go by. The latest one was bigger than the others. Probably 100 people walked extremely slowly in very close order, almost shuffling along to the strains of a haunting musical accompaniment played by what sounded like a New Orleans jazz band. I could see a tuba among the gathering. In the front, an old hearse with a badly cracked windshield (guess there's no car inspection here) carried the casket, and behind the mourners, a truck inched along carrying flowers.

In mid-February my sister Julia, from Taos, New Mexico, arrived for her first visit to SMA, but not to Mexico. The plan is for Julia to stay with me for a week and then transfer to a sort of combination B&B and retreat center. My Nova Scotia friend Karen, whom I met at UUFSMA last year, also came into SMA about that same time.

My daughter, Suji, and son-in-law, Geoff, arrived several hours later. They were supposed to have arrived a few days earlier, but when Suji got out her passport as part of her packing, she discovered that it had expired in January. She immediately went online and found that it is indeed possible to get a passport renewal in one day, so they would have been all right, but Monday was that federal holiday, remember? So she spent the next six hours on the phone and sending emails, changing their flight and shuttle pickup date and time, and contacting the manager of their rental, making an appointment online with the Philadelphia passport agency for Wednesday, etc. In spite of having this appointment, she appeared on Tuesday at 8 a.m. so as to be the first in line for the 9 a.m. opening of the agency. She was prepared to beg and plead. It went very well for her, and several hours later, she had her new passport. She called friends of theirs who were coming to SMA later in the week, to tell them of her misadventure, and so they were prompted to look at their passports. Theirs had also expired in January! Since their flight wasn't until Friday, they had several days to sort it out.

We all had a raucous dinner together at a place I visit regularly called El Tomato, and met an artist who lives in Mt. Airy, our former neighborhood in Philadelphia.

On Friday, Julia and I hiked up to the hotel hosting the annual SMA Writers' Conference to hear the keynote address by author Barbara Kingsolver. All 800 seats in the auditorium were filled. Barbara's talk was inspiring, informative, funny, and interesting.

The following day, all of us went on the Saturday Adventure. Our first stop was at Casa de las Ranas (House of the Frogs), where Anado McLaughlin and his partner—both very large men about my age with huge white beards (they look like twin Santa Clauses)—live and have a studio. There, they create art pieces using a staggering number of empty wine bottles in unbelievable ways, plus about a trillion other found objects, to create what the *New York Times* described as "… divinely elevated kitsch."

After that tour, we moved on to the home of Robin and Beto Díaz, owners of the popular SMA restaurant El Pegaso. Their son, Aáron Díaz, is a breathtakingly handsome and sexy Mexican soap opera star, and photos of him, including a life-size cardboard cutout, dominated the place. The home of the restaurateurs is quite lovely and not at all over the top in the way of some places I've seen here. On the property is their own private ancient chapel. They also have something I've not seen or heard

Anado with his likeness in mosaic above.

of anywhere else in SMA—a pond stocked with tilapia and koi. They continuously recycle the water, pumping it around and down a small waterfall. Aáron had it dug and stocked recently for his parents as a gift.

MARCH 2010

EVERY SATURDAY IS A NEW ADVENTURE

Sister Julia and I taking a snack break.

The weather is definitely warming up. I now wear sleeveless shirts and 3/4 pants exclusively during the day and a spring nightgown for sleeping, although a light blanket is still required. One avoids the direct sun midday by always walking on the shady side of the street, and it's no longer necessary to tote a jacket for the evening. In the shade, it's still a little cool and a light shawl or wrap may be needed. There is zero humidity and no mosquitoes. I love it!

If it's Saturday, that means another Adventure, and Karen and I took a long ride with the group out to the elegant El Rancho Ojo de Agua (Eye of Water Ranch). This working ranch, where they breed, raise, and train Andalusian horses, is owned by a Mexico City family that comes here only on weekends and holidays. As we neared the spread, I saw a helipad. A helipad! That told me everything I needed to know. We toured the main house. No family member was in residence, even though it was the weekend; however, a staff of housekeepers and grooms held down the fort. We walked to the paddocks and to the pool house, where we were served soft drinks and cookies, as is customary on all of the Saturday Adventures. The pool chairs showed the family's crest, which we noticed again in the horses' brands, on flower pots, and on the grooms' T-shirts. We had ample opportunity to see the crests when one groom put a horse through its paces for us as we sat in shaded bleachers. The family also raises bulls, which we didn't see, and has its own private bullring, complete with the family crest. And all of the mares are pregnant!

As has become traditional after the Saturday Adventure, Karen and I went to La Palapa—"the fish taco place," as I call it, since I only recently learned that it even had a name. This place seems to me what Jimmy Buffett had in mind when he sang "Margaritaville." It's nothing but a shack, really, shaded with a barely thatched roof, and the best meal for me is the steamed fish or shrimp tacos with killer carrot cake, its only dessert offering.

That evening was a dinner for 11 of us (whom Suji dubbed "FOC," Friends of Cynthia) to say farewell to some of our number. The month of February had run out and many gringos were heading home. We had a lovely, delicious, fun meal at La Posadita, one of my favorite restaurants, which has a remarkable view from its terrace, particularly at sunset. We bid a sad goodbye to Alex and Cheryl, and to Carol and Yoram and their son, Todd, and met a new friend of theirs, Gary, who had just arrived. Suji, Geoff, Julia, Karen, and I rounded out the party.

A few days later, a picture-perfect day, although most of them now fall into that category, Julia, Suji, and I had a ladies day out at La Gruta, one of the several hot springs here. We swam from the main pool into a hotter grotto. Hardly any people were there, but those we saw were *muy amable* (very friendly). We finished off several hours of soaking with lunch in La Gruta's restaurant.

Julia left for home, and I attended a truly extraordinary lecture on "Aging in SMA," given by a geriatrician whose name I forgot to note, who is in SMA doing research on the aging patterns of estadounidenses living abroad. He started out with some eye-opening statistics: The fastest-growing cohort in the U.S. is the over-90 population! Over 50,000 centenarians are living in the U.S. One-third of hospitalizations in the U.S. among the elderly are prescription-related. Taking an elderly friend or relative for a walk is the best way to gauge his/her general health as you observe speed, distance, gait, and how out of breath the person becomes and how quickly.

He joked that people go to Florida to die but that they come to SMA to live. The intensity of creativity in SMA, he said, helps to impede the aging process. He said he felt that many doctors of the aged act more like cheerleaders for the oldsters to keep going rather than helping them to accept the inevitability of aging. In the most glowing terms, he spoke of Cielito Lindo, an independent and assisted living facility here, and said that the good human hands-on care one receives there is often of more benefit than the care found in some of the high-tech, youth-oriented societies in the U.S. He called the age span of 55 to 80 "the recreational stage," and the years following those "the fourth age," which he defined as more self-reflective, and which is the last gift we give to our children as we show them how to age gracefully and how to die.

Around this time, I received word from my son, Ajay, that he and his family would not be coming to Philly for Christmas 2010. They had purchased a new condo in Helsinki, and need the money—and, even more, the time they would have spent traveling—to renovate their new place. While the thought of not seeing my grandchildren is not a happy one, and the thought of Christmas in Philly without them plunged me into a funk, I quickly recovered when I realized that I could come to SMA six weeks earlier than planned! Meanwhile, Suji and Geoff saw a house here on Calle Animas that they want to rent for a month next winter, and told me I should run over to see it, as it would be perfect for me for December. (I had re-upped from mid-January through March at my current rental, but it was already rented for December.) Well, I fell for the house, too, and immediately signed up. I got the contract for my current rental rewritten to have it start on 1/1/11 and terminate 4/1/11.

I went out with a friend, Brenda, for dinner at Planta Baja. I was prevented from getting to the restaurant, however—I could see Brenda across the street—by a short religious parade. Because I was going only one block from my rental, and wanted to lighten my backpack, I hadn't taken my camera. So here were the participants in the parade: It began with firecrackers all around my neighborhood for about a half hour before, then there were tiny girls dressed in angel costumes with fluffy wings strewing flower petals on the street from baskets they carried, followed by a group of musicians that looked a lot like a military band. Close on their heels came older women holding high on their shoulders a statue of the Virgin sitting on a platform. Next were about a dozen of the indigenous dancers like those in the Feast of Our Lord of the Conquest last year. Right behind them was a sizable group of all ages carrying pink and blue balloons and tiny pastel tissue paper flags with something written on them. I recognized the priest from the Blessing of the Animals ceremony! Bringing up the rear was a Dixieland-style band playing the same haunting tune as I'd heard for some funerals. Wow! When I was finally able to cross the street, Brenda said that sometimes here in Mexico she felt as if she lived in an alternate universe. She was madly scribbling notes, as she'd left her camera at home, too. When I asked Carlos about the parade the next day, he said that he didn't know what it was for and that sometimes the Mexicans themselves don't know what the parades are about.

Saturday morning, I appeared bright and early at the Instituto Allende with about 20 other people for a day trip. Our first stop was Bernál, in the nearby state of Querétaro, where the third-largest natural monolith in the world (after Gibraltar and Sugarloaf in Rio de Janeiro) is located. It's made of granite and called Peña Bernál. It's not volcanic, but rather it is the result of the movement of tectonic plates 65 million years ago. César, our fascinating guide, with whom we traveled to see the monarch butterflies last year, told the Mexican creation story, that of the gods at Teotihuacán and how they tried five times to create the world and had to destroy it the first four times because of the misbehavior of the creatures created. (This is where the belief among some comes that 2012 will be a judgment year for the humans created on the fifth try. This date appears in both the Aztec and Mayan legends.) On the fourth try, according to the legend, giants were created but then became petrified as punishment. The belief is that the monolith in Bernál is part of one of these giants, and thus sacred. Huge bones were found in the area, which led credence to this belief, but of course we now know that they are dinosaur bones.

San Miguel is at 6,500 feet; Bernál is 900 feet above that, and the top of the monolith is 1,000 feet higher than the city of Bernál. The monolith is believed to be an area of high energy, and during the spring solstice, huge numbers of people flock there for ceremonies. Interestingly, a very high percentage of the city's population lives to be over 100 years old. Also, mountain climbers from all over the world come to Bernál to practice, particularly those preparing to climb the Himalayas. It is possible to hike up about two-thirds of the way without equipment. In the 1500s, Bernál was on the Camino Real, and a bright blue cross was placed at the summit of the monolith. Each year, in May, the cross is brought down and there is a huge fiesta.

In 1647 the first building was erected in Bernál, but it's been repurposed big-time. The area around this building is now a small traffic-free pedestrian walkway, with all types of interesting shops, many selling semiprecious stones such as opals, which are mined locally. Bernál is a major sheep-producing area, also, and thus there are many weavers and magnificent woven items for sale. SMA is considered by other Mexicans to be really expensive (of course, the gringos think it's dirt cheap), but Bernál had prices about one-third of those of SMA.

Then it was on to the much-larger capital city of Querétaro (which translates as "the place where people play ball"). Since the devastating earthquake in Mexico City in 1985, many people and industries have moved to Querétaro, and it has grown exponentially. Querétaro is the

A man in traditional garb, but with a cellphone clipped to his waistband.

place where the Spaniards started to evangelize the indigenous people. It was their training center, and from there, priests were sent to the north of Mexico and into the southern U.S. as far up as Santa Fe.

One of the biggest attractions in Querétaro is the aqueduct, built in 1726-36. Before the building of the aqueduct, there was *agua pesada*, "heavy water," that is, filled with minerals, and many people became ill and had to abandon the city.

An example of the creative weavings that are made in addition to the more standard rugs, shawls, blankets, sweaters, vests, pillow covers, etc.

The town leaders called upon an old aqueduct engineer from Mexico City, and there is a charming story about the fact that he accepted no money for his services, but instead asked to meet "the pretty nun," a very attractive young nun who had been given by her family at the age of three(!) to the convent to be raised, according to the tradition of the time that the first-born boy became a soldier, and the first-born girl, a nun. In this extremely strict order, the nuns were never allowed to see any people in the outside world. They were allowed to see (but not speak to) their families only once a year through a small grilled window. However, this young girl would crack open the door to the church during Masses to gaze upon the faithful, and thus people caught a glimpse of her and named her "the pretty nun." Because the engineer was going to save the town, the order relaxed the rules a bit and allowed him to meet her. The engineer asked the nun to marry him. She said she would when the aqueduct was completed.

Dogs were used to locate underground water in the nearby mountains. There are a total of 74 arches in the aqueduct, stretching more than a mile. Gravity brings the water down from the mountains through clay pipes. When the water was again good to drink, the people returned to the city. And at that time, the engineer returned to the convent to collect his bride. However, the nun insisted that the engineer build them a beautiful house first. During this process he died, and the pretty nun stayed true to her religious vows. The house that was built for them, the House of the Marquesa (as he was a marquis), is now a luxury hotel. It's an endearing story and, according to César, a true one.

We also visited the Cementerio de los Hombres Ilustres, the Cemetery of Illustrious Men. César told us the incredible story that when one of the three big names in the War for Mexican Independence from Spain—Doña Josefa Ortiz de Dominguez—died, her daughter tried to get her

This girl is not a bride, but a quinceañera with her escorts.

mother buried there, but it was for hombres only. After much pressure, the town fathers agreed, but with one caveat. They erected a statue of Doña Josefa at the entrance to the cementerio—with a mustache!

Then it was on to the Hill of the Bells, where stands a stunningly tall statue of Benito Juarez, along with the Chapel of Archduke Maximilian at the exact place where he was executed. Juarez, born of Mesoamerican parents, who was a national hero and president of Mexico (1861-72), fought against foreign occupation under the Emperor Maximilian, and sought constitutional reforms to create a democratic federal republic. This park is a mecca for brides and quinceañeras wanting a beautiful backdrop for their keepsake photos.

Our final stop on the trip was in the downtown area of the city, where we had about 45 minutes to wander around. It was late afternoon on a Saturday, and mobbed. Many costumed people were strolling about, advertising a play being staged that evening: readings by impersonators of famous people in the struggle for independence, as part of the bicentennial celebration. We had margaritas served on board the bus (can you imagine?) and returned to SMA about 11 hours after we'd started, tired but happy.

Suji told me the next morning that she and Geoff had gone to the restaurant San Augustín, called Chocolate y Churros by the locals, quite late on Saturday night and were the only gringos in the place. The owner, Margarita, a former soap opera star, made an appearance. She stopped to schmooze at each table and have her photo taken with the guests. Churros are a pastry made by extruding a very thick batter into hot fat (somewhat like a funnel cake) and then rolling them in sugar before serving them hot with spicy hot chocolate—a delightful combo on a chilly night.

It's All New to Me from This Point On

Since I left SMA mid-March last year, everything that takes place from here on in is all new to me. The first thing I experienced was allergies. I have never had any allergies to plant material in Philadelphia, but in San Miguel, OMG. My friend Satomi, the Japanese woman I met here last year at our Spanish language school, arrived for a week's visit on Sunday. By Tuesday, we both were laid low by allergies. We sneezed repeatedly and blew our noses nonstop. Eyes itched. Throats were sore. We were told that because of the deluge in January, the blossoms were particularly lush this year, thus creating more than the usual amount of pollen, particularly the jacaranda trees, which come into vivid purple bloom around this time. A pharmacist suggested a saline spray and it actually worked!

Teaching English at Ojalá Niños

Monday brought my first day teaching English to the kids at Elsmarie's after-school program, Ojalá Niños, in only the second class of this type ever taught there. I walked to a designated corner in my neighborhood to meet a fellow teacher, Amy. We hopped a bus for the Bodega Aurrera (Walmart by a different name), where we were met by yet another teacher, Marilyn, who came on a different bus, and Elsmarie in her car. Elsmarie drove us all to her house and we set up on her patio for the first class, at 3 p.m. In came about eight students ages 10 to 12. After a quick warm-up, we had a review of the first lesson, "What's Your Name?" and "My name is _____." We then launched into the day's lesson, numbers from 1 to 15 (we weren't sure how old the kids were going to be), and "How old are you?" and "I am _____ years old." We split into small groups and helped them to fill out worksheets, which they were invited to take home to show their parents and to aid them with practicing the language. With the three of us, it went pretty well.

At 3:45, we dismissed those kids and geared up for the second class at 4 p.m. There were only six students, and we repeated the lesson exactly as the first time. As I was working with individual kids, I asked how many brothers and sisters they had. No one had fewer than three, and others, many more. At the conclusion of the second class, I was on a total high, but by the time we retraced our route by car and bus and foot back home, I was utterly exhausted. Suji and Geoff came over and they, Satomi, and I had wine and cheese on my terrace. A bit later, we had a farewell-to-SMA dinner at the Hotel Sierra Nevada, as they were departing for home the next morning after their month's stay.

I went to yoga for the first time at Bellas Artes, the former convent near my rental. I loved the class, even though it was very large and much more crowded than I like. Alejandro, the teacher, provides mats, straps, blocks, and blankets. The space is amazing: cool, with a hugely high *boveda* ceiling (a technique where bricks are built up over the walls of a room to form a vaulted ceiling that is self-supporting –*Wikipedia*), and lovely wood floors and *barres* all around, as it's also used for dance classes. And then there's the soothing sound of cooing *palomas* (pigeons). I pictured nuns in that space for centuries before I showed up on the scene.

I am in awe of the many things that Alejandro can do at once. The class is overwhelmingly made up of gringos, but there are some Mexicans, and so he calls out the instructions for getting into the *asanas* (poses) in both English and Spanish, and sometimes even calls the poses by their original Sanskrit names. While facing us, he demonstrates the poses in a mirror image of what we're to do, and he is constantly scanning the room for people who need a little adjustment or correction. He can call each student by name. And he is keeping an eye on the clock!

On Thursday, I met with Marilyn to plan our lesson for the following Monday. Amy and her husband had gone to the beach, so we viejas were on our own. Marilyn is an older woman from the Bronx with an attitude and nary a word of Spanish. We decided to do parts of the body with the kids, concentrating this week on the head.

On the first day of spring, early in the morning, there was the annual parade of the youngest children, dressed as birds, bunnies, butterflies, beetles, etc., all things reminiscent of spring. The costumes—not to mention the hairstyles and makeup on the girls—were incredibly elaborate. They marched up the street to a church in their school groups, accompanied by many proud parents. Each school was identified by banner carriers or by trucks that preceded the groups. This is such a feel-good event! Everyone is smiling. Beautiful children in charming costumes parading on a magnificent day to welcome spring. What more could one ask?

I was happy to see some of the special-needs children totally in the swing of things.

Friday also brought the opening of the first-ever SMA Environmental Fair at Parque Juarez. All of the money raised will go toward care of the environment in local public parks and gardens. There's a project now underway to partially light Parque Juarez via solar power. It is being proposed to City Council that this lighting program be implemented throughout the city, at a cost of 18 million to 20 million pesos. The savings in electric bills will pay off this amount in time. If there's ever a place to harness solar energy, SMA is it.

Another Saturday, another Adventure. I was so excited to read in *Atención* that the trip was going to the home of Mayer Schacter, a well-known and accomplished ceramicist, now the owner, with his wife, Susan

Page, a highly successful writer of relationship books and the director of the SMA Writers' Conference, of a world-class museum (their home) of Mexican folk art, plus a gallery next door. Mayer is the representative for dozens of the artists. He posts a photo of each artist next to his/her work, which adds a personal touch. I had been wanting to go to this treasure in Atotonilco. Well, the joke was on me, as the moment the bus pulled up to the home, I realized I had been there last year on a Saturday Adventure but hadn't known where I was. I was not nearly as "with it" last year as I am this time. Anyway, I didn't mind going again, as their house, built on the site of a former rattan furniture factory, is beyond fabulous, as are the crafts. This eight-acre property was remarkable for all of the water on it. They have a pool, a meandering aqueduct leading from it, a lake, and a river. Because of this, everything was quite lush, a real treat to the senses here in the desert.

This was my favorite of the items for sale.

Unfortunately, no one bought anything, which made us all feel bad, but our hosts were undeterred. We moved on to their home, which is filled with some of the best crafts in the world, and not only from Mexico. They have about six rescue dogs that were lolling everywhere, so you did have to watch where you were walking (but then that's nothing new in SMA). They also had some rescue burros.

Darkness and Light

Sunday at UUFSMA was a contrast in darkness and light. Here's the light part: Instead of a morning message, we had Bill Day and Tajali from the Children's Global Peace Network to teach the congregation the Dances of Universal Peace that I had done twice earlier with the kids out at Ojalá Niños. As a surprise, Elsmarie brought 15 or so of the kids from Ojalá, ages about two through 12, to share the dances with us. They had forgotten cameras—and I don't know how they would have taken photos anyhow, as they were very busy with the teaching and the dancing—so Sandy, knowing that I always travel with my camera, asked me to document the morning. It's a good thing I had that assigned task, because I was reduced to tears seeing these tiny kids teaching us gringos viejos the dances of peace.

A sweet pairing for one of the dances.

The kids voted unanimously for us to start with an African dance that required Tajali to call in all of the tribes in her amazing voice. The windows were open, and I suspect that the people in the hotel's swimming pool below could not figure out what they were hearing from above! We listened to and watched how to do one of the dances. We had both guitar and drum accompaniment, a big plus. And then we danced! And danced!

While all of this wonderful activity was taking place, darkness also reigned at UUFSMA. The service ended at the completion of the dances, and two women immediately discovered that they had been robbed of their wallets. None of the niños could be blamed because they were all busy dancing—and captured on film.

We had had a collection as part of the service, so the thief was easily able to see where various people kept their money in their purses, which were left on seats as we danced. Not all danced; some watched. And one took the opportunity to steal. One woman whose purse had been stolen, Ruth, had been sitting next to Sandy, who insisted that the police be called. The hotel resisted, as it looked bad for it. But the police were called. Janice, the other woman who was robbed, did not stick around for the police. The police asked Ruth and Sandy to go to the state police headquarters on Monday to make a statement, as the local police do not have that under their jurisdiction.

Janice, meanwhile, did her own detective work. She immediately called her credit card company, which told her that 900 pesos had been charged at an OXXO gas station on the outskirts of town not long after the theft. After canceling her card, Janice, knowing the exact place and the amount, went to that OXXO, and saw the receipt. The clerks identified the purchaser as a small, dark, young Mexican woman who bought cigarettes with the card. Janice posted all this on the Civil List.

When Sandy and Ruth arrived at the state police headquarters

Monday morning, the police had evidently read the Civil List postings, because they knew all about what Janice had discovered. Sandy's recounting of her two hours at state police HQ sounds like something out of a Fellini movie. They were told when they arrived that it would be 30 to 40 minutes until a translator was free. Sandy said that was not acceptable, and within 10 minutes, one was found. Sandy said he was the largest man she'd seen in her life; he must have weighed in at about 400 pounds, but was sweet and gentle. He took the two ladies into a small office where there were a Mexican lawyer, wearing a face mask for health reasons, and a typist. The lawyer would ask a question in Spanish, the translator would do his job, and Sandy and Ruth would answer. Then the translator would translate the answer into Spanish, and the typist would record it. Can you imagine this scene? Then the translator said he had to read back their entire statement (four 8½-by-14 pages) so that they could agree that it was accurate and sign it. Finally the translator said that they needed two witnesses to the crime. Sandy said that no one witnessed the crime; if anyone had, they would have stopped it! But still, two witnesses were needed, to verify Ruth's identity and the veracity of what she and Sandy had reported. Ruth found another woman from the congregation, and they all returned another day. Meanwhile, Janice never made an official police report, depending, instead, on her postings on the Civil List. What a weird experience all around!

The next afternoon, I met Marilyn so she could show me where to wait for the bus to Bodega Aurrera, our pickup point for getting to Ojalá Niños. It's a good idea here to always inquire of the driver if he's going to your destination, regardless of what's posted on the bus window. Marilyn asked our driver three separate times (although in very bad Spanish) if he was headed to Bodega Aurrera, and he said yes every time. When we had gone about two blocks, the bus turned, and Marilyn said it wasn't the right bus. Thank goodness I was with her, because I would not have known. We immediately got off. The driver would not refund my five-peso fare, and I didn't make a fuss. Marilyn lucked out, as she was still digging in her purse for hers. We walked to the next stop and caught the right bus. Wendy, the co-chair of the board of Ojalá, and Elsmarie were waiting for us.

Because work had begun on the patio space behind Elsmarie's house, where the lessons usually take place, we had to move into the house. Many more students showed up at 3 p.m. than we'd had the week before, and many weren't even on the roll. We decided to carry on, but there were way too many students and a few too many rowdy boys, and we two oldsters were a bit overwhelmed. The 4 p.m. class went much better. This was Marilyn's final class, as she was returning to New York. She handed over all of the ESL materials to me. Amy, a much younger teacher, was away at the beach, so I am on my own for next week as to planning, getting materials copied, etc. I will call for backup, though, in the actual teaching.

Things are really starting to wind down here now. Many friends have returned home. I had my final Spanish conversation class with Chely, and she said that next year, she'd prefer to do an *intercambio*, with us speaking Spanish for an hour, and then English, with no money exchanged. I like that idea.

I went to an extremely helpful lecture/slideshow with handouts on "Negotiating Semana Santa." Semana Santa, Holy Week, the week between Palm Sunday and Easter, is huge in the state of Guanajuato, and particularly in San Miguel. Since it's not such a big deal in other parts of Mexico, throngs of people come to SMA to participate. It's celebrated very differently here than in the United States. The lecturer, Charlotte Bell, is the author of a book on Semana Santa in SMA called *Tears from the Crown of Thorns*. The handouts included a day-by-day plan as to what time which ceremony was taking place at which church. Then there was a map of all of the participating churches (10 of them!), and all of the procession routes. It's invaluable, as are her hints on how early to go, or where to stand for the best views or to be in the shade, etc. This lecture took place at an old hall I'd not been to before, called El Sindicato. It was formerly a union hall for the workers at La Fábrica de la Aurora, a textile mill a short distance outside of Centro. El Sindicato is now used as a cultural center.

 Charlotte explained that when the Catholic priests first started to evangelize the illiterate indigenous peoples, they frequently used plays to illustrate Bible stories, and that some of them would be re-enacted as part of Semana Santa. She further told us that Mexicans believe that pain and suffering promote spiritual awakening, and that the feeling of "It's my fate" is rampant, thus there is an acceptance of their lot in life. She explained some of the symbolism we'd see throughout the week.

On Saturday, I went on the last of the Adventures for me for the season. First, we went to a *fábrica* (factory) where the workers make *papel-maché* fruits, puppets, rattles, napkin holders, appetizer picks, and a host of other fun, brightly colored items. Three women were at work when we arrived, and one of them gave a demonstration of making a rattle in the shape of an animal's head, while our leader narrated in English. The process is extremely labor-intensive, and I was surprised to learn that all materials are natural. They do this because they ship their creations all over the world, and with all-natural materials, there is no problem in meeting or not meeting some country or other's rules. The workers are paid on a piece-rate basis. The operation is not an assembly line, à la Henry Ford. Each worker does all of the steps from start to finish to make a particular item. We learned that the objects inside that create the rattling noises are tiny pebbles that ants bring to the surface when they build a colony.

The worker is showing an animal's head that has just come out of a mold.

After the visit to the papel-maché factory, we headed out of town to Puerto de Sosa, a 16th-century ex-hacienda that is owned by an SMA family that also has a home in Mexico City. They were not in residence, but their staff made us feel welcome and even prepared cheese quesadillas with a choice of three salsas for a light lunch. What I loved about this place was that they had made minimal changes to the original structures. Our guide told us that some of the old haciendas are so tricked out inside by their modern owners that they have lost all sense of original design. These owners, on the other hand, live quite simply here, and their decorations are tasteful and perfect for the spaces.

There was a granary on the property with a boveda ceiling, built by the Otomí Indians for the original Spanish hacienda owner. As I mentioned earlier, every hacienda has its own chapel, and this one is no exception. The magnificent grounds included a lagoon, lots of flowers, and my favorite, pampas grasses, waving in the breeze.

We had been encouraged by UUFSMA to turn off all lights for an hour on Saturday night at 8:30, in recognition of Earth Hour, standing in solidarity with others around the world at this same time in our desire to work on environmental concerns, including climate change. Was I ever surprised when at 8:30 sharp (right away that's a surprise!), almost all the lights in the jardín and at the parroquia were shut off. At first I didn't know what was going on, but others reminded me of Earth Hour. It was a little tricky to see, and I decided to stay at the performance of the troubadour-style singing group La Tuna (the fruit of the cactus) until the lights came back on, which they did after only a half hour. I was touched by this gesture on the part of the SMA government.

April 2010

The Days Dwindle Down to a Precious Few...

Monday afternoon took me back to Ojalá Niños by the same tortuous route, and I was thrilled to see that a young Spanish-speaking friend of Elsmarie's was in the car that came to pick me up and that she was ready to help me teach, if needed. Because it was Semana Santa and the kids had off from school all week, perhaps they thought there was no English class, because there were only eight or so for the 3 p.m. class, which was actually a relief for me. Not wanting to repeat the claustrophobic experience of the previous week, we set up on a shaded patio just outside the front door. Between Elizabeth and me, we had a good class. We taught more parts of the body, helped them fill out worksheets, and then did faster and faster renditions of the song "Head, shoulders, knees and toes, knees and toes…" We reviewed numbers (and they know them cold, but still have trouble pronouncing 12), then asked them what words or phrases they would like to know. They were writing like mad in their new notebooks.

On the Saturday before Easter, a day when no Semana Santa activities took place until the evening, I went on a trip to Victoria and Pozos with the Instituto Allende. I was the first to sign up, and was told that the trip would be canceled unless at least six people wanted to go. When I arrived at the Instituto at 7:45 a.m., there was only one other couple, so we three plus three staff (I guess there is a certain logic that says that's six)—the guide, César, with whom I'd gone on a number of other trips both this year and last; the van driver; and a "shepherd," probably not needed for such a small flock. The brochure warned of "several species of succulents whose nip can be unpleasant," and recommended jeans and shoes with a good tread. When I got dressed to go, I put on my jeans and immediately took them off again as I knew they would be way too hot later in the day. (I cannot fathom how the Mexican men wear jeans here year-round, but they do. You can see Mexican workers even in Philadelphia in the hot and humid summer wearing jeans.) I substituted a much lighter weight pair of long pants and wore sneakers. The other woman was not dressed appropriately at all, including 3/4-length pants and open shoes.

On our not-too-long ride, we passed several signs that declared "Jesús por Presidente." I got a really big laugh out of that but soon concluded that a man other than the biblical Jesus was running for president, and indeed, later signs proved it was Jesús Rivera. César told us that the contest was really for mayor of the little town we were passing through, that the Mexicans use "presidente" not only for the president of the country, but for mayor, also.

We drove to a natural shamanistic center (used as such for centuries, and now because of the petroglyphs and what they might teach, and also because of the energy at this particular spot) seemingly in the middle of nowhere, where we climbed to three levels to observe the rock art. The climb and viewing areas were not for the faint of heart. The man of the couple, somewhat older and not in the best of health, quickly bowed out. It was nearly midday and the sun was fiercely hot. We crouched to keep our centers of gravity low, sometimes got from place to place on our behinds, and wriggled through a very tight spot, but as they say here, *vale la pena* (it's worth the effort). The 360-degree views from the top were well worth the tortuous climb and the sweat.

The petroglyph on the lowest level is thought to be from about 1200 A.D. Another is probably from the 1500s, and shows men with guns. The Spaniards had arrived!

We took a different and easier route down, but it involved going through someone's yard. A fiercely barking dog and a snorting pig greeted us. César tipped a boy a few pesos to call off the dog and allow us to

*It's a good thing someone was at home,
as that dog was not letting us enter its territory.*

walk through his property. The boy told César, when asked, that he is one of eight brothers and sisters, and that his mother is only 30 years old!

From that climb, we went into the pueblo of Pozos. Usually, César told us, it's pretty much of a ghost town, but because it was the Saturday of Semana Santa, it was rocking. There were lots of tourists, way too much traffic on roads never meant to handle cars, and many booths set up to sell all manner of foods and trinkets. We had a spectacularly delicious lunch at a restaurant called Los Famosos de Pozos, owned by a couple of extranjeros. The couple also have an art gallery in town, featuring the very fine paintings by one of them.

We gringos sat at a table for four and the Instituto staff at another. Since my tablemates did not speak a word of Spanish, I became the interpreter for the table to the waitress. After the meal, César came over, saying he had overheard my Spanish and was quite impressed. He asked all kinds of questions about how long/where/with whom I'd been studying. He praised my accent, and I about died of happiness. It's nice to know that two years of hard work and lots of time and money have paid off handsomely.

After lunch, we walked to a tiny store that had a back room. We were treated to a concert of three original songs by two couples (two brothers who have married two sisters), all of whom are composers, on instruments of the indigenous peoples, such as turtle shells played with deer antlers and a three-foot dried squash.

César told us that Pozos is in about the same condition SMA was 50 to 60 years ago. A renaissance has started. There are currently 56 expats with properties in Pozos, including several B&Bs, one of which César said is the nicest he's ever seen anywhere. We then walked around the city, including visiting the church, since it was Semana Santa.

Then it was on to the now-closed but formerly extremely active and prosperous metals mine at Santa Brigida. On the way there, we had to stop to let a herd of goats—and the goatherd—cross the street in front of us. The road into the mine was dangerous, with a drop-off on one side and no guardrail. I didn't dare to look in that direction the whole time we were driving on that road.

A narrow wind tunnel had been constructed to increase the force of the fire built to extract metals from dirt brought up from the mine. At one end was a flue open to the sky, and the intense winds in this area howled through the tunnel, feeding the fire raised on a grate at the opposite end. Mules would carry bags of soil to the grate to be exposed to the extremely hot fire. This mine was producing immense amounts of precious metals in the 15th, 16th, and 17th centuries. The indigenous people, who were treated like slaves by the Spaniards, lived with their families right on the grounds so that production could continue around the clock.

It is a must to walk around this property with a guide, as there are open mine shafts all over the place. We were also warned about a swarm of killer bees in one area. Talk about an adventure!

In the distance, you see Los Tres Picos, the three giant hearths built by the Jesuits in 1597. They are possibly the oldest on the continent. Their height is 60 feet, so large that they are a puzzle. They were capable of handling 50 tons of ore per day, whereas the usual capacity for a 16th-century hearth was 5 to 10 tons. The ore production included gold, silver, copper, lead, and mercury. César told us that the working life of a miner at that time was only about two years. They went blind from working totally in the dark, and they got mercury poisoning.

I was scheduled to go to two Semana Santa activities on Saturday night, but I was too exhausted by my 10-hour trip, the sun, and the climb. Plus, I'm a bit procession-ed out. I remembered to put the clocks ahead for daylight saving time (always on the first Sunday of April in SMA; the border towns stick with the American timetable) before I fell into bed at 9:15.

The final Semana Santa activity, called "Blow Up Judas!" took place at noon on Easter Sunday. (You'll have to read my final posting about Semana Santa in Chapter 3 to learn about this quirky custom.)

Los Tres Picos.

The next morning, I had my last Spanish lesson, and it was very difficult to say goodbye to Carlos. We have become great friends and have shared a lot. Then I took some books and things to the biblioteca for its weekly book sale and to the Bodega de Sorpresas, a sort of garage sale of donated items of every stripe (but mostly clothing), and bought some apples and granola bars for my trip home. My regular produce guy was effusive in his good wishes for my safe trip, rapid return, etc.

That afternoon, on my way to meet my ride out to teach my last two classes at Ojalá Niños, I stopped at my rental from last year, as I knew Eleonor would be working that day. As a marked contrast to our meeting three months earlier, she held out her hands to me and responded with tears to mine when I told her I was leaving the next day. She told me that Carla had complained that she didn't get to see me this year except for our brief gift exchange when I first arrived.

Eight students showed up for the English class that day. It was the second week of vacation from their regular school for spring break. On the other side of Elsmarie's wall was a flock of sheep, which sometimes made so much noise that we could hardly hear each other. And the odor was a little ripe, but actually I didn't mind it so much.

The previous weekend, a whole bunch of gringos, including me, attended the regular Saturday night performance of La Tuna for the last time. They appear under the portal across from the jardín every Saturday about 8:45 p.m. Pablo, the sort-of-MC, sort-of-worker-of-the-crowd (in Yiddish, a *tummler*, as Sandy explained to me), is gifted, and brings much joy to everyone, myself included.

As we tearfully said goodbye, one of the musicians said in perfect English, "Come back. We'll be waiting here for you." And so will all of SMA. It has been a rare and wonderful gift to have lived here for four months, shared in the culture, spoken the language, made friends with many people, both Mexicans and expats, eaten spectacular food, gotten sick only twice, and minimally at that, had adventures every day, and learned a great deal about myself. I cannot believe my good fortune, and I am filled with gratitude.

One of the joys of returning to SMA this year has been to see how different my experience of the place is this time compared to a year ago. I no longer need to carry and refer to a map constantly. I know the location of almost everything I need, although I continue to learn about and discover new places daily. And I recognize faces of both Mexicans and extranjeros: the owner of my favorite ice cream cart, waiters/waitresses in restaurants I frequent often, the produce store man, the checker at Bonanza, people I've gone on tours with or seen at my UU fellowship. When I walk out of my door, I no longer feel as if I live in a foreign country; nothing feels strange anymore. I feel now that it is home.

I have promised myself a couple of things for next year: yoga at least two mornings a week, hopefully three; fresh flowers in the house always, as it is so inexpensive here to be surrounded by beauty; attendance at some of the workshops at the Writers' Conference; and a return to the short-story discussion group.

Pablo is shakin' his bootie here, for sure.

Only in San Miguel

A representative Mexican story, this is how things sometimes work (or not) here: I had finished all of the books I had brought with me and then some, and needed something to read on the flight home. I bought probably the only Anita Shreve book I hadn't yet read from a bookstore on Calle Hidalgo that gives credit for used books. I finished the book in one day, and took it back Saturday night, but it was closed. You have to walk through the bookstore to get to a restaurant behind it, so it didn't look closed. And a patron at the restaurant looked like the woman I had bought the book from, so I started telling her that I wanted to return it for credit and get another one. Well, the chef rushed out from the back and explained that this was not the salesperson, although he admitted they did look similar, and said I should take the book I wanted, come back on Sunday and tell them what I had done and pay then, but I shouldn't tell them that he suggested that. I decided not to do that but to return on Sunday.

When I returned, I asked for credit from the same salesperson I had purchased from originally, and she said I couldn't get credit for books I had bought there, only for books I brought from home. ¿*Que?* OK, so I said, "Forget that I told you I bought this book here. I brought it from home and I'd like to have credit for it," so she writes it all up in duplicate and says, "Can you come back tomorrow, because the owner has to give you the credit and he's not here today." At that point, I said I'd donate the book to the biblioteca for its weekly sale, and I bought another book.

"Devotion runs deep and true." – *Atención*

Chapter 3

March 26 – April 4, 2010

Semana Santa

Semana Santa, Holy Week, is the time between Palm Sunday and Easter. It is celebrated decidedly differently in San Miguel than in the U.S. "Week" doesn't really encompass the activities that take place as a preamble to Semana Santa. The first event, two Sundays before Easter, was one in which I didn't participate as a spectator due to the early hour: the ceremonial moving of the statue *Nuestro Señor de la Columna* (Our Lord of the Column). This statue—a beaten and bleeding Jesus, bearing a scar representing Judas' kiss, and with some ribs exposed—is tied to a column (or "resting his arms on a column" or "his body bent over a column," depending on the source material), and is credited with miraculous powers. It's kept in a glass case at the Shrine of Jesus the Nazarene in Atotonilco, about seven miles from SMA.

"This tradition dates from 1823 when, according to the chronicles, a plague infested the Village of San Miguel el Grande, and the Christ was brought out in hope of a miracle," *Atención* tells me. Since that time, the statue is taken down from its place of honor on the fifth Sunday in Lent, wrapped in hundreds of silk scarves and then in canvas to protect it, and carried on foot from Atotonilco to SMA. Two other statues, that of a sorrowful Virgin and the apostle St. John (San Juan), accompany it. The story of this miracle is enshrouded in mystery. The existence of the plague in 1823 in this area and this story are not backed by hard evidence, and at least two other conflicting stories exist as to why the statue makes the journey annually on this date.

The silent procession starts at midnight Sunday, lit only by torches and lanterns. At about the midpoint in the journey, 3 a.m. Monday, at *La Cruz del Perdón* (the Cross of the Pardon), a stop is made for a Mass. While this journey is taking place, in SMA the residents of Avenida Independencia decorate their street with *alfombras*, carpets made from colored sawdust. Chamomile and fennel are also strewn on the ground, palm leaf arches are constructed and decorated with multicolored flowers, and white and purple balloons and *papel picado* (cut paper) are strung everywhere. Fireworks are shot off in SMA around 5 on Monday morning to let the people know that the *santo* is coming. At 6 a.m., the pilgrimage arrives at Avenida Independencia, and there the statues are uncovered while praises, chants, and prayers are said. *Cojetes* (firecrackers) are set off. After a religious ceremony, the procession continues straight to its final goal, the church of San Juan de Dios, where another Mass is performed for a huge crowd of the faithful.

On *el Viernes Santo* (Good Friday), the statues are returned to Atotonilco in another procession, which I also didn't watch because of the press of attending two other, larger ones that day. It's a busy time! When I took the trip with the Instituto Allende to Victoria and Pozos, of which I wrote in Chapter 2, our guide, César, told me that he and his wife had made the journey on foot all night from Atotonilco with the statue. I was mightily impressed!

The activities began for me on the Friday before Palm Sunday, March 26, with *Viernes Dolores*, Friday of Our Lady of Sorrows. This is the one night a year to visit altars erected around town in private homes, in storefronts, and in many public fountains to focus on the sadness of Mary at the death of her son, Jesus. By the next day, they are all totally dismantled.

Some common elements in all of the displays were bitter oranges, to mark Mary's grief; chamomile, which imbued the whole city with a delightful scent; little tubs of wheat grass signifying resurrection; small gold pennant flags (the implication of which even Carlos, my Spanish teacher, didn't have a clue); candles; figures of Mary herself contemplating Jesus on the cross (these statues are frequently hundreds of years old); and fruit waters, to also signify her tears.

Those fruit waters are often in the form of *paletas* (similar to Popsicle ice pops), and some families even bring small coolers to hold all of the paletas they collect from the many altar sites. When I laughingly told Carlos of this, he admitted that his family had done the same thing, and that his son got to enjoy paletas for about a week after the event!

In the late afternoon, I spent a contented hour or so watching the assemblage of a huge altar in front of the San Rafael church, which is adjacent to the parroquia. It seems that designated families take over the construction of these altars.

A large sheet of plastic was placed at the bottom of the decorated stairs, huge bags of colored sawdust were emptied out, and the sculpting began in earnest. With the brisk wind, I was afraid it would blow around, but it didn't.

I believe that this is the heart of Mary with the crown of thorns superimposed on it.

I liked this man's quiet moment of contemplation and assessment after completing the altar.

And in true Mexican style, one huge activity at a time in a space is not enough. Adjacent to the area being used for creating the altars, and in the midst of throngs of people in town for the week, a *telenovela* (soap opera) was being filmed. Perhaps Semana Santa was included in the story, as the actress posed directly in front of the parroquia with all of its purple draping.

Later that evening, I began my trek to visit as many altars as I could. Happily, my attendance at the lecture on "Negotiating Semana Santa" had furnished me with the route for best viewing. However, cars were not stopped on this route, and on the poorly lit streets, with crowds of people and traffic, I found it quite stressful to see my way safely.

The next big event, and the one that ultimately had the most impact on me, was *Domingo de Ramas*, Palm Sunday. You'll remember that when the Spanish priests were evangelizing the illiterate indigenous people of Mexico, they often used plays to illustrate Bible stories. The re-enactment of this day of Jesus entering Jerusalem, to be met by palm-carrying devotees, is one of those plays. I walked to the top of steep Calle San Francisco, on my way to the Calvario church, one of over 20 in town!

I particularly liked this altar, which I watched come into being on Calle Insurgentes, one of the busiest streets in the city. With the image behind the sheet and because of the wind, the cross took on various ghostly appearances.

Visiting palm weavers await customers.

This tiny church is rarely used but is the starting point for the Palm Sunday procession.

On my way up to the church, I walked through the public space between the parroquia and the jardín, and saw the most amazing display of woven palms. Specialists in palm weaving come to SMA from the neighboring state of Michoacán just to sell their wares on this one day.

The route of the procession would go down Calle San Francisco and take a right to the Oratorio church.

This couple struck me as true believers.

I really liked Jesus' face as he schmoozed with the crowd, as he might have done in Jerusalem.

The crowd patiently waited for Jesus to appear, and then there he was on his burro. He looked as I think Jesus might have looked: dark-skinned (what's with portrayals of Jesus as white, anyway?), bearded, small, with rough white garments for a desert setting. An interview with him had been printed in *Atencíon*, and he spoke of growing out his beard and hair, of the deep honor that it was for him to do this re-enactment, and of what he would be thinking as he rode down the street.

These women were waiting to throw rose petals down in front of those carrying the statue.

As the procession began, Jesus turned pensive. The faithful followed along, carrying their palms, as did I. I couldn't stay for whatever happened next because I had to rush to get to the next procession! It was sort of a repeat of what I had just seen, except it came from Parque Juarez and its destination was the parroquia, plus it wasn't a Jesus portrayer this time, but rather believers carrying a statue of Jesus on a donkey. The street on which this procession traveled, Calle Sollano, was fabulously and brilliantly decorated with garlands of greens and flowers hooping over the street. I was enchanted.

This time it all began with altar boys and incense. What appeared to be members of various societies, wearing ribbons with medals around their necks, came next, carrying elaborate palms, followed by drummers. Finally, the statue of Jesus on his donkey appeared in the background. Periodically during this entire time, firecrackers were being set off all around us. I have an extremely low startle reflex, so I was constantly jumping and flinching, and I seemed to be the only one doing so. Some kids even laughed at my reaction to the noise.

Boys will be boys!

The girls were demure and serious.

When the statue of Jesus reached the parroquia, the bells pealed loudly for a long time.

I don't think I've ever taken so many photos as fast as I did during this procession. This had been quite a morning and it was just noon. And there was a full week of Semana Santa events yet to go.

At 5 p.m. on Wednesday, I went to the Oratorio church (where I had witnessed the Blessing of the Animals very early in my stay) to watch the beginning of the procession of *Las Cruzes del Señor Golpe* (the Crosses of the Whipped Jesus). It was such fun to see the kids dressing in costumes for the procession, with anxious mothers buzzing about them, adjusting this and that to perfection. The boys were hamming it up for the photographers and being, well, boys, while the girls seemed more restrained (nothing out of the ordinary in that scenario!).

Very authentic-looking Roman soldiers.

First out of the church, in full regalia, were the Roman soldiers.

Then the acolytes. And then the statues began to pour out, held on the shoulders of those, I was told, who are the cream of

Perhaps a dozen men bore this huge statue of Jesus carrying his own cross.

Many of the women wore very high heels for this hours-long procession, walking on cobblestones. I think the heels are just part of their dress-up "uniform."

Limpia camaraderie.

the crop of religious SMA society, as this is a distinct honor. Some of these statues also are centuries old.

Before the procession began, a priest came out and announced that there were insufficient bearers (and I understood what he said!) so that anyone who wanted to could help. Those who volunteered were assigned to fill in with lesser statues.

What was amusing to me was that the *limpia* (cleanup) crew marched directly behind the procession, sweeping up all of the chamomile that had been thrown in front of the marchers, and other debris. I've never before seen such rapid cleanup after an event.

In addition to the weight of the statue and the tough walking conditions, harsh light was a problem, as it was late in the day and the sun was very low in the sky. Interestingly, very few Mexicans wear sunglasses (or regular glasses, either). The cost of glasses may be out of reach.

These darlings were distributing chamomile on the statues' route.

I walked all along the procession route, which went up a street that led to the parroquia and then down another street to return to the Oratorio church.

The priest would stop now and then to say something to the assembled masses along the route, so that everyone would get to hear his message, causing the entire procession to grind to a halt.

On Thursday, Maundy Thursday to gringo Christians, was the re-enactment of the Last Supper in all of the churches. The first one was at 2 p.m., and then there were successive ones every hour or so at different locations. I went to a couple of the churches, and all of the pews were moved to the sides to accommodate the crowds coming through. The re-enactment was not done by people, but by figures in tableaux. Altars inside the churches were decorated with the now-familiar symbols of chamomile, bitter oranges, and candles, and the faithful prayed. I was told that this is the time when the priests did foot-washing, to emulate Jesus doing it, but I didn't see any of that.

And outside the Oratorio church, a series of street restaurants sprang up, virtually before my eyes, to tempt the many worshippers coming through. From my observation, most Mexican tourists in SMA seem to consume an inordinate number of street snacks. For the most part, they don't eat in the restaurants, but subsist all day or all evening on street food, which can be very filling. Steamed yellow corn on the cob, smeared with mayo and topped with hot chile powder, is the #1 favorite, I'd say.

Happily, there appear to be fairly strict guidelines for the fleeting street-food establishments, as they were immaculate and the workers all wore aprons.

At 5 p.m. all the church bells stop ringing and all the statues in all the churches are covered. I was told at the "Negotiating Semana Santa" lecture that years ago, people would not wash around this date so as to appear to be covered in ashes, as an indication of their grief. Then they would go to the churches on Saturday and the priests would throw cleansing water on them. Because of the recent drought of several years' duration, that practice was outlawed.

El Viernes Santo was the day to be in SMA. Bells rang for many minutes from every church every 15 minutes. No cars were allowed into El Centro; they had to park in remote lots, and buses brought their passengers to the jardín. It was a brilliantly sunny and hot day, and vendors were doing a steady business selling gorgeous light cardboard parasols for 20 pesos ($1.60 USD) that looked very Chinese to me. Of course I bought one; I never would have survived the daytime procession without it. There was very much a carnival atmosphere, with all kinds of food, drink, and toys being hawked, that is, until the beginning of the religious aspect of the day.

Atención spoke of this day in these words: "Good Friday is the culmination of weeks of non-stop pageantry with a long, unbearably slow and tortuous dragging of crosses through cobblestone streets to the dispirited beat of a single drum. As they perspire in the hot afternoon sun, solemn men in suits and ties brace heavy statues of saints on their shoulders and press forward. Children through seniors represent angels and mourners, and wave after wave of their faithful parishioners tread onward in the depths of despair. Parade watchers are stacked along the route in hushed silence. Devotion runs deep and true." I thought that was so exquisitely expressed and summed up the day perfectly.

Those who came early got a rare seat in the shade in the church's courtyard, quite a coup.

CHAPTER 3

Jesus, dragging his own cross.

Mary moves through the crowd.

Santo Encuentro (Holy Encounter) kicked off at 11:30 a.m. from the San Rafael church, where I had watched the altar-building a week earlier. The size of the crowd was amazing. Once more, I positioned myself and my camera at the door of the church from which all of the participants in the procession emerged. Again, things got started with the Roman soldiers. So here's my question: are these the same Roman soldiers from yesterday, or does each church have its own wardrobe of costumes worn by different people?

The strain of the work was beginning to show by this time on the faces of both the men and the women.

Jesus (not a real person in this part of the re-enactment) was brought out to hear the charges being read to him by Pontius Pilate, who recited them with the aid of a microphone. This was very dramatic, as after the charges were read, Pontius Pilate asked if anyone were present to speak for the accused, and no one did. Then he said, "I wash my hands of him," and actually washed and dried his hands.

And then came Mary, and again I wondered if it was the same statue from yesterday's church and yesterday's procession. Today's route was roped off from the crush of spectators.

Next were the three thieves who were crucified with Jesus, carrying their own crosses. Then came statues of three women. I didn't know who they were, but learned that one is Veronica, as a Latina woman from Texas proudly told me; her name was Veronica, also. She told me that she was a member of an evangelical congregation in the States and that they never showed Jesus on the cross. She said they've moved on from that point to his resurrection and beyond.

The Encounter between Jesus and his mother—the main event of the procession, which I wasn't able to photograph for reasons that I now forget—was extremely moving. The entire procession paraded around the square block surrounding the jardín and wound up back in front of the parroquia. The statue of Mary, which was ahead of Jesus in the procession, was actually backed up so that she and Jesus faced each other when he caught up to her. Jesus' head was hinged in some way, and when a cord was pulled, his bowed head was raised so that he and Mary were looking directly at each other. And then a priest read words saying that Jesus asked his mother to forgive him for causing her this sorrow, and apologized for any wrongs he had done her in his life. The statues went back into the church, and Part I of Good Friday was over.

But even that majesty and emotion couldn't begin to compare with the procession of that evening, *Santo Entierro* (Holy Funeral), Jesus' funeral. This is the biggie. Whoever organized this procession, in which literally thousands of people participated, is a genius. So many different age groups, so many varied costumes, religious objects, statues, and on and on. It was scheduled to begin at 5 p.m. from—again—the Oratorio church, so I left my house at about 4:30 to walk the few blocks there.

When I got to my corner, I saw that the streets were cordoned off and that people were already seated to await the procession. So I chose a piece of curb, plopped down a cushion, and happily sat next to a well-educated Mexican couple—Martín and Lourdes—and their teenage son, Emilio, with whom I passed the next several hours chatting in both English and Spanish and asking them questions about aspects of the procession that I didn't understand. Martín is a broker at Santander Bank, and said he was pleased to have an extended opportunity to practice his English since many of his clients are gringos.

Again came the Roman soldiers, but these were different.
They were the biggest men I've ever seen in my life.
I don't know where they found so many of that size.

And then, an hour and a quarter after I left my house, the procession finally made it to where I was sitting. This was because it moved at a snail's pace, and, again, made frequent stops for the priest to deliver his message to the crowd. This was the most formal procession I'd seen all week, and, as Martín told me, staffed by SMA's elite.

Every group of children had a matron accompanying it. The women kept the groups together and kept them under control when they stopped. They also made sure that the statue bearers rested their shoulders and changed sides periodically.

At last came the entombed Jesus. Supposedly the tomb weighs a ton and 36 men are needed to transport it. Because of the extreme weight, they have to shuffle along, and you can hear that noise from far away.

And then it was over.

On Saturday night, I had planned to go to the *Misa de Gloria* at 10 p.m. at the parroquia for songs and bells, but I was just too wiped out from my excursion to Pozos and Victoria—the climbing, the sun, the long day—and so skipped it.

Everyone wondered who the red-haired woman was. Could she be Lucy Nuñez, the mayor of SMA? While many like her, many do not. What else is new?

On Easter Sunday came the catharsis after more than a week of mourning and grief: Blow Up Judas! This unique celebration started at noon. My UU service was still going strong at 11:45, but I ducked out along with a new friend, Ruth. I did not want to miss Blow Up Judas!

So we hightailed it up to the jardín and could hear the explosions as we neared. In past years, they blew up only Judas, but recently, other figures—mostly unpopular current political ones—were added, and so there were several dozen life-size papel-maché figures to be blown up.

They were strung on wires between some buildings and the trees of the jardín, and men in the buildings did something to them to cause them first to twirl one way, and then another, and then explode with a deafening bang, pouring out smoke and bits of paper. Often the heads remained intact, and enterprising youths scooped them up and sold them to eager buyers for 200 pesos each. My Spanish teacher told me that when George W. Bush was in office, he was among the papel-maché figures, and the gringos cheered loudest of all when he popped.

And so with that release, Semana Santa ended. I attended only about three-fifths of the events, and still I found it an intense and grueling week. Easter was pretty early this year, allowing me to partake, but like the trip to the monarch butterflies last year, it was a once-in-a-lifetime experience; I'm really glad I did it, but I probably won't ever do it again.

The next day, when the visitors had gone home, we all breathed a sigh of relief to get our sleepy, quiet San Miguel de Allende back again.

And thus my trip to Mexico for winter and spring 2010 ends. I eagerly await my return later this year, on December 1, for four months next winter—and more adventures.

> "In Mexico, frequently things don't work,
> but they almost always work out."
>
> Carol Merchasin, author of hilarious books about Mexico:
> *This Is Mexico: Tales of Culture and Other Complications*
> and *How It Goes in Mexico: Essays from an Expatriate*

Chapter 4

December 2010

First Dispatch from Third Visit to SMA

It is said that constantly learning new things is a possible deterrent to Alzheimer's disease. (I'm not so sure about this, as no one kept his brain more active than my father, and he succumbed at a young age to that dread disease.) Anyway, if it's true, I probably earned myself at least one more nonbefuddled year as a side benefit of coming to Mexico, as I am learning by the minute every day I'm here.

I'm in a new rental on Calle Animas just for this month, and in only a few days after returning to San Miguel on December 1, I have mastered two remote controls, one for the TV and one for the DVD player so I can practice yoga each morning along with the yogi on the disk I brought with me. I have learned how to light and extinguish the two gas fireplaces without shutting off the pilot light. I have figured out the myriad keys required to get into the "compound" (of two houses) and into my house in particular, into the shared laundry area, plus onto the three separate outside sitting areas, each having its own key (and each turn of the key is counterintuitive, except for the one or two that aren't, and then there's the question of whether the key is put into the lock right side up or upside down).

I have decoded which switches turn on which lights and which fountains, and the minutiae of the working of the stove, washing machine, microwave, and all those other appliances we take for granted but which are slightly different in each house. In my first six days here, I have dealt with the housekeeper, Marí, who is amazing and lovely, solely in Spanish; with a representative of the property management company, Delfino, also lovely, half in Spanish and half in English, to troubleshoot a couple of things; and with three cable guys, each on a different visit in trying to activate Internet access, also half Spanish and half English.

This house hasn't had anyone in it for a very long time, and thus the problems I encountered with no English TV channels and no Internet hadn't been reported earlier. The first cable guy came in response to a call from Delfino, but he didn't know where "the box" was, and thought it was in the other house, which is unoccupied, and I didn't have keys to that. Delfino arrived early the next morning to give me the keys to the other house, but cable guy #2 found the box right by the front door to the compound. When he unscrewed the cable, water poured forth and he pointed out the corrosion present. I wondered aloud how it was possible to have water in the cable when it rarely rains here. Guy #2 dried the connection with the help of a paper napkin I gave him and established temporary Internet access until cable guy #3 could come out and totally replace the damaged cable.

The cable company gives a fairly long window during which the workmen can come, and of course that means I have to stay in the house, but they do come within that window. Yesterday, #3 replaced not only the connection from my house to the street cable, but the street cable also. Problems solved. I can listen to the news on CNN while I get dressed in the morning and I can send and receive emails and check the Internet. These possibilities, by the way, enable me to be in SMA for as long as I choose. I'm able to do all of my business via the Internet. What an amazing thing it is!

CHAPTER 4

As I was coming home from the market one day, an attractive, obviously middle-class Mexican woman my age was standing on the sidewalk near my house, holding an absolutely stunning-looking baby girl. I admired the baby and we got to talking. Suddenly, out of nowhere, she switched to English and asked me, "What is the plural of veterinarian?" Say what? She didn't pronounce veterinarian correctly, but I got it anyway. After I told her the plural and helped her to pronounce that very long word, she told me that she is trying to teach some English to her grandchildren. Starting with the word veterinarian?

Biker and grandma: you've got to love it! Only in SMA!

One of my favorite things here is the Sunday Danzón—public dancing—in the jardín. Formerly, when times were better and the municipal treasury

161

was flush, live music accompanied it, but now it's all recorded music, enlivened by a gringo DJ/MC who has been living in SMA forever and is married to a Mexican woman. He speaks incredibly clearly and slowly in Spanish so that I am able to understand 95 percent of it. He plays a wide variety of dance music, from salsa to fox trot to cumbia to James Brown and more. Every shape, size, age, and nationality gets up to dance. I photographed what I considered "odd couples." I particularly liked the biker dude in complete regalia dancing with the much older woman (perhaps his grandmother? I don't think so). None of the odd couples were "together"; they just wound up dancing arm in arm in the bright, warm sunshine on a glorious Sunday afternoon. What could be bad?

Atención runs a color photo in each week's issue, submitted by the gringo readership to illustrate "Only in Mexico." It invites submissions, and because I've gotten very favorable feedback to my photos, I'm going to send in some.

In the Thick of Things

I now have a schedule of regular activities, which always makes me feel better. On Mondays, Wednesdays, and Fridays, from 9:30 to 11, I have yoga at Bellas Artes, now an arts center but formerly the cloister area of the Convent of the Immaculate Conception, built in 1755-65 and deemed the "most ambitiously landscaped cloister in all Mexico." I really belong in the intermediate group, but that meets at 8 a.m., and I just can't do that, so I attend the beginners' group.

The instructor, Alejandro, is a Mexican Rodney Yee. It's sometimes a little hard to understand him with his slightly accented English and the weird acoustics of the room, but I make sure to station myself very close to him, and that seems to work. Alejandro has a "frequent-flier" program, where for 350 pesos up front, you get 10 one-and-a-half-hour lessons and use of a mat, blanket, block, and strap, so I don't have to either buy or schlep any of that stuff.

Alejandro, my yoga instructor.

On Tuesdays, I attend the weekly discussion group of my UU congregation, followed by lunch and a Spanish lesson, and the following day, I go to the Wednesday Comida, another UU activity, which meets for lunch and fellowship at a different restaurant in a different neighborhood each week. On Thursdays, I have another Spanish lesson, this time in the morning. With my mornings filled, I have the afternoons to do laundry, shop for groceries, have lunch with friends, go to some of the rich cultural offerings, or just sit in the sun and read.

The weather, while nothing like what is going on in the States, is still darned cold. Recently, it has been below freezing at night, and rising to the high 70s in the daytime, a spread of 50 degrees, which is pretty hard to believe. I use the second bedroom in my rental, which you access by going outside (the layout of the houses in this compound defies simple explanation), as my computer room. It has a space heater with a thermostat, and in the mornings, when I check my email, it reads in the low 50s. If I'm in there for a couple of hours, it can get as high as 60; it's never gone above that. I think most of the heat from the faux log gas fireplace in the living room/dining room/kitchen space goes two places: up to the extremely high ceiling and up the stairs to the second floor. It's quite cozy up there; it is only just tolerable on the first floor. The second floor also gets an infusion of brilliant sun each day. There's a gas fireplace up there, too, but I need it only when I first get up in the morning.

I asked my housekeeper one particularly cold morning when she arrived if she had any kind of heat in her house, and she said no, that they can't afford the electricity it would take to run a space heater. I don't know how they stand it. And for the people out in the campo, where it's much colder, and where they have dirt floors on which they sometimes sleep, I can't even imagine. None of the houses in SMA—even those owned and rented by gringos—have central heat or air conditioning, as it's usually not needed, but at least we have fireplaces, space heaters, and overhead fans.

December 12 is the day to venerate the Virgen de Guadalupe, a major religious figure in Mexico, and thus is a holy day of great significance. It happened to fall on a Sunday this year, and at UU, we heard a talk by a Mexican professor about the legend of the Virgin's appearance to a poor peasant, Juan Diego, outside of Mexico City on December 9, 1531. When he told his bishop about the apparition, the bishop did not believe him, and asked him to bring some proof. Again the Virgin appeared to Juan Diego and told him to go and pick some roses nearby (which were seemingly an impossibility in the dead of winter and in the desert) and take them to the bishop as proof. Three days later, on December 12, when Juan Diego opened his cloak to show the bishop the roses he had picked, the image of the Virgin was imprinted on it. This cloak is on display in the Basilica of Guadalupe, and the church is one of the most visited religious shrines in the world.

Mexico's first president changed his name to Guadalupe Victoria in honor of the icon. Many boys are also named Guadalupe, and the nicknames Lupe and Lupita refer to that name. Hidalgo and Allende, SMA heroes of the Mexican fight for independence, carried flags with the Virgin's image on them in order to rally troops to the cause. In our order of service was printed this quote from Mexican author Octavio Paz: "The Mexican people, after more than two centuries of experiments, have faith only in the Virgin of Guadalupe and the National Lottery."

On all holidays, political or religious, firecrackers are set off very early in the morning, presumably to awaken people to get the celebrations started. (I've also heard they are to give God notice that something important is going on here.) I was awake already when I heard the first blasts around 6 a.m. on December 12. Usually, after a half hour or so, they stop, but on that day, they continued sporadically all day long! The last thing I heard that night before I fell asleep at 10:30 was the firecrackers. In the dark and stillness of early morning, when the bursts echo in the nearby hills, it's quite wonderful. Most guidebooks warn visitors about this custom, as the firecrackers do sound like gunfire and could lead some gringos to think that the next revolution had started.

I had a funny experience involving a crèche scene at the biblioteca. It had been newly set up and I went over to look at it, only to discover that there was no Baby Jesus. When I went into the office to buy a movie ticket, I told the director of programming, José Luis, of the absence of Jesus in the manger, and was told, "He hasn't been born yet! When he is, he will appear in the crèche scene." I told him that in the U.S., Jesus is always in the manger from whenever the scene is set up.

A girl cradling her beautifully dressed Baby Jesus doll in a posada.

Another encounter with a Baby Jesus came a few days later, when I saw a *posada*, a parade of children each of the nine nights before Christmas, representing the nine days that Mary and Joseph traveled until they found lodging. The children stop at various homes along the way, and a script is sung back and forth between those outside, asking for a place to sleep, and those inside, refusing them, until at last they find shelter.

✳ ✳ ✳

I lost Internet access a few days ago, and the same CyberMatsa technician returned. He found yet another cable box where the cable was dripping water, so I offered to get him another *servilleta* (napkin) with which to dry it. I asked him if he remembered the word in English for servilleta, which I had taught him the last time. He thought for a minute while I went to get it. When I came back, he proudly said "kidnap!" I totally understood how he could have mixed up those two words. I explained the meaning of that word and told him about napkin again.

Christmas in SMA

I met my neighbor with the gorgeous granddaughter again on the street, and again we spoke. I learned that her name is Mercedes. She asked if I'd like to do an intercambio with her. I jumped at the chance. We had our first meeting at her house the next Tuesday, early in the evening. I didn't know what to expect. I knocked on her door, and a woman who I now think was the housekeeper let me in and led me to a small sitting room. Mercedes soon appeared, and we had a really fun time with her reading me a silly story in English from a book she had, and asking me questions about words she didn't understand. Then I suggested that she ask me questions in Spanish. It went very well. We decided to do it again on Thursday, same time, same place. That evening, she asked if two nieces and a nephew, ages around 8, 9, and 10, could sit in with us. I agreed, and this was even more fun than when we were just the two of us. We read a story in the same book about ducks hatching and there was lots of new vocabulary, like beak, webbed feet, hatch, egg, shell, down, feathers, etc. During the Spanish part, the kids enjoyed asking me questions such as what is my favorite color (then we practiced all of the colors in both languages), do I have any children, when is my birthday, etc. We planned to meet again the next Tuesday. This is so much what I enjoy doing.

Added to the exhilaration of this experience was that of having a photo that I took in 2009 or '10 published in *Atención*. When I sent it in for a contest this winter, I said I wondered how much the shoeshine man enjoyed polishing the boots of the beautiful young woman, as she seriously skewed the age of the gringo population in SMA.

A photo of mine that was published in **Atención**.

It was suggested that I go to Tianguis for an anti-mall Christmas experience. I'd been to the Tuesday Market several times on other SMA stays but decided to go again. Lots of things were for sale for celebrating Christmas, including all of the figurines, in a variety of sizes, to make a crèche. I found out that each family sets up a crèche in their home. They dress the Baby Jesus in any number of lavish costumes, and I saw women trying to make up their minds among several different outfits for their Baby Jesus dolls. On Christmas Eve, they bring the dolls to the Mass, either cradled like a real baby or in a basket, for the priest to bless. Once blessed, the doll can then be added to the crèche scene at home.

On Christmas morning, I attended, along with about 50 other gringos, a historical walking tour of San Miguel. I had taken this tour nearly two years ago when I first arrived, and knew much of the information and all of the places, but it was good to hear the fascinating history again, and I did learn some new things. I returned to my rental and, with an eight-hour time difference, Skyped with both of my kids, their spouses, and my grandchildren, all of whom were in Helsinki together. Really, the technology is a miracle—and it's free! Imagine! My Christmas was complete. However, I met Sandy and Marge at 3 p.m. to take a taxi to a spectacular hotel/restaurant called La Puertecita for a lovely fixed-price, fixed-menu meal in a charming setting.

YOGA MOVES

I showed up at the appointed time on the Wednesday after Christmas for morning yoga at the Bellas Artes and saw one of my classmates exiting the facility. I asked her what was going on, and she told me there was a sign on the door directing us all to go across the street to the Arthur Murray dance studio. It turns out that Alejandro, our instructor, received a phone call at 6:30 the previous night informing him that as of the next day, Bellas Artes was closed—for a year! He had to scramble for a place to hold the class. Ordinarily we could have done our yoga on the huge dance floor on the first level at Arthur Murray, but not that day, as they were setting up for a fiesta that night. We had to go upstairs and divide ourselves among three small, adjacent rooms, with poor Alejandro shouting instructions and moving from place to place. All of the mats, straps, blocks, and blankets were still over at Bellas Artes. We were cheek by jowl in the three rooms, but Alejandro was cool as a cucumber. Starting in January, the dance floor is already booked for Mondays,

Wednesdays, and Fridays for its own yoga program, so maybe yoga will be changed to Tuesdays and Thursdays, but those are not days I could attend. Then there's a chance for a spacious second-floor space a few blocks away, but it will take time to get leases, etc., straightened out. I'll be most disappointed if I have to give up this yoga class. Yes, there are others, but this is the best and certainly the least expensive.

At yoga on Friday (again squashed together in three adjacent small rooms on the second floor of Arthur Murray), we got the full story about the closing of Bellas Artes. An emergency situation caused the entire place to be closed in such a hurried manner. Chunks of roof were falling onto the second floor, and the management feared that the whole place was unstable and would fall down, so they closed it. They are calling in engineers to assess the condition of the facility, and they hope they will be able to reopen at least the first floor in about a month. However, I'm not holding my breath. Meanwhile, yoga is changed to Tuesdays and Thursdays at Arthur Murray for the next two weeks. By then, Alejandro hopes to be using a very large space, bigger even than the room at Bellas Artes, at another nearby facility. That large space is not available until mid-January, however. He took our email addresses and will let us know what's happening.

One day when my housekeeper was in my casa, the doorbell rang. I wasn't expecting anyone. Since the door is quite a long walk away—and for security—there is a video system so that one can see who is at the door in addition to being able to speak to him/her. Marí spoke to the person but didn't go to the door. I asked who it was and she said a man with a burro selling potting soil. She said these men live way out in the campo, and start walking to town with their soil around 4 a.m. Sometimes their wives and children come, too. They then go door to door selling their product. They stay in town (I have no idea where either they or their animals spend the night) until all is sold, and then they walk the six hours back. What a way to earn a living—and how much of a living could it possibly be?

San Miguel has been a mob scene since a few days before Christmas. The cars in the streets are often in gridlock. One can't find a seat in the jardín. Thousands of Mexican tourists have come here for the holiday and the gringo snowbirds have returned, so things are really hopping. I'm so glad for SMA that at least for a while, tourism is in full swing. You can tell the Mexico City visitors in an instant. They're wearing high heels and pushing strollers and carriages (and often lifting them over the cobblestones), neither of which the sanmiguelenses usually do. Some people will leave after the New Year's weekend, but others will be staying through January 6, Three Kings' Day. The kids are off from school until after that important gift-giving day.

There were no gringo cultural activities during the week between Christmas and New Year's, so I used some of that time to go to two museums. The first was the former home of Ignacio Allende, hero of the war for independence from Spain, in honor of whom the city changed its name from San Miguel el Grande. Seniors get in for free all the time, and it's free for everyone on Sundays. While the furniture exhibited is not original to the Allende family, it is true to period. I commented that from the furnishings, there was no way to tell that that family lived in Mexico; everything was Spanish and quite lavish. I've learned about the *peninsulares*, those living in Mexico who had been born in Spain. They were the wealthiest and held positions of power. When peninsulare women found out they were pregnant, if they could they'd hop the next ship back to Spain so that their children could be born in the home country and thus enjoy all of the advantages that came with that distinction. Next came the *criollos*, the children of Spaniards, but born in Mexico. Then there were *mestizos*, the children of marriages between Europeans and indigenous people, and finally the *Indios*, the indigenous themselves.

Next up was the toy museum, which is new this year. The toys in the museum are the collection of one woman. The building housing them is bright and light and beautiful; it was a former home. It's not a please-touch museum, however, and I could imagine that for a child, it would be very frustrating to have the glorious, brilliantly colored toys right at hand but not be allowed to touch them or play with them. One guard was wearing a gun. I was horrified by this and asked her why, in a toy museum, populated mostly by families with children, it was felt a necessity to have a guard with a gun. She explained that she was a municipal police officer and, if needed, could be called outside at any moment to deal with whatever situation presented itself. We talked to several people working at the museum to express our reaction to this. I'm guessing the museum can't afford a guard and thus the city assigns an officer to the museum. Hopefully, someday soon there will be a guard without a gun.

I had another session with Mercedes and her nephew and two nieces, and we read *Goldilocks and the Three Bears*. I read it aloud in English, pausing to point out slang, idioms, whatever I felt needed additional explanation, and Mercedes translated it into Spanish for the kids. Periodically, I stopped and asked them questions about the story in

Spanish to test their comprehension. It was a good session and the first time they'd heard the story; it is not popular in Mexico.

I had to cancel our Thursday session because Sandy and I had tickets to a flamenco show. There were 12 in the troupe: four dancers, three guitarists, a couple of percussionists, and some *palmas* (rhythm clappers) from Mexico, Spain, and Brazil. The place was packed, and the show was extraordinary. I am a real fan of flamenco, and had had my interest reignited on my trip to Spain last fall.

JANUARY 2011

My Moving Day

On New Year's Day, I moved to a new dwelling for the remainder of this visit, and finally, in my third year here, I am in the building I want to be in. It's right next door to where I rented last year, and I have the same landlady, Heather. I had three suitcases, three plastic bags, and my backpack to move. Since this new apartment is on the third floor, I asked the cab driver if he would carry my heavy suitcases up for me if parking was available. Because it was a holiday, there was parking, and he did. As we entered the complex, we were met by Heather; my housekeeper from last year, Reyna, who will also be helping me out this year; and Sandy. What a welcoming committee! All helped to carry my stuff up.

Being a third-floor apartment, it is flooded with light and is delightfully warm. A tiny balcony off the bedroom has a close-up view of a four-story-tall Norfolk Island pine. I've never seen one that tall or in such pristine condition. I can also see the tippy-top of the parroquia with its cross. Also, I can go up to the huge terrace on the fourth level, which is for anyone in the complex to use, but Heather said she's never seen anyone up there. It has a clothesline, so that's where I'll hang my laundry. There are also a table and chairs and several chaise longues, and we're working on an umbrella. The place has a stunning street-level central courtyard with fountain, still lavishly decorated for Christmas. I know several of the people in the building. It's centrally located, and it's the perfect spot for me.

Heather left me two bottles of wine and one of champagne, and about 10 pounds of fruit of all kinds, already disinfected. Among the fruits were six golden delicious apples, not my favorite—so, in a fit of domesticity, I made applesauce. I had no cinnamon but used some craisins I had on hand, plus a little sugar, and the result was delicioso! Then I made up a half gallon of *jamaica*, a tea brewed from dried hibiscus blossoms. I was served this deep red brew at a fundraiser last year and was immediately hooked. I had it again this season, made with cinnamon and a small amount of cloves, but I prefer it straight with just a touch of honey. It's quite tasty either hot or cold—and such a splendid color! A few days later when I offered some to Carlos, my Spanish teacher, he told me it's a diuretic that should be consumed within a day after making it. Mine has been in the fridge for three or four days. Sigh.

Three Kings Day

Almost every part of the move between my two rentals had gone smoothly, except that I was unable to remove my yoga DVD from the player at the Animas rental. I had inserted it the first day and played it faithfully every morning, never needing to remove it. Marí, my housekeeper there, and I tried to remove it together with no luck. She promised to tell Delfino, the representative of the management company, about it on Monday. (No one was working on my moving day since it was New Year's Day.) After a few days, when I hadn't heard anything from Delfino, I called the management office and spoke to Maribel, who said she was going to the house the next morning on another matter and would look into the

DVD problem. When I didn't hear back from her in two days, I called again. She said she had gone to the house and tried herself to get it out, to no avail, and that an electrician was going that very morning at 10 to work on it, and she'd get back to me. So far I've heard nothing. If I get it back and it's playable, I'll be very surprised. But I'm remarkably calm about it. I miss doing my yoga each morning, but I rearranged one of my two weekly Spanish lessons so that I could attend yoga with Alejandro on Thursdays on the dance floor at Arthur Murray until another site for the classes on Monday, Wednesday, and Friday can be arranged.

And speaking of Alejandro, I went to a party one evening last week at the home he shares with his partner, Jorge. It was given for several reasons: for Three Kings Day, January 6; to welcome back a woman who had taught yoga with Alejandro last year and who had just returned from the States and successful surgery for a brain tumor; and to kick off a new season of yoga with the snowbirds. They live in a gorgeous rented house with a large patio in a neighborhood I'd never been in. He had made the finger food and there was lots of wine. Soon after I got there, a huge pizza-like box was delivered, but it wasn't pizza, but rather *rosca*, a special bread prepared only for Three Kings Day in hundreds of shapes and sizes, in which has been baked a teeny, tiny plastic Baby Jesus. The tradition is that whoever gets the Baby Jesus in his or her slice has to throw a party on Candelaria, February 2, providing tamales and *atole*, a corn drink, for all those at this party. I'd be scared to either break a tooth or swallow Baby Jesus, so I was pleased that a man in my yoga class and his wife got it.

The night before Three Kings Day is comparable to our Christmas Eve, a time when the children are so excited, awaiting the three kings who will put gifts in the shoes that they've put out with great expectations. In order to keep the kids of SMA occupied throughout that long day, the city had activities for them in the jardín—inflated things to bounce on, clowns, dancing, etc. I would have stuck around to watch and take more photos, but the music was so loud that I fled.

Earlier, I had asked Mercedes' nieces, Alicia and Diana, what was on their gift list, and both had told me boots. Miguel, their brother, wasn't there that day—I really missed him because he knows some English and is far less shy than his sisters—since he was on a school holiday and had gone with his father to another state to work. (When school is in session again on January 10, he won't be part of our group anymore because he'll be attending school from 2 to 8 p.m., and I'm there from 6 to 7. The schools are so crowded here that they have to go on split session.)

Alas, on January 6, when I went to Mercedes' house for our session, I found that the girls did not receive the hoped-for boots. They were both wearing lovely new clothes, however, and seemed happy. They were also very tired. Mercedes told me that kids in Mexico don't sleep much on the night before Three Kings Day.

Here's a rundown on a recent morning of mine: Javier, trusted all-around handyman, wearing his plumber's hat, is due at 9 a.m., so I am sure to be up, dressed, exercised, and fed, with the bathroom stripped of most things, as he's going to be doing some major plumbing work and will need to turn the water off for at least three hours. He and his father have already been in my apartment for a full day earlier in the week (with the water turned off only briefly). Now I know why Mexican houses—at least those owned and rented by gringos—have so many bathrooms; it's because at least one is under repair at any given time.

It's 10 a.m. and still no Javier, so I prepare to go out to buy *Atención* and some fruits. (Javier has keys to my apartment and is totally trustworthy.) The doorbell rings; I think it's Javier at last, but, no, it's the flower lady, Lupe. This woman comes on Tuesdays and Fridays, carrying many bunches of flowers in a large metal tub filled with water, and stops at each apartment in the complex to see if anyone wants to buy. Sandy had directed her up to me, a newcomer in the building. Fulfilling a promise to myself to always have fresh flowers in the house while I'm here, and because she is so charming and persuasive, I buy two bunches. Of course that means I have to abandon my plan of going out, because I now must arrange the flowers.

I find some vases and start clipping long stems, and almost immediately the ultra-cheap scissors break. So now I have to stop arranging so I can fill the vases and the sink with water because soon Javier will come and turn it off. As I'm doing this, Javier arrives, and I leave to buy some scissors as well as fruits and *Atención*. I'm successful except for *Atención*, and return to the apartment. I can't disinfect the fruits because there's no water. I use my new, supposedly stronger scissors to cut the stems of the flowers I have bought and arrange them around the apartment. Now it's time to go out front to wait for a ride to Ojalá Niños.

Another morning a few days earlier, I was awakened at 7 by the most ungodly mechanical screaming noise I've ever heard. I traced the sound to a silver cylinder above the washing machine. There was absolutely nothing I could do, because I didn't know what the cylinder was and I couldn't reach that high anyway. My landlady, Heather, who lives directly under me, called to say that there was no water because the pump on the roof had malfunctioned and that the pump in my apartment—the silver cylinder that is part of the water purification system—was screaming its outrage at not having any water being pumped into it. Saint Javier appeared within about 15 minutes, checked on my apartment, and then got onto the roof, where he fixed whatever was ailing the pump PDQ. Then he came back to my place to check on another noise the pump was making. I was grateful that the sound didn't happen in the middle of the night, and Heather was grateful that she didn't need to put out 9,000 pesos for a new pump.

I have decided that this year, I will not sign on to any regular volunteer position, but rather wait to see what needs present themselves and help out on an ad hoc basis. Of course this does not include the twice-weekly visits to the home of my now-former neighbor Mercedes, to teach English and learn Spanish; being on the welcome committee at UUFSMA, greeting folks and giving out orders of service each Sunday; and taking over a small (or so I was told) weekly administrative task for Ojalá Niños, which can be done completely on the computer, while the woman who usually does it travels to Ecuador.

Ojalá is the after-school program in San Miguel Viejo, an extremely poor community just outside of SMA, where I taught English last year. I was invited to assist with a thank-you luncheon for the 42 mothers of the kids in the program who had provided snacks for the kids since October. The program meets on Wednesdays with classes in art, music, dancing, and English for about 125 kids. Volunteers—mostly gringos—staff these classes and bring healthy snacks for the kids. Elsmarie, the amazing woman who started the program in her home, thought that providing snacks was something the mothers of the kids could do that would help to organize them. (The people in this community are not united in any way, and Elsmarie, a sort of one-woman Peace Corps, is determined to get them organized for their own well-being. There are many issues in which having an intact, organized, and vocal community could stand the people in good stead.) Well, the whole idea of simple, healthy snacks ballooned, and the mamas started doing major cooking and bringing comida for all the kids—a huge undertaking. So, in thanks for their labors of love, we threw them a luncheon where we prepared all of the food and served them at nicely set and decorated tables outside in the shade—an experience Elsmarie is sure they've never had before.

Of the 42 women who received an invitation, 24 arrived and seemed to enjoy themselves. Of course, we had prepared food for 42 women, plus the 12 or so volunteers, so after the lunch we packed lots of lasagna and salad for the women to take home. I participated by going two hours early to help set up and chop veggies. Then I helped to serve the women and clean up. I was on my feet for much of four hours, but I had a lovely lunch and a chance to interact with women that I would probably never meet in any other way, as our lives are completely different. I also got to meet again a couple of the students I taught in my English class last year. They had grown! And they remembered me. It was a poignant moment.

The party for the mothers also marked the end of the big weekly meals they were preparing. It had been decided that only on the last Wednesday of each month would there be snacks after the classes and that time would be used to celebrate the birthday of any children born in that month. This will give the classes more time to finish their projects, as they were having to dismiss early in order to accommodate the eating.

At Times My Apartment Is like Grand Central Station!

You will remember the water pump problem of a week or so ago. Even though Javier thought he had fixed it, water continued to drip from it, happily just into my utility sink. He concluded that the seals had been damaged when the pump tried to work with too little water, so he and his father returned to my apartment one morning just before I had to go to yoga. Javier stopped in downstairs to talk to Heather, and sent his father up with the tools. His father at one point in his life suffered some kind of brain damage, and so he is compromised. He was standing in my hall, waiting, so I invited him to sit in my living room, and I tried to converse with him a little. He is missing almost all of his teeth, so when he did speak, I had trouble understanding him. It was a long five minutes or so. I left him sitting there when I went to yoga.

When I returned, Javier and his father were still there and just finishing up with the pump. Soon Reyna arrived for her twice-weekly cleaning visit. And shortly after that, again my doorbell rang, but it was a friend of Reyna's—probably another housekeeper or she couldn't have gotten into the complex—who had some quick business with her. I needed a new garrafón, so I gave Reyna the necessary 20 pesos and asked her to get Ruben, the *mozo* or general factotum for the complex, to bring a new one up. I had a few other problems in the apartment, like not being able to turn on one of the gas heaters—which had not been necessary until today when it turned quite cold again—and a lamp was not working. Javier got to work on the lamp when Ruben came up with the garrafón. So now I had four people working in my apartment!

Then the outside doorbell rang, and it was Delfino, from the management company of the house I rented in December, with my yoga DVD in hand. What a pleasant surprise. We'll see tomorrow when I do my yoga practice if the DVD is playable. (Later report: It is in perfect working order!) Really, I had just about written it off entirely, thinking I'd never see it again. I need to be more patient and give these things time. I couldn't wash up and change out of my yoga clothes before Carlos arrived for my Spanish lesson because there was too much activity in my place. I did manage to eat a quick lunch on my balcony to keep out of Reyna's way.

CHAPTER 4

You know, telling of all these things happening to me and in my apartment makes for a good story and a laugh. I wonder, though, if, over the long haul, they would become tiresome nuisances. I remember wondering about that last year, too.

Recently I caused a minor disaster. The fourth-floor terrace has a wrought iron table with a thick circular glass tabletop cover. It's impossible to be up there midday without an umbrella because the sun is so strong, so Heather hired Javier's brother to bring in a special tool that sprays water while cutting a circular hole in the glass; the water keeps the glass from breaking. Heather gave me an umbrella and up I went to put it in place. I decided not to leave the umbrella in the table after I lowered it, but rather to store it on the landing with the cushions for the lounge chairs. Unfortunately, the top-heavy upper part of the umbrella slipped when I was trying to disengage it from the pole. It hit the glass and caused two cracks to form from the center hole out to the edges. I was pretty hysterical, as you can imagine. I immediately told Heather and said I'd pay for a new sheet of glass and the cutting of another hole. She told me where I could go to make that happen, but I decided that my Spanish was not up to that task, so I will ask Javier to do it. I told Heather that I will never again use the umbrella because it's just too easy to lose control of it and cause another round of cracks.

I continue my twice-weekly sessions with Mercedes and her two nieces, and my time with them has become a cherished part of my week. Alicia has a repaired cleft palate and wears braces on her teeth (called the English word "brackets" here), so it is somewhat difficult for me to understand her, and she has trouble saying some of the English words I'm teaching them. We do a lot of singing and dancing ("The Farmer in the Dell," "Hokey Pokey," "Head, Shoulders, Knees and Toes," "If You're Happy and You Know It," etc.). This week I'm going to teach them "The Itsy Bitsy Spider" and "The Wheels on the Bus." I made a boo-boo the last time I was there that caused much hilarity. As I was leaving, with Mercedes seeing me to the door, instead of saying, *"Hasta miércoles"* (goodbye until next Wednesday), I said, "Hasta Mercedes." What a wonderful laugh she and I shared; it was a special moment.

I am beginning to tentatively ponder the notion of moving to San Miguel. The numbers are legion of folks who come to visit San Miguel and after three days buy a house. That is so not my style! I want to take my time, sample various periods of the year and their celebrations, and make absolutely sure that this is a step I want to take. For me, there is no denying that moving here would be a major upheaval, a huge change in my life; why would I rush into something that monumental?

Mercedes with some of the kids in the ever-changing cast of characters who attend my English class in her home.

So, after a lot of thinking and admittedly some hesitation (for reasons I was not able to identify for myself), I have decided to rent here for three months in the fall. For the months of September and October, I'll be in the apartment next door to where I stayed last year, and in this apartment for November. It's broken up like that because both apartments are already rented for different periods of time.

Supposedly fall has the absolute best weather (although I don't know how anything could be better than it is now) and there is a profusion of flowers because of the summer rainy season. September is filled with Mexican fiestas of all kinds, and there is a Cervantes Festival in nearby Guanajuato in October, which has a wealth of cultural opportunities. I'll do my yoga, have my Spanish classes, volunteer, and enjoy the less-crowded atmosphere. In December, I'll go home for six weeks to celebrate the holidays with my kids and grandkids, and then return here on January 15, 2012, for the rest of the winter. The fall is a good time to leave my house in Philadelphia unattended, as the garden won't need watering anymore, there will be no need for air conditioning or heat (except perhaps the last couple of weeks), and I can rake all of the leaves after they've fallen rather than some each week.

Frequently, when I'm at home, people ask me what I do all day in Mexico, and I tell them that I live there, but recently I came across this perfect reply: "I do the same things that I do when I'm home, except everything takes longer."

I have become very interested in the sound of three vendors' voices, and it will challenge my writing skills to try to describe them for you, as capturing sounds with words is quite difficult. On the corner near my apartment, the first man has a small kiosk that he can somehow pack up and take away. He stocks and sells so many different things that it's hard to believe. He periodically advertises maybe eight to 10 of his products, always the same few (I think) very, very quickly in a loud voice. I have challenged myself to try to isolate some of the items. So far I've gotten Chiclets, cigarillos, and *cacahuates* (peanuts).

Another of the voices I love is from a huge man (in all directions) who sells newspapers in the jardín. He has a basso profundo voice that matches his girth, and when he shouts his quite short pitch (I have yet to discern what it is he's actually saying—perhaps "newspapers," but I think I'd get that, or perhaps he names a few of the papers that are available), the sound seems to reverberate in the air after he's finished. I'm thinking that under different circumstances, he'd be an opera singer.

And the last hawker, who walks through the streets with his wares, seems to be on a rigid schedule, because every single time I walk over to Mercedes' house at a few minutes before 6 p.m., he is coming toward me on the same street. He has a completely different style from the other two men. He accents and elongates the final vowel of each food that he's selling, even though the accent is not actually on the final syllable in any of the words, and in a voice loud enough to pierce the thick adobe walls of the homes to pique the interest of the housewives within to purchase his offerings. I've heard *elote* (corn on the cob), *jícama* (Mexican yam bean or Mexican turnip, an edible tuberous root), and cacahuates. I look forward to hearing his cry as I proceed to my intercambio.

January 21 was Ignacio Allende's 242nd birthday. Although it is a holiday in all of Mexico, SMA does it up proper for its heroic native son. I missed the parades of the military and the schoolchildren this year, as I was at my short-story discussion group, but I did attend a free outdoor evening concert. As I sat enjoying the classical music provided by an excellent army orchestra numbering about 50, with a chorus of about 20, I was wearing only a light jacket. I recalled the many layers I had to wear this time last year, not to mention socks, a heavy scarf, and gloves, as the weather then was most unseasonably cold.

An homage to Allende was set up in the gazebo in the jardín (where the crèche scene had been a month earlier).

Yesterday we had a cloudy day. This is so unusual in SMA in the winter that it is actually a news item (in this piece, anyway). And at an event I attended last night, there was even a whisper of the possibility of rain. That didn't happen, and today is back to perfection: brilliant blue sky, sun shining brightly, not a cloud in sight, and 78 degrees. Unfortunately, that fine weather doesn't extend northward. Friends that were expected here Tuesday from near Chicago were still in their home on Friday. Their Tuesday cancellation was rebooked for Thursday, which was also canceled, and they hoped to get out on Saturday. They are in a deep funk.

The event I attended last night was run by the SMA Literary Sala, a group that works to give exposure and encouragement to local writers. It was a panel discussion on "When Cultures Blend: An Intimate, Personal Look at Bicultural Life." This was part of the gear-up for the SMA Writers' Conference later this month, which features Sandra Cisneros, author of *The House on Mango Street* and her newest (2002) book, *Caramelo*, as the keynote speaker. Many in town are reading *Caramelo*, including me. There are discussion groups all over.

At the event, which was extremely well attended, there was a panel of six, half Mexicans and half gringos, of various ages and life stages, who had lived—or were living—a bicultural life. During the introductions, it became clear that the life experiences of the panelists were vastly different, and as the evening progressed, the answers to the questions posed first by the moderator, and then later by audience members, were quite extraordinary.

How would you describe being bicultural?

One Mexican stated that all Mexicans are already bicultural because of the Spanish conquest. I had never thought of that. Another Mexicano commented that when he saw his *paisanos* (countrymen) in America, they were more Mexican than they had ever been in Mexico! A very wise person pointed out that he looked for the positives in both cultures, and that the experiences of the well-educated and/or those with legal status differ from those of the laboring class and/or those without papers. He also said we have more in common than we have differences. A woman from the U.S. shared that she had had to give up part of herself. She also said that she perceived thinking in the U.S. as linear, and in Mexico as circular.

Have you personally experienced a clash in values?

Several described noting a far different perception of time and space in the two countries. A few thought that those in the U.S. were driven in terms of productivity and agendas vs. living in the moment in Mexico, embracing what destiny has in store for you. "The present is the most important," one said. A Mexican doctor said she felt that Mexicans have a very loose sense of time and that if they are to compete globally, they will have to be more aware of punctuality.

One gringa who moved into her in-laws' home after she married a Mexican disclosed that the idea of having her own space wasn't even a consideration. A Mexican professor divulged that when she went to the U.S. to teach, she bought and wore a watch for the first time in her life, and bought a cellphone for the alarm feature. One Mexican man told of how he was getting ready to leave for the U.S. to study at the exact time that his grandmother was dying, and he was prepared to go ahead, until his wife jerked him back with a values check. He said you should really listen to women, which I thought was an extraordinary thing for him to admit. Several contended that in Mexico, there is happiness even without money. And the woman from the U.S. who had married a Mexican professed that she has "backed away from striving. My kids will find their own way." Another expressed, "I've reinvented myself wherever I've gone; it's just about being."

How do you think Mexicans feel about the Americans/Canadians in SMA?
A Mexican man stated that when Americans come to Mexico, they are welcomed, but that there is a different experience for Mexicans going to the States. Another said there are good and bad outcomes. Prices are higher in SMA than in other places in Mexico (for example, their children are being priced out of the real estate market because the Americans have driven up the cost of homes in El Centro), but there are many more jobs, and because of the high rate of volunteerism and NGOs (non-governmental organizations, like U.S. nonprofits) that do an enormous amount of good, in balance things are better with the Americans and Canadians here.

What are some stereotypes of other cultures?
The older, retired Mexican woman doctor, who had practiced in public health in the U.S., said she thought Mexicans imagined that life was easier in the States, that machines do all the work, and that the things you needed just fell from the sky. She talked about having to rake the leaves and shovel the snow and the difficulty of keeping a family life going with both parents working and no domestic help.

How has being in another culture changed you personally?
This same doctor felt that her life had been enriched.

All on the panel agreed that when you move into a different culture, you must learn the language.

After the panel, I purchased a copy of *Solamente in San Miguel,* a compendium of short stories written by members of the Literary Sala. The foreword was called "San Miguel Writers: Diverse and Notorious." Thought you might be interested in knowing about some of these writers who spent time here or who live here now:

Ken Kesey

Allen Ginsberg

William S. Burroughs

Vance Packard, author of *The Hidden Persuaders*

Clifford Irving

Gary Jennings, who wrote *Aztec,* which is "regarded by some historians as one of the most significant novels ever written in English about Mexico"

Acclaimed screenwriter **Bill Wittliff,** who adapted Larry McMurty's *Lonesome Dove* for a TV miniseries and wrote the screenplays for *Barbarosa, Legends of the Fall, Black Stallion, The Perfect Storm,* and *A Night in Mexico*

Joseph Persico

Soledad Santiago

Tony Cohan, author of *On Mexican Time*

Beverly Donofrio of *Riding in Cars with Boys* fame

Also, in **Jack Kerouac**'s *On the Road,* SMA is never mentioned by name, "but this is the Mexican town he was referring to in his hipster classic," the book told me.

※ ※ ※

When I took a seat in the jardín a week or so ago, a Mexican man on the bench next to mine said hello, and we started a conversation in English. He told me he had recently escaped from the corporate life in Distrito Federal (more commonly known as Mexico City), where he had worked for TelMex. He had been the account manager for the Mexican government's telephone needs, which sounds like a very stressful job. He and his wife had moved to SMA just four months earlier, although his wife was still in D.F. receiving physical therapy after an automobile accident. He now runs tours for the Audubon Society and his wife has a flower shop here. We talked about recycling (or the lack thereof) in SMA, and I told him about Recycle Bank's groundbreaking incentives approach in Philadelphia, to give points to people for the amount of recycling they have, these points to be used to purchase groceries and other goods. He was very interested in this concept. I gave him my card, and later that evening, I received an email from him thanking me for the thought-provoking conversation and saying he had already Googled Recycle Bank and was going to take the idea to the city department that handles *ecología*. I wrote back with some ideas for his floral business.

Friday a week ago, three friends and I took the Primera Plus bus (and very "plus" it was, with movies, unique leg rests, and a bathroom onboard) to the Expo Bicentenario in Guanajuato, about an hour and a half away. It looked ever so much like the World's Fair in NYC where I spent my honeymoon in 1965.

There was a huge line of schoolchildren waiting to get into an exhibit. Happily, an awning overhead provided some sun protection. We, as viejas, were able to jump to the front of the line at each exhibit and walk right in. Yes! The Mexican government subsidized the admission for all schoolchildren, which was wonderful, but of course brought them out on class trips in droves. The admission was kept low at 15 pesos (current exchange rate is 11.8 pesos = $1 USD), but we got in for free by showing our bus tickets. All of the school groups were led through the exhibits by guides.

We stayed four and a half hours (you had to indicate when you purchased your round-trip tickets which return bus you wanted; they ran about every two hours) and thus we could see only a fraction of what was available. I was really perplexed that there had been no advertising about the Expo in SMA. I would have returned two or three times to experience more of it, but it was closing at the end of January, after being extended for two months. A friend who had been to Mexico City several times recently to visit her ill father said she hadn't seen any notice of it there, either. What a shame! It was marvelous!

We saw only three exhibits. The first was a collection of artisans' works from around the country, the best of the best, owned by Banamex, Mexico's national bank.

The next exhibit, called the Identity Pavilion, was about crafts made by the various indigenous peoples. It included examples of the crafts, and photos of the people, with some rather shocking statistics (birthrates, for example). Most of the indigenous people have 10 times the population that they had just 100 years ago.

The last exhibit we saw was the Pavilion of Tomorrow, which focused on climate change, population growth, and sustainability. I noticed that the kids were paying serious attention to the exhibit about trash. But what stopped them and everyone else in their tracks was an exhibit of bags of ever-escalating amounts of rubbish surrounding one of the colossal heads of the Olmecs, who were the earliest-known major civilization in Mexico (1200 BCE to 400 BCE). They lived in the tropical lowlands of south-central Mexico in the present-day states of Veracruz and Tabasco.

There were about 30 additional pavilions, the most perplexing of which were the ice-skating rink, the Santa Claus House, and the European Union exhibit (at the Mexican Bicentennial Expo?). One person who'd been to the Expo earlier said that every single person who went out onto the ice on skates fell down immediately because of course no one has had any experience with ice underfoot. And they don't do Santa Claus here; the gift-bringing persons are Los Reyes Magos.

This enormous display of a well-known Mexican icon caused a major stir.

FEBRUARY 2011

SOME UPDATES ARE IN ORDER

Working with Mercedes and the children.
It seems that every time I go to Mercedes' home, another child has been added. It's fine with me. We have so much fun. I've researched lots of children's songs that incorporate motions and teach words in English I think they should know. This week's song was "Here We Go Round the Mulberry Bush," which teaches the days of the week, and then, just for fun, I taught them "Bingo," where you clap instead of saying the letters, one by one, in the name B-I-N-G-O. As Mercedes was showing me to the door on Thursday, she told me that she'd spoken to a friend of hers

about our lessons and that the friend wanted to join us. I said why not; the more the merrier. It will be interesting to see where this goes.

Waiting to see what develops in the volunteering department.
You'll recall that I kept my scheduled volunteer activities down to only three modest ones, just waiting this year to see what came along, and sure enough, something interesting did. Chely, a sanmiguelense and Spanish conversation partner of mine since my first year here, who is now also my friend, told me in one of our sessions that her husband, André, would have an exhibition of his photographs at the biblioteca during the month of March. André, born in Paris to Hungarian parents, then raised in Argentina, is a sociologist, a professor of French, a published author, and a harpist in addition to being a fine photographer. He and Chely divide their time each year between SMA and Montreal.

Because André is dedicating his exhibit to a mentor and friend who committed suicide, he wrote an incredibly poetic dedication to her to be hung with the photos. He wrote it in French. Chely then translated it into Spanish, and then into English. And here's where I came in. She asked me to read it over and put it into perfect English. Of course I agreed. I was overcome by the beauty of what André had written. I changed all the lines except one from the passive voice to the active voice (I kept one in the passive voice to vary the cadence) in order to give the piece more vibrancy and life. I had to refer back frequently to both the French and Spanish versions to make sure that I was keeping André's choice of words and feelings intact. I sent it back with many compliments on André's writing and also with misgivings. Would he like what I did to his piece? He loved it!

Chely then asked me to write an article for *Atención* advertising the exhibition, so I sat with André and Chely for about an hour to get more information. André spoke to me in his charmingly French-accented Spanish, which I understood most of. Chely was at the ready with a translation to English for those things I didn't catch. Because the deadline for the article was coming up soon, I went right home and wrote it and attached a photo that André had emailed me because I suggested we run one with the piece. There were a couple of back-and-forths until everyone was satisfied with the article. Then, because *Atención* is a bilingual paper, Chely translated my article into Spanish.

The other evening, I had only my second "ugly American" experience here in three winters, and it was indeed ugly. The Pro Música concerts are held at 5 p.m., and afterward, a large number of the concertgoers walk about two blocks to a very popular restaurant called Hecho en Mexico, one of my favorites. Last Sunday evening after the concert, many followed this pattern, and I was in the crowd. Because all the seats were taken by the time I got there, they offered me a table in the bar, which I was happy to take. A gringo couple were eventually seated there also. Because I got there a few minutes before the couple, I already had my menu. The couple waited a few minutes and then the woman asked the bartender in a very loud voice in English where their menus were. Immediately, a waiter came over and explained to them in English that the restaurant was overwhelmed by the recent influx and that menus would be coming forthwith. He asked if, in the meantime, he could take their drink order. The woman replied by screaming, "Eat! Eat!" Then another waiter came in with menus for them, and they ordered with many changes.

My food had arrived by this time. When the waiter left, the woman complimented the bartender on his English and then said, "You know what's wrong with San Miguel? Not enough people speak English." Well, duh. San Miguel is in Mexico, and anyway, that's so not true. Most waitstaff and store clerks speak far better English than the tourists speak

Spanish. When their meals did not arrive after a few minutes (you can imagine how busy the kitchen was at this point), she insisted that the bartender leave his post and check on their meals. He returned to say that they were coming right up, and the food did arrive soon thereafter. At no time did I hear the woman use the words "please" or "thank you" in either language. By that time, I had lost my appetite, and I asked my waiter to wrap my food to take home. I was so angry that I knew if I stayed any longer, I would have to confront this woman. By the way, the husband uttered not one syllable. Unfortunately, a few days later I encountered the same woman in the restroom at the biblioteca, and she started in again. "Look at this disgusting filth. This is absolutely the worst thing I've ever seen. Being from New York, I'm just not used to this," and on and on. Because there are communal toilet paper dispensers on the wall outside of the individual stalls, from which you tear off paper to take in with you, some shreds of clean toilet paper were on the floor, and that was about the extent of the mess. I've certainly seen a lot worse, both at home and in other countries. Clearly it didn't deserve all that vitriol. I guess she hasn't been around much if she thought that was bad. I didn't say a word in reply and left as soon as I could. She's an extremely attractive older woman with perfectly coifed hair, full makeup, and lovely clothes. I'm hoping she'll be so upset by SMA that she'll never return.

I have finally finished *Caramelo* by Sandra Cisneros, just in time, as the Writers' Conference is coming right up, with the author's keynote address on the first evening. If any of you are going to read it, I recommend you not skip the chronology in the back. I learned some very interesting facts. Among them: Mexicans earned more medals of honor than any other group during WWII, and in the Vietnam War, Chicano soldiers, per capita, were awarded more medals for bravery than any other group. They also died in disproportionate numbers.

Sandy and I were having dinner one night at Vivali (the name now changed from Vivoli due to a divorce settlement), an Italian place around the corner from our rentals that is among our favorite restaurants, when the waiter rushed over and told us to go out to the street immediately, as an interesting parade was going by. It was to advertise the fact that the Cañada de la Virgen (the Gorge of the Virgin), a pre-Columbian Mexican archeological site not far from SMA, was reopening to the public after a long time spent on excavation and conservation. There are seven enormous pyramid structures of different sizes and shapes. The main monument was for sky observation. Only 200 tourists a day are going to be permitted in, and all services will be at the entrance and people will be bused to the site. I'm really excited to go there, but it may have to wait until next fall.

A parading dancer representative of the indigenous who built the pyramids nearby.

The first Danzón of 2011 was held in the jardín, and I wouldn't miss it.

A group from a dance studio showed us all how it's done.

Something interesting happened as a sideshow to the dancing. An obviously *borracho* (drunk) guy was up on the bandstand dancing and in danger of tumbling off, so two police officers came to intervene. The crowd called out that he wasn't hurting anybody and not to remove him, and they didn't. The officers just got him down and he wandered away. I liked that method of dealing with a nonthreatening situation.

Quick Hits

One day, I was standing at my window that overlooks the courtyard and something caught my eye in the clear morning sky: a hot-air balloon drifting slowly over El Centro, taking in the sights.

These two danced so smoothly together!

When a hot-air balloon is close, it sounds like a dragon breathing.

When Alex, Carol (another friend for the past three years here), Chely, and I had the first meeting many weeks ago of our re-formed Spanish conversation group, I teared up. There we were once again, four people from totally disparate places and with completely diverse lives, who enjoy each other's company immensely and who meet up for just a few weeks together each year in SMA to speak Spanish and to laugh. Oh, do

Chely, André, and I at the opening of his exhibit.

we laugh! And today at the end of our session, when I bid Alex goodbye (Carol left a few days ago), again I wept a bit. Many things can happen in a year. I only hope that next year in SMA, we can all come together again.

The article I wrote about André Mayer's photography exhibit at the biblioteca during the month of March was published in *Atención*. André, Chely, and I were all pleased with it. In thanks, they took me to lunch at a great seafood place called La Sirena Gorda (The Fat Mermaid). It was a fun time with unique tacos and drinks and three languages being spoken.

I had tiny ants in my kitchen (just like at home in Philadelphia). At Bonanza, my nearby supermercado, I found sprays for everything but ants. I was telling Reyna, my housekeeper, about this, and listed all the different insects for which there were sprays, but I made a mistake and said there was one for *mascotas* (pets) instead of *moscas* (flies). We shared a good laugh over that one!

As part of my job as transportation coordinator for the volunteers who staff Ojalá Niños' weekly after-school art classes, it has been necessary for me to occasionally speak Spanish on the phone, as there are now some Mexicans volunteering who do not have Internet access, just cellphones. Yikes! It's so difficult to understand, and the cellphone reception certainly doesn't help matters. I have taken to repeating what I have thought I've heard and praying that all of the connections I've set up materialize.

Many times here, life is a three-ring circus. Take this morning. The short-story group was meeting in Sandy's apartment, which is in my complex. I told her I'd stand outside the main door to open it for the guests so that she wouldn't have to keep running to buzz people in while simultaneously greeting others as they arrived at her apartment door. Just as I was going out to do that, Heather and our shared housekeeper, Reyna, showed up, along with two movers who were struggling up to the third floor with a Chinese chest Heather had bought and was installing in my place. Heather wanted to consult with me about placement of the chest. I gave my quick opinion as I sidled toward my door. Then, as I neared the front door, the flower lady appeared and I wanted to buy from her, but I needed to be outside acting as door person. So I grabbed some flowers, paid her, then ran back up the three flights of stairs, thrust the flowers at Reyna, and asked her to arrange them in a vase for me. And I can't tell you how often things like this happen here.

Writers' Conference

Let me sum it up by saying that it was extraordinary and exhausting. I met dozens of wonderful, smart, funny people of all ages and several nationalities. Because all the presentations of the featured speakers had simultaneous translation into Spanish (those needing that service wore headphones), and because the conference organizers had hired a PR person from Mexico City to sell the conference to Mexicans, and because a good number of the presenters were Mexicans themselves, there were many Mexican attendees. In addition to three full days, there were excursions, intensive workshops, and lectures during the two days prior to and the two days after the main conference. Thank goodness I did not elect to take any of the intensive workshops; believe me, the conference itself was intensive enough for me. I'd leave the house by 8 a.m., walk a half hour to the hotel housing the conference in time for breakfast before the first address at 9 a.m., and not get home until nearly 11 p.m., after whatever party concluded each of the three days. But I did take three of the four offered excursions, which were included in the price of the conference.

On Thursday, I walked to the Hotel Real de Minas to meet up with the group that was to have a tour of historic homes from the colonial period. I was a little early, so I went out to the pool area to wait. Because only one shady seat was left, I asked the woman sitting on half the bench, reading, if I might share it with her. This, of course, led to spirited conversation, and Nancy and I became conference buddies. Nancy is not a writer, but she read 120 books last year; that's a new book every three days, folks! I am in awe of this accomplishment. But the conference's title was "A Bilingual Conference for Writers & Readers," so she was in the right place. At nearly the appointed hour for the tour, not seeing any group forming nor bus arriving, we walked to the hotel's entrance and met a conference staffer who apologized for the misinformation, and handed me 20 pesos with instructions for us to take a cab to the jardín, where we'd meet up with our group. I had just walked from that area! Anyway, we found our group of about 16, and after introductions had a fascinating tour. I never did find out how that many people knew that we were meeting at the jardín and not at the hotel, and how it was that Nancy and I didn't get the memo.

The first house, on Calle Hospicio, was 450 years old and was the former orphanage of SMA. The current owner of the house started the Writers' Conference six years ago. She had flown in just that morning from Aspen, Colorado, where she now lives, since the house is up for sale for $2.1 million USD as part of a "friendly divorce." The walls are three feet thick. There are five bedrooms and four and a half baths. She said the property was in grave disrepair when she and her husband bought it.

And then we walked just a few blocks to the second house, which was built in 1729. The owner of this house rents it out almost all the time, but there was no one in residence when we were there, maybe because it rents for $3,950 USD PER WEEK. But there are at least four bedrooms, each with its own terrace, so the idea is that four couples could rent it together. They'd probably never even see one another, the place is so immense. And that price includes a housekeeper, cook, and gardener.

It was quite a hot day, so Nancy suggested to me and a younger woman, Christy, that we all go out for a beer. I don't drink beer, but I was game for a margarita. I took them to a favorite spot of mine for sunset drinks, La Azotea, and we spent a couple of relaxing hours telling our life stories and sharing lots of laughs. From then on, we were a trio. I couldn't resist taking a photo of the bartender with his humongous bag of limes. I think of this every time I buy my four little limes at the fruit store.

Probably just one evening's cocktail orders' worth of **limones.**

Each of the three days of the conference, there was a common schedule: buffet breakfast provided by the hotel, a presentation by a featured speaker, a one-and-a-half-hour mini-workshop with about seven topics to choose from, and a box lunch provided by one of the restaurants in town, during which there were author readings and individual consultations with professionals. After lunch, there was another presenter, then mini-workshop #2, with all new choices, a break with open mic for authors to read from their books, and again individual consultations.

Just before the 6 p.m. keynote speaker, Sandra Cisneros, we had a special presentation by one of the vendors in the conference bookstore, purveyors of silk rebozos. These world-class, top-of-the-line rebozos play a large role in *Caramelo*, so the demonstration of all of the ways in which they can be worn was timely. Afterward, hundreds of extra folks filed into the ballroom for the keynote. Sandra's topic was "Living in *Los Tiempos Sustos*" (Living in Frightening Times).

Following a short Q&A (there was to be a much longer one the next morning for which we were invited to write questions on 3x5 cards), we walked en masse about three blocks to the Instituto Allende, which had been transformed into a Mexican plaza for the Viva México fiesta. I don't think I've ever been to such a party!

As we entered the magnificent, ancient courtyard of this venerable institution, we were given little hand-painted clay mugs on a ribbon, which we could wear around our necks when the mugs were not filled with straight tequila (with lime slices) that smiling waiters poured with abandon! A decorated burro was present with which to have our photo taken. Bustling waiters passed hot (in both senses of the word) *botanas* (appetizers). Huge puppets called *mojigangas* danced to a mariachi band playing and singing their hearts out.

The burro and I get friendly (with a little help from a shot of tequila).

Then it was on to the back patio, which was festively decorated and dotted with stands serving tamales, hot poblano soup, tacos, traditional Mexican drinks (such as *horchata*, a sort of super thin, sweet and cinnamony rice pudding-tasting beverage, which I didn't love), and then fresh fried churros with—and this is really gilding the lily—chocolate or butterscotch sauce to ladle on top. Guests just wandered from station to station, eating and drinking as much as they liked, while a fire juggler did his thing, and other mariachi bands entertained.

I was so very pleasantly surprised to see that my favorite mariachi group, La Tuna, had been hired to entertain us. The leader, Pablo, recognized me and gave me a warm hello. Spirited dancing ensued.

And then the grand finale—fireworks.

Another highlight of the first day was making a new friend, Enaid. We had met coming in the front door of the hotel and immediately clicked. She lives in Guanajuato, and I'm going to visit her for a week in the fall when I'm there to experience Cervantino, the world-renowned Cervantes festival in the capital city. I'll be a guest in her home and she'll get the tickets I'll need. I am so humbled by this act of generosity and friendship.

Where else in the world could an author have the name of her latest book lit up in fireworks?

On Day Two I enjoyed more lectures, Q&As, mini-workshops, breaks talking with new friends, and gaining lots of new knowledge and strategies for my writing. For the evening part—a *Carnitas* Fest (literally "little meats," a dish originally from Oaxaca made by braising or simmering pork, served shredded as a filling for tacos, burritos, etc.) and Talking Gourd Campfire—we were bused about an hour out of town to Simple Choice Farm, the home of a very interesting couple, both of whom are chocolatiers. The man, whose name I regretfully can't remember, but whose chocolate factory is now closed down, used to make chocolate by special order for Vincente Fox and George W. Bush. His wife, poet Judyth Hill, still has her business, the Chocolate Maven, in Santa Fe. She also writes cookbooks, and her most recent one was *Geronimo*, done in concert with the chef at that famous restaurant, also in Santa Fe.

After we'd eaten, we assembled around a fire and watched and sang as the full moon rose over a nearby hill, a highlight of the conference for me. Then we passed around a decorated gourd and when it came to each person, he or she was free to read a poem, sing a song, or just say something, or not. A new friend, José, shared deeply from his life experience and I was extremely moved. I didn't speak, because at that point, I was really overwhelmed with all that was happening.

On the third day, after the usual schedule concluded, the main conference ended, but there was still more fun to come. One of the really valuable mini-workshops I attended was "What It Takes to Write Personal Stories and Memoir: Writing About Things You Don't Remember." The excellent teacher of this course, Laura Davis, now sends writing prompts to my email once a week, at my invitation.

On the Monday after the conference, I went on another excursion, this one to Charco del Ingenio, SMA's incredible botanical garden. I think people were either totally wiped out or had gone home already, because only five of us were on the bus. We were given a two-hour private tour toward the end of the day by the director himself, Mario, who was so *guapo* (handsome) that I could hardly pay attention to what he was saying and showing us.

The final excursion—very well attended—was to La Gruta (The Grotto), one of the hot springs here. We had about three hours to unwind in the various temperatures of water, plus we talked and lay about on chaise longues. The perfect end to a unique and exciting several days. I'll definitely return next year!

Mario Hernandez, the director of Charco del Ingenio.

March 2011

Music, Music, Music

The three-ring circus that usually holds sway here has been reduced lately to only two, but what rings they are! The eighth annual Cuba Fest is in full swing for 10 days. There is free, very good music, sometimes accompanied by dancing, almost every evening in the jardín, free movies, and a nice selection of Cuban DVDs, books for both adults and children, jewelry, T-shirts, and musical instruments, etc., for sale in an outdoor setting.

And then there were two...

I attended a one-night-only show of Cuban music, an homage to two famous members of the Buena Vista Social Club, Compay Segundo and Celia Cruz. It was very loud and very high-energy. At the finale, anyone who wanted to boogie was invited onstage, and many did! A good time was had by all.

At the very same time, the Baroque Festival, celebrating its fifth anniversary in SMA, is going strong for six days. Its numerous events are held in churches all over town. I attended one concert, Polyphonic Passions in South America, performed by Mexico's foremost baroque ensemble joined by a baroque orchestra to perform music from the Christian missions of the Chiquitos Indians in eastern Bolivia. The music by Ennio Morricone that accompanied the 1986 movie *The Mission* (which I love!) was pooh-poohed by the announcer. This concert, he said, was the real thing.

I also attended a screening of *Farinelli* at a brand-new, very upscale hotel and condo development somewhat out of town. Ten a.m. was a tad early for this movie of an 18th-century castrato, due to its subject matter, but it was fascinating and based on historical fact.

Two other musical performances took place right before these two festivals. The first was a free evening concert in the jardín in celebration of International Women's Day. I didn't know anything about it, which is a continuing problem. *Atención* frequently doesn't get the news of things going on in the Mexican community, and there were no flyers up about it. It was only because of Chely that I even heard about it. And was I glad! The singer, Dolores Canta (which translates to "Dolores sings"—surely a stage name), had an extraordinary voice and a stage presence unlike any other. Also, her keyboard accompanist was on fire! The audience was about 98 percent upper-middle-class Mexicanas.

For her final number, she lit candles for all women, for those who suffer, and for other things I don't remember now, put them on a plate, and then put the plate on her head, and walked around singing, slowly and regally.

Now here's where the two-ring circus comes in. The day of this concert was Mardi Gras, and the last hoorah before Ash Wednesday the next day and the beginning of Lent. During Dolores' performance, the adolescents in the jardín were totally out of control, racing around and around, screaming and smashing cascarones willy-nilly. The municipal police station is just across the street from the jardín. Why didn't they station a couple of officers there to nip that behavior in the bud? I felt very bad for the singer. She showed no sign of annoyance, and when I told a friend here about my dismay at the lack of respect for a well-known performer, she said that maybe because the singer is Mexican herself, it was not disturbing to her, but just the way things are.

Last Saturday, the long-awaited American Roots Music extravaganza, featuring Maria Muldaur, of "Midnight at the Oasis" fame (recorded 37 years ago, she told us—yikes!), took place as a benefit for the programs offered to the youth of SMA at the biblioteca, which has the second-largest collection of books in English in Mexico, and which is the heart and soul of the cultural life of the gringos. The celebration of our U.S. musical roots took place about 15 minutes out of town at Rancho Arcángel, an immense private property that also contains the Mayan Baths, a series of pools filled with water from the hot springs there. We were invited to bring our bathing suits and enjoy the baths.

Buses ran about every half hour from a central point in town out to the concert, and although that type of music is not my favorite, the musicianship was of such a high caliber, I enjoyed myself immensely. I met lots of friends there among the 600 concertgoers. It was extraordinarily well planned and executed, primarily by a man in my UU congregation, Jon Sievert, who was a photographer for *Rolling Stone* magazine and knew all of the musicians. The food was catered by about six of the town's best restaurants, all seats were covered, it was a gorgeous day (well, when isn't it in SMA?), and a fine spirit prevailed throughout.

Last Sunday night, I attended one of the Pro Música concerts staged as a garden party. There must have been 300 people present in a magnificent garden with grass (grass!) and an Olympic-sized lap pool, which formed an aisle of sorts between the rows of chairs. A friend described the music played as "Top 40" (classical) and turned up his nose, but I enjoyed such familiar favorites as the overture to *The Barber of Seville*, Largo from Dvořák's "New World" symphony, Bizet's *Carmen* Suite No. 1—you get the idea. The last piece played before the intermission was Johann Strauss' "Champagne Polka," and the bartenders timed their popping of the corks to correspond with the music. During the break, we enjoyed that champagne and fabulous botanas as evening fell. Several birds accompanied the music and it was altogether a magical evening.

CHAPTER 4

Four Months in San Miguel Come to an End

Mercedes' kids are now speaking in English sentences. It's so thrilling for me. While I'm in Philly these coming five months, I'll be cutting out tons of photos from magazines and brochures to bring back and looking for books to help me teach them English, although the Internet has been a fine resource. Next visit I'm going to buy a printer here, as it's been a challenge to do this work without one.

After yesterday's class, Mercedes asked if I had some time to speak with her daughter in English. I did. Paula, age 23, wants to go to the U.S. as an au pair, and she had found a website that matches families and au pairs. We did a trial interview in English, as that is the first step in the process. When I got home, I read the whole website (in Spanish) and found it to be very solid; it's been in business since 1965, and 70 percent of its parent applicants are repeaters. The au pairs stay for one year and can re-up in three-month blocks if all are in agreement. The workers get excellent support, starting with a four-day course at the company's school on Long Island, and then from regional directors. Monthly meetings with all of the au pairs in that area and a director are mandatory. There is a study component, too, for which the family has to pay; this is a rule of the U.S. government. I knew about this because over the years, I have had any number of au pairs in my ESL classes in Philadelphia, all of whom needed special documentation that they had attended regularly and had successfully completed the course. When I go to Mercedes' home tonight to teach my last lesson, we will discuss what I learned from my research on the site.

The Princess Drinks Coca-Cola

I learned that frequently, folks drink Coke as an alternative to water, since they have no potable water available to them. A retired doctor friend of mine who volunteers at one of the medical clinics has told me that he frequently sees five- and six-year-olds with a mouthful of totally rotted teeth from the consumption of Coke. Coca-Cola would be in a position to pay for the infrastructure to deliver potable water to the campo, but of course it would never do that because that would cut into its profits.

This Coke-drinking princess was parched after processing in the annual Welcome to Spring parade.

Some very good news: The jacarandas, which cause a huge percentage of those in town to sneeze, get watery, itchy eyes, and even have asthma attacks, are now in full bloom, and I wasn't affected as I was last year. Perhaps my symptoms then were just coincidental. The spectacular long-lasting display of purple flowers is almost worth the distress of so many, I can say now that I'm not among the sufferers.

I saw a documentary recently called *Letters from the Other Side*. The filmmaker helped Mexican families left at home and husbands/brothers/boyfriends/fathers who had gone to El Norte to look for work to make video letters to those "on the other side," which the filmmaker then hand-delivered and caught the emotion they engendered on film. As you can imagine, it was pretty heavy-duty. In many towns in Mexico, there are virtually no men, and the women are left to run everything. Sometimes this is very good for the women, as they learn job skills, form cooperatives, and come to depend on themselves rather than others. Often, of course, when the men come home, they want things to revert to how they were, and that is not going to happen. (It reminded me of what happened to the women left at home while the men went off to fight WWII—Rosie the Riveter never went back to the kitchen.)

I learned that a staggering 16 percent of Mexico's workforce is in the U.S. During the Q&A after the film, someone asked if the Mexican government was encouraging (or at the very least turning a blind eye to) this huge migration north as a way to keep the same demographic of young, undereducated, unemployed men that's demonstrating all over the Middle East, out of Mexico, because if they stayed, there would probably be another revolution. The moderator, whose educated opinion I value and trust, said yes. This was the first time that I saw the Mexican government as part of the problem and it was really eye-opening for me.

Although I haven't attended all of the Baroque Music Festival, I went back to another concert that I'm pretty sure was the highlight: a concert in a canyon of El Charco del Ingenio, the botanical garden, featuring "Música para los Reales Fuegos de Artificio" ("Music for the Royal Fireworks") by Handel. A wooden platform was built for the musicians and a boardwalk constructed for them to walk down with their valuable instruments. Concertgoers were to choose a rock and settle in for the show. There's an expression here, "*No vale la pena*" (it's not worth the trouble), and I'd have to use it to describe this extravaganza, for me at least.

A friend and I arrived by cab and then walked a long time to be in a good spot to both watch and hear. Happily, teenagers were hired to extend a helping hand to seniors and others who needed help jumping from one rock to another. We finally got settled in with our pillows, binoculars, and sunscreen. The music was supposed to start at 5:30, but so many people continued to stream in, and the sun was in the eyes of some of the musicians, so things didn't get started until after 6. The orchestra played only two pieces. The first selection, "Pulcinella Suite" by Stravinsky, we could barely hear. Because the "Royal Fireworks" suite, which ended the program, had a lot of brass, we could enjoy it more.

We had been promised fireworks to coincide with the music. When the second piece began, there was a terrific boom of firecrackers very, very close to where we were sitting that scared the life out of us. Later in the piece, unfortunately when it was not yet dark enough, a few fireworks lit up right over our heads. Completely surrounding us was dried grass. All I could think was what would happen if a burning ember fell onto that grass and set the whole place on fire. Luckily, a stiff breeze blew the spent fireworks in the opposite direction. Whenever there was an explosion, hundreds of ducks—which, I later found out, are in their mating season—would rise into the sky in fear.

This is how things looked at the end of the day.

When it was over—and it had to be over quickly in order to allow folks to get back out of the canyon before dark—we retraced our steps, hopped on a free shuttle bus to the entrance to the park, and compared notes with others who had different vantages. We just about all agreed that, while it probably raised a huge amount of money for the botanical garden, they also spent a lot of money on the construction of the stage and boardwalk. It was a happening for sure, and I guess I'm glad I went so I can now say I was there, but really, in my heart, *no vale la pena*.

The Final Chapter

I had been arranging rides for four months for the other volunteers to get out to Ojalá Niños, the marvelous after-school arts program that my friend Elsmarie runs (with tons of help) out of her home in San Miguel Viejo. Very limited public transportation goes there, and it was my job to hook up those with cars with those who required rides, making sure there were seats for all who needed them. The names and numbers of the helpers changed every week. I had taught English at Ojalá last year with other volunteers, and Elsmarie kept asking me when I was going to come out to see all of the changes at the place, and to visit with the kids, so on my next-to-last day, I went. I was picked up at the house of a friend. We stopped at Bodega Aurrera, the usual spot for the rendezvous of volunteers. The driver left her car door open for a very long time while she was talking to someone, and I thought I'd go nuts with the dinging. Someone in the back seat said, "Take the keys out of the ignition," so I did. When the driver came back and tried to start the car, it was stone dead. She tried pushing something called a kill switch, but nothing worked. I felt horrible. Could I possibly have disabled her car by pulling the keys out of the ignition? Anyway, all of her passengers got into another car, she found somebody with a cellphone, and she called her housekeeper's husband, who, she said, could fix anything. She never made it out to Ojalá. When I got home, I wrote her an email inquiring what was wrong with her car and apologizing again.

I spent three hours at Ojalá, meeting all of the people I'd arranged rides for over the past four months, whom I'd not met, and seeing all of the different projects going on. It was amazing stuff, much of it made with trash: a mural crafted from pieces of broken tile; miniature houses fashioned from shoeboxes; creation of a sea scene, complete with salt(!) and paper fish (I wondered how many of those kids have ever seen or will ever see the ocean); birdhouses constructed of scrap wood; and pocketbooks and change purses created out of many empty potato chip bags, using either the foil inside or the brightly colored outside, depending on the look desired, cleverly folded origami-style to interconnect. I asked a teacher how long it took her to make one of the bags, and she said a month! They are beautifully lined with material and have a zipper. There was bead-making out of Sculpey, a polymer clay, and perhaps one or two more activities. Pretty incredible!

For me, the most exciting and eye-popping project was the mosaic mural that was taking shape.

I helped out with the littlest kids making the sea scene. Bubble wrap was used to make the look of bubbles in the painted sea. Of course the bubble wrap was also used by the kids to make loud pops. Since that day was the last Wednesday of March, all birthdays during that month were celebrated with a meal that the mommas prepared and brought. I couldn't eat anything because I wasn't sure they'd disinfected all of the veggies, and I certainly didn't want to get sick two days before leaving. What they brought looked delicious! There were about eight purchased cakes, and I was going to eat a piece of one of those, but someone was leaving and I needed an early ride back so I could get to Mercedes' house on time.

When I finally got home from working with the kids from Mercedes', I answered a phone call from Eleonor, my housekeeper from my first year in SMA, with whom I've kept in touch. Before Christmas, when I had taken some presents over to the house where she works to give to her niece, I gave Eleonor my card with my dates in SMA written on it. She said Carla had been asking her why they never saw la señora, so we made a plan to meet up the next day because they wanted to give me a gift. Oy! They always do that, and I keep telling them that it is so unnecessary, but Carla got her mother to crochet me two lovely bureau scarves that she presented to me beautifully wrapped when we met up. I suggested that we go to the jardín to sit and chat, and I bought ice cream for all.

I was very touched by my gift, and it was difficult to say goodbye. The day before I had said farewell to Alejandro, my yoga teacher, and I actually broke down crying. I had said adios to Carlos that morning as both of us shed some tears.

Then it was off to Mercedes' house for our final English lesson of this visit. They also gave me a small thank-you gift, two little angels made of glass and metal that the father of one of the girls makes. More tears were shed over them and as we said goodbye for a while, I promised to pick up where we left off when I returned in September. These were difficult days!

Eleonor and Carla on our outing to the jardín.

ADIOS, SAN MIGUEL!

On the first day of April, after a final goodbye to both Heather and Reyna, off I went to return to my other life in Philadelphia. The trip home was uneventful except for the fact that my plane left an hour late out of León, and so I nearly missed my flight in Houston to Philly. Because it was the last flight of the day of any airline to Philly, they held it for those on the flight from León, a lucky break for me!

Y así pasan los días... *(And like this the days pass...)*

Now that I'm back into my Philly routine, I've realized that I am happy in both locations. My life seems "right" both in Mexico and here. I surprised myself by falling in love with small-town life, even though I very much like what a big city has to offer, and its anonymity. Frequently during this stay in SMA, I emailed Suji the sentiment, "Why don't I live here?" Finally she wrote back, "Well, why don't you?"

I'm going to be in Mexico for six months next time, going down in September, right after my nephew's wedding during Labor Day weekend, to experience autumn there. I'll come home for six weeks on December 1 and host my son and his family for the holidays. Then on January 15, back down I'll go until April 1. I am, as always, filled with gratitude for the opportunity to have this experience.

Only in San Miguel

A few doors down from my rental is a bakery. One day as I was walking by, a woman came out carrying a huge sheet cake on a piece of cardboard. It was not in a box, but open to the dusty air. I thought this was strange. Not an hour later, I was reading in Sandra Cisneros' book *Caramelo* these words: "Birthday cakes walking out of a bakery without a box, just like that, on a wooden plate." I was floored. The book was written in 2002 about the writer's memories of her early life in Texas and Mexico. She was born in 1954, so this method of taking home birthday cakes goes way back.

> "San Miguel is a version of paradise."
>
> Juan Villoro, well-known Mexican intellectual, journalist, and writer, quoted in *Atención*

Chapter 5

September–November 2011

El Grito and El Dia de la Independencia

During my summer in the States in 2011, something significant happened as I returned to Philadelphia after a visit to Suji and Geoff's New Jersey beach house, riding with their friends Dave and Heather. On the two-hour drive, Heather mentioned that they were considering moving from their house in Germantown and that they liked the Art Museum area in which I lived. Heather casually said, "If you ever feel like selling your house, we would be interested in buying it."

I had occasionally been thinking about the possibility of moving to San Miguel almost year-round, and had been spending more and more time there, testing different seasons to make sure I enjoyed each one as much as I did wintertime. I also worried about leaving my house in the Northeast for months at a time during the winter. But here was the possibility of a nearly painless way to unload my house without the usual concomitant agonies involved in selling it. Now I've begun to ponder this possibility in earnest.

※ ※ ※

Since I arrived in SMA in early September, vendors have been selling virtually anything you could imagine in the colors of the Mexican flag—red, green, and white—to be used or worn on Independence Day, September 16. Also, decorations, which to me look awfully similar to those that went up for La Navidad, are hung on the streets.

Flags, blouses, sombreros, you name it—it's all for sale for Día de la Independencia in San Miguel.

After the presentation, girlfriends and wives joined the riders as they galloped out of town. Not the best riding gear on that lovely lass, I'd say.

During the day of September 15, as a build-up to El Grito, a re-enactment group rode their horses into El Centro for a short commemorative speech in the jardín. I was totally impressed with the condition of the animals; to a horse they looked well fed and well taken care of. Groups of runners from various neighboring towns made a symbolic lap around the jardín carrying *fuegos simbólicos*, torches similar to the Olympic flame.

Elsewhere in the jardín, the length of one entire city block was given over to vendors selling tchotchkes for the fiesta. (The word *tchotchkes*, which means baubles or cheap souvenirs, has Yiddish and Polish roots and is surprisingly similar in Spanish: *cháchars*.)

You gotta love this hat!

The ceremony of El Grito commemorates that moment around 6 a.m. on September 16, 1810, when Father Miguel Hidalgo exhorted people gathered for the morning Mass at the parish church in Dolores (since renamed Dolores Hidalgo) to join the revolt against the Spanish government, which is considered the beginning of the Mexican War for Independence. Now, El Grito is celebrated in every city in Mexico on the night of September 15, here in SMA at 11 p.m. I was warned away from this celebration by at least three sanmiguelenses. I was told that more people than you could ever imagine jammed themselves into the relatively small jardín space and that many were very drunk. Pickpockets were rampant. Think Times Square on New Year's Eve on a smaller scale, or Carnival in New Orleans. Fireworks rain down on the attendees, and one year, one of the elaborate structures called *castillos*, built to deliver fireworks in place, fell over, although I noticed stout guy-wires on all of them this year.

A castillo at the ready to thrill the crowd with its fuegos artificiales *(fireworks).*

I was told that sanmiguelenses stay home that night and that the city is turned over to Mexican tourists. Basically, it's a bacchanalia; many of the attendees are young adults who act as if they're on spring break. It's such a double-edged sword, because it's advantageous for the hotels, restaurants, shops, and street merchants, but the tourists make so much noise long into the night and create tons of trash on the streets. The gringos do not act like this at all, and I hope the citizens of San Miguel have taken notice.

I took the advice I'd been given and, at close to 11 p.m., went up onto my rental's communal terrace, where I met others, both a gringo and a Mexican family. Since I rent just around the corner from the jardín, I could clearly hear the historical grito, traditionally delivered by the mayor (who, for the first time in SMA history, is a woman), and see the fireworks, coming from both the castillos and overhead displays.

That's the very attractive door to the condo development where I rent an apartment, in front of which are those awaiting the parade.

On El Día de la Independencia, I walked out of my apartment at 11 a.m. to try to find the promised parade route (none was given in the newspaper), and found that I was on it. Hundreds of people were lined up, waiting for the parade to pass by.

I really liked this man's outfit as he walked with one school group.

The parade consisted primarily of the students of every school in San Miguel, each dressed in a different, distinctive uniform. There were also reenactors, playing the part of local revolutionary heroes, and representatives from other states in Mexico in their traditional garb.

And you always know when the parade is over, as the limpias (the cleaning crew) bring up the rear, in this case mostly to pick up horse droppings.

Celebration in Honor of San Miguel Arcángel–Part I

The final fiesta of the month—and, my housekeeper assures me that there is not another for quite a long time, *gracias a Dios*—is the celebration of the birthday of San Miguel Arcángel, the patron saint of SMA. Festivities got started early on a Friday evening with the usual four-ring circus in the jardín.

First up was a drum and bugle corps of schoolchildren.

As these groups left the scene, a colorfully outfitted company of *voladores*, literally "flyers," first made sure that all of their ropes were in proper order. (The Danza de los Voladores—in SMA called just los voladores—is an ancient Mesoamerican ceremony/ritual still performed today, albeit in modified form, in isolated pockets in Mexico. It is believed to have originated with the Nahua, Huastec, and Otomí peoples

The voladores preparing to "fly." What stunning, undoubtedly hand-embroidered outfits for their flight.

in central Mexico, and then spread throughout most of Mesoamerica. —*Wikipedia*)

Then they danced around their pole to the music of a tiny drum and flute, both played by the same man at the same time. One by one, some of the men climbed to a minuscule platform at the top of the pole and spent quite a long time creating harnesses for themselves out of the rugged ropes, while a couple of others remained below to keep the pole steady.

Pretty impressive, those voladores, let me tell you. The crowd was rapt!

When they were all sure of their harnesses, down they came, unraveling around the pole like a maypole dance in reverse.

While that was going on, another "ring" was occupied by what looked to me to be whirling dervishes in beautifully embellished costumes. They did a sort of twist dance, and I hadn't a clue that day what they were or where they came from. Although they wore men's masks, there were women among the dancers. I later learned that these dancers are meant to represent the Spanish conquerors.

And then—right between these other groups—were the Indian dancers, whom I've seen several times before at other fiestas. Because of that, I resisted the urge to photograph them all over again, except for one amazingly tall (by Mexican standards), handsome specimen I couldn't take my eyes off. And I wasn't the only one.

After the dancing stopped, many female tourists asked to have their photo taken with this muy guapo (very handsome) dancer, to which he graciously agreed.

Mystery dancer.

And to add to the cacophony, the bells in the parroquia were being rung almost constantly by hand by men right next to them! I hope they hire deaf people, because if they weren't deaf when they went up there to work, surely they are by the time they come down. They just keep flipping the enormous bells over and over. It must take some real brute strength until they get them going.

When it was completely dark, a small religious parade came through, bringing what I assume was an icon of San Miguel Arcángel. And finally—devils! And this was only the night *before* the celebration!

CELEBRATION IN HONOR OF
SAN MIGUEL ARCÁNGEL—PART II

The festivities for the actual birthday of San Miguel Arcángel had begun much earlier that day at the ungodly hour of 3 a.m. in a ceremony called *La Alborada* (the dawn, but it was waaaay before dawn), which included processions starting at different points, but meeting up in front of the parroquia at 4. The celebration combines Christian and pagan symbols and rites. When the processions meet, those walking and those waiting for them sing *las mañanitas* (happy birthday) to the patron saint, firecrackers go off (called "the burning of the powder"), and church bells ring. Trust me when I tell you that not a single person in SMA was sleeping after 4 a.m. that day.

One of the xúchiles being carried in.

Can you imagine how many hands and hours it took to fashion this?

That evening around 5, a huge parade for San Miguel Arcángel began. People came from all over the region with individual offerings to the saint, but the main reason for the parade is the bringing in of huge floral offerings called *xúchiles*. They are constructed of *cucharilla* (green desert spoon, which is nearing extinction because of indiscriminate use), giant reeds, and *cempasúchil*, the Aztec marigold, native to Mexico.

They are then stood upright around the entrance to the parroquia. Each one is more magnificent than the next.

The marchers all came up Calle Canal and hung a right to proceed to the parroquia. They just kept coming and coming and coming, for over two hours. I wondered, more than once, where they were all going to sleep and eat and go to the bathroom.

The parade ended with the arrival of the mojigangas, the giant puppets. After dark, fireworks were shot off (endlessly). They like their celebrations long, loud, and colorful here.

Ojalá Niños Art Walk

On a Sunday, I offered to help out Ojalá Niños with its second annual fundraising art walk. The art walk is a favorite activity here in SMA, usually confined to El Centro. You publicize your event, display your art at your gallery, have refreshments and drinks at the ready, and await the folks, and it worked just that way for Ojalá Niños, except that this art program for children in Viejo San Miguel is not in El Centro, but way out along a dirt road in the country, and it rained—hard—on Saturday, making the only access road impassable. A call went out for an emergency truckload of soil, and many willing workers made the road as good as new—until it rained again in the wee hours of Sunday. More soil, more workers, and the road was ready when we arrived. In fact, we were the first car to roll over the repaired section at about 11 a.m.—and the art walk was called for noon to 4 p.m. Whew!

And then we were open for business. All afternoon, I worked at one of two cashier stations, got to sit down the whole time, and was in the shade, chatting with interesting people. This is work?

A magnificent mosaic mural was done by the oldest group of kids, and has the famous quote "Be the change you wish to see in your life" (in Spanish, of course) from Gandhi. This and other murals they've done at Ojalá Niños have gotten them much attention and potential business. A woman who taught groups in Guatemala about the cooperative model is going to come to the program to help them start one up. These kids could soon be contributing to their families' income and perhaps even finding their way to a lucrative profession in their adulthood—all because of the volunteers who teach skills such as this one at Ojalá Niños. Of course that was not the original intention of the program—rather, it was to give kids from very poor families a chance to express their innate creativity—but, hey, if you can turn your art talent into income, that's all to the good.

Fewer people attended the art walk this year, I was told, perhaps out of fear of what the road would be like after the rain, but those who did come bought generously. Everyone seemed pleased.

A photo I took near my house that I just love. The flag and papel picado *(cut paper) were still up from Día de la Independencia several weeks prior.*

Cervantino—Part I

Way back in February at the SMA Writers' Conference, I met Enaid, who lives in Guanajuato, the capital city of the state with the same name (SMA is in this state, also). She had come to Guanajuato from Chicago via Costa Rica. I had been thinking of going to Guanajuato this fall for Cervantino, the International Cervantes Festival, now in its 39th year—a smorgasbord of the performing arts over about a three-week period—and when I expressed interest in renting her casita, she pooh-poohed that and invited me to be her house guest instead. We agreed on a week and, before I even got there, she provided me with incredible services: walking me through the complicated events schedule by phone and email, helping me to zero in on the programs I wanted to experience, then standing in lines to buy my tickets. Wow, that's hospitality!

Early one morning in mid-October, I boarded a bus for the slightly more than one-hour trip to the state's capital. Then, following the careful instructions Enaid had given me, I guided the cab driver to her house. And what a house it is! I learned that it is only a year old, and that in the year before that, Enaid had moved to the city, rented an apartment, found a building lot, hired an architect (although she already had the whole place planned), and had her house built—all in a foreign land and in a foreign tongue.

After a sumptuous brunch, Enaid led me on an orientation tour of the city. There is excellent and cheap bus service, as well as taxis for really out-of-the-way venues where a few of our programs were to take place.

Guanajuato is situated in a narrow valley with cramped, winding streets, called *callejones* (alleys). Cars can't pass through many of them. Constant flooding from water pouring down from the hills led to the construction of large ditches and tunnels to contain and divert overflows during the rainy season. In the 1960s, a dam was constructed that controlled the flooding, and the tunnels were converted into a warren of underground roadways.

Cervantino had its birth when college students presented readings of Cervantes' work in the streets. Now, each year, Cervantino honors a country or countries and features a different Mexican state by inviting them to send performers. To my delight, the guest countries this year were Denmark, Finland, Norway, and Sweden. I mean, what are the chances, with my son and his family living in Finland, that this would be so? The highlighted Mexican state was Nayarit, a small state on the west coast located between the forested mountains of the Sierra Madre Occidental and the Pacific Ocean.

Among the buildings holding Cervantino events was the famous Teatro Juarez. Built in 1872-1903, it is the only theater in Mexico to have maintained the original furnishings. I would soon learn that charm does not mean comfort.

We went to a display/sale of Mexican folk art assembled especially for Cervantino.

Right across from the imposing Our Lady of Guadalupe church

At the Cervantino art show, I fell hard for this paper piece, which was selling for the ridiculous price of the peso equivalent of $50 USD. I was especially taken by the corrugated cardboard box bent to fit the mask perfectly. I resisted temptation and did not buy it.

was the stop for the bus that took us back to Enaid's neighborhood, so I got to look at the church up close quite often during my stay. The area in the foreground is Plaza de la Paz. The cast-iron benches there are the

Plaza de la Paz.

most uncomfortable things I've ever sat on (and they are identical to the ones in SMA's jardín), so while waiting for Enaid to go to the bank, I folded my fleece jacket and sat on it. When she came back, I stood to join her, forgetting about the fleece. By the time I remembered it and came back, it was gone.

My first Cervantino performance was the Inauguration at La Alhóndiga. (The first battle in the Mexican War of Independence was fought at La Alhóndiga de Granaditas—public granary—between the insurgents and the loyalist troops.) The group performing was Orquesta de Jazz de Estocolmo, from Sweden. I expected there'd be long-winded speeches in Spanish before the music began, it being opening night, but at precisely 8 p.m. the music began, to my delight.

The second night, also at La Alhóndiga, turned out to be my favorite performance of the week. It was the Ballet Folklórico de México. I'd seen this group in Ciudad de México over 50 years ago, and several times at the Academy of Music in Philadelphia in the intervening years, and was surprised to see that the dances had not changed. The costumes were brilliant, the music lively—and loud—and the energy and joy projected by the performers were catching.

La Alhóndiga is an outside performance space. I was impressed to learn that all the seats behind a certain designated point are free. It's first come, first served, and people start lining up hours before curtain time. Directly in front of that point is general seating, where you can sit wherever, and closest to the stage is assigned seating at a slightly higher price. None of the performances was expensive at all, though. The six tickets for evening performances that Enaid bought for me cost a total of $68 USD.

Another interesting custom is that there are three calls, starting about 10 minutes before the show starts. A recorded voice says, "*Primera llamada, primera llamada*" (first call), and people who are milling around start to take their seats. Then there is a "*segunda llamada*" (second call), and just moments before the curtain opens, "*tercera llamada*" (third call). At this point, any unclaimed assigned seats are fair game, and people sitting in general seating (not in the free seats, however) or even in less-desirable assigned seats are free to move into them. If you're holding an assigned seat for a friend with a ticket for it, you cannot hold it past tercera llamada. If they come late, they cannot insist on having their seat.

Because this is an outdoor venue, lots of people just stood on a bridge next to it and watched, and people in a private home across the street put up folding chairs in their third-story enclosed porch and filled them for every performance. It was quite chilly in the evenings, and I was glad Enaid warned me to bring warm clothes.

Cervantino—Part II

Since the majority of the Cervantino presentations that Enaid and I chose to experience were in the evening, we had our days free to explore. One day Enaid hosted her bridge group, and since I don't play bridge, I was off on my own. I walked around a bit, taking photos, first of the giant statue of the famous Pípila. *Pípila* means "hen turkey" in Spanish, and Juan José de los Reyes Martínez Amaro (1782-1863) had some mental and physical defects that caused him to walk like a hen turkey, thus the nickname. He was an object of ridicule. As a young man, he worked as a miner and had come to Guanajuato from San Miguel. He became famous for an act of heroism near the beginning of the Mexican War for Independence, on September 28, 1810. The insurrection had moved from Dolores to Guanajuato. The Spanish barricaded themselves—along with plenty of silver and other riches—in a grain warehouse known as La Alhóndiga de Granaditas. It was a stone fortress, but with a wooden door. With a long, flat stone tied to his back to protect himself from the muskets of the Spanish troops, Pípila carried tar and a torch to the door of La Alhóndiga and set it on fire. The insurgents—who far outnumbered the Spanish inside—stormed in and killed all of them. (*–Wikipedia*) I knew the story of the door burning, but I was glad to learn what the nickname Pípila meant.

One evening, we went to a fairly new venue outside of the center of town, the Auditorio del Estado (the State Auditorium), to see a modern dance program called "Now She Knows," presented by the Zero Visibility Corporation from Norway. Others liked it pretty well; I, not so much. The auditorium, however, was splendid, and quite a change from La Alhóndiga.

While attending programs, I had two adventures that are worth reporting. On Saturday morning, I decided that I wanted to go hear Magos Herrera, an extremely well-known Spanish blues singer who has earned many awards and who was performing in the ex-hacienda de San Gabriel al Barrera. Although I didn't have a ticket, I took a cab to the somewhat-outlying place, and when I got there it was completely sold out. My heart sank. One of the ushers saw my disappointment and told me to speak to a bunch of other ushers closer to the entrance. I told them my problem and that I'd been sent to them for help. They told me to stand on the side for a minute. After a short while, one said, "*Pasale, señora,*" and gestured that I was to go in. I said, "*Sin entrada?*" "*Si, si, pasale.*" I have no idea how I got in or why, but I was thrilled.

The other adventure took place while I attended the last performance on my list, by the Orchester Wiener Akademie, from Austria, playing "La Viena Clásica: Haydn, Mozart, y Schubert" in Teatro Juarez. They were stupendous; the seats were not. You'll remember that this theater is the only one in Mexico that has all of the original furnishings. My seat was on a bench without a back in a small box in the third balcony, which I shared with three others. Behind us was another bench, also seating four people. There was so little leg and foot room between the bench and the wrought iron guardrail that I couldn't put my feet flat on the floor. Mexicans over 100 years ago, I guess, were a lot shorter and had smaller feet than mine. I don't know how the taller, bigger man next to me managed. My back was killing me, and during intermission I told an usher that I had to have another seat, one with a back on it. Since the theater was only about two-thirds full, that was not a problem. She showed me to another box, farther around the curve from the center, with a vacant chair, and I shared that box with two other women. But, being in the back row, I couldn't see the orchestra (the women in the front row had to lean way out over the railing to see); I could only hear them. Luckily, the orchestra was very, very good, so it wasn't too bad.

No visit to Guanajuato would be complete without a peek at the *Callejón del Beso* (Alley of the Kiss), featuring two houses facing each other on the narrowest of all the streets that make up the city, so narrow, in fact, that the occupants can kiss each other from their balconies.

Run-Up to El Día de los Muertos

When I returned from Guanajuato, I discovered that a tent city had been erected in the Plaza Cívica in my absence. I didn't know what the booths were selling or why they needed to be so protected. Then, when I got closer, I saw that they offered some of the elements needed to decorate altars to the deceased for Día de los Muertos, Day of the Dead, and held two things that could not stand up under the daily onslaught of the sun: figures made out of sugar, or *alfeñiques*, and candles. The alfeñique is of Arab origin. The Spaniards adopted the custom and, sometime later, with the Conquest, it reached all of Latin America. To bring this custom more joy and color, the Mexicans modified the alfeñiques' appearance, using decorations like colored pastes and chocolate, I learned in *Atención*.

Some alfeñiques, tiny creations one might place on an altar to a deceased loved one, all made of sugar.

These tiny Day of the Dead dancing ladies were a favorite of mine.

At the organic market on the Saturday before the holiday, lots of stalls were selling pan de muerto tradicional *(traditional bread of the dead, the sugar-coated one at the top of the basket). They come in smaller, individual versions, too.*

Día de los Muertos is not a morbid, sad occasion, but a joyous—even raucous—celebration of the lives of those who have gone before. Families erect sometimes simple, sometimes elaborate altars to remember the deceased. On these altars, you will see more marigolds than you've ever before seen in one place. I was told that the scent of those flowers can bring back the spirits of the dead. Indeed, in the jardín, with so many altars awash in marigolds, their unique odor permeated the air.

Typically on the altars, besides marigolds, are hygiene products such as soap and cologne, so the visiting spirits can clean up before the fiesta begins. Tiny re-creations in sugar of their favorite foods are frequently a part of the altars. There are sometimes cans of Coke or beer or bottles of tequila so the spirits will have a good time at the party. And usually you will see a photo of the deceased. I am enchanted by these miniature creations.

Amid the anticipation leading up to El Día de los Muertos, race cars in the *Carrera Panamericana* (Pan-American Race), the most famous rally in the world, came through town. Each driver made a short stop in front of the parroquia to receive a bottle of water, a medal on a ribbon, and a packet of materials, then stopped for a meal and service on the car on a street on the outskirts of town.

According to *Atención*: "The Panamericana was run for the first time from 1950 to '54, when the Mexican government inaugurated the *Carretera Panamericana* (Pan-American Highway), which runs through Mexico from Guatemala to the U.S.

"In 1988 the Panamericana was reborn as a rally by a group of car enthusiasts headed by Eduardo León, current honorary president of the event. Since that year, the race has begun in Chiapas or Oaxaca and ends in Nuevo Laredo; however, this year it will end in Zacatecas due to the problems along the border. The rally lasts seven days and the cars run 4,000 kilometers through cities such as Oaxaca, Puebla, Querétaro,

Morelia, SMA, Aguascalientes, and Zacatecas."

What I didn't know until they appeared was that this is an event for antique cars. There are drivers from Sweden, Switzerland, Germany, Finland, and Mexico. Last year's first-place winner was from Finland and second place from Mexico, with a difference of only 20 to 30 seconds!

Meeting an Exceptional Individual

One of the things that makes me love San Miguel so is that I have many peak experiences here. A recent one was meeting the most extraordinary, unusual, and fascinating man ever in my life. I attended a documentary called *El Pianista de la Sierra Madre*, and the subject, Romayne Wheeler, was there for a Q&A afterward. He was incredibly warm, open-hearted, and deeply spiritual. His unique story is this, in a nutshell: He was born in California in 1942 and studied piano as a child. When he was eight or nine, he traveled with his father to Puerto Rico for a piano competition. He heard Andrés Segovia play *"Recuerdos de la Alhambra"* ("Memories of the Alhambra"), by Francisco Tárrega, on guitar, and at that moment young Romayne decided to dedicate his life to music.

As an older teen, he went to Austria (he loves the mountains) and studied for 12 years, graduating with one degree in performance and another in composition. His professors suggested that he record the music of the indigenous people of his own country before it disappeared forever. After spending numerous years on that project, he decided to travel to Mexico to study the role of music in the spiritual lives of the Tarahumara Indians, who live in caves in the Copper Canyon area. (I saw the Tarahumara and visited one family in their cave when I traveled to that region some years ago with Elderhostel.) Wheeler was enchanted by the Sierra Madre and the gentle Tarahumara character. He returned annually, bringing a prototype of a solar piano with him.

Eventually, Wheeler and the Tarahumara bonded, and he decided to settle permanently among his adopted family, where he could compose, paint, and write in serenity. He lived for two years in a cave with a family before having his own house built, totally adapting to their lifestyle. He speaks fluent Spanish as well as German, English, and French, and is working to master the language of the Tarahumara.

One of the most amazing parts of the documentary was the tale of moving a concert grand piano, which had been played by Anton Rubinstein at the opera house in Guadalajara, to the very rim of Copper Canyon. It got to Creel, the gateway to Copper Canyon, by train, I believe, and then the challenge began. Wheeler hired a truck and 18 men. He used two tons of potatoes as ballast on the truck to secure the piano. When the truck could go no farther, the men took over, carrying the piano on their shoulders. The whole operation took 18 hours. The men were paid in potatoes.

The Tarahumara live a subsistence life, frequently going hungry. They have no medical care and a child mortality rate of 50 percent; advanced education is unaffordable. Wheeler undertakes worldwide piano concert tours annually. The money he raises is used to meet some of these needs. He gives scholarships and buys food and medicines for the Indians. He has built a modern House of Healing and hired a nurse who provides care to 400 families. Wheeler dresses in the Tarahumara style, which includes a loincloth (although he was wearing pants in SMA), a belted tunic, and sandals made out of tires. The Q&A probably lasted longer than the documentary as we just wouldn't let this unique individual go. I asked if he had Internet access where he lives and, unbelievably, he does. He said it would be impossible to arrange his tours without it.

The following night, he played a concert in the biblioteca, which I attended. The room was packed. The piano was not the best in town (the best—a Steinway at St. Paul's—was booked for another use at the time scheduled for the concert), but he rose above it. He plays like an angel. The man sitting next to me was sobbing. I recommend that you go to your computer to learn more about this exceptional man, and hear him play the piano. Try to hear him or someone else playing "Recuerdos de la Alhambra." The way Wheeler plays it sounds exactly like a guitar.

El Día de los Muertos—Part I

At Fábrica la Aurora, this little witch and her father captured my heart.

Another witch—another Cynthia—from my UU congregation.

Talk about peak experiences! El Día de los Muertos has to be at the top of my list. The festivities kicked off with a blow-out party at Fábrica la Aurora, Centro de Arte y Diseño, on Saturday night, October 29, for the benefit of *la Cruz Roja* (the Red Cross). At the entrance to this gigantic factory repurposed as a collection of artists' studios and galleries, we were met by a marimba band. Most of the artists had put up altars in their galleries or in nearby halls, and their creations were really something to see.

Just a few of the many catrinas and catrins in the jardín on November 1.

I went to the jardín on November 1 and was met by one of the most cheerful displays I've ever seen. A mixture of pastel and all-white papel picado hung across the expanse between the jardín and the parroquia, creating captivating shadows below. On the ground in that space were submissions to a contest for students of the University of León (which has a campus in SMA) to create "carpets" made of seeds, rice, beans, and other natural materials like those found on the altars. One display was an homage to Steve Jobs.

Catrinas of all stripes were making the rounds. *La Calavera Catrina* (the Elegant Skull) is an icon of El Día de los Muertos. They are skeleton-inspired images or costumes, usually humorous, doing a seemingly endless variety of activities.

Also on November 1, I went to the shop Camino Silvestre to see the altar to extinct Mexican birds, featuring the imperial woodpecker. The owners' original business was the manufacture and sale of glass hummingbird feeders, and now in their store, in addition to dozens of models of feeders, they have bird- and nature-related jewelry, pottery, notecards, candles, glassware, and on and on. The owners had teamed up with the Audubon Society so that everyone who bought a membership or renewed got a free hummingbird feeder. The place was a madhouse! People were spilling out onto the sidewalk. A musical group was playing as the owners served tiny tamales, atole, and white wine.

In the evening, in the jardín, a group of youngsters, along with their teacher from La Casa de la Cultura, entertained the audience with a concert played on all-natural instruments. It sounded just like a jungle, with bird noises, big cat sounds, drumming, a rain stick, etc.

El Día de los Muertos—Part II

I was totally unprepared for the intensity of emotions that greeted me on November 2 when I went to El Panteón Guadalupe, the municipal cemetery, for El Día de los Muertos. There were police just to handle the foot traffic. The road to the cemetery was completely filled with vendors—mostly of flowers, but also of big, empty, restaurant-sized food cans that they'd saved for months to sell for either fetching water from the fountain or in which to put flowers (the more enterprising folks even painted the containers), and a variety of foods and beverages.

As we neared the entrance to the cemetery, a waist-high rope was strung in the street to separate those going in from those coming out. We were packed in the line to go in. I felt I had to move my backpack to the front for safety. As we entered the cemetery, it was a riot of color, activity, music, food and drink, and people of all ages. I was completely overwhelmed. In every aspect of life here, including in the cemetery, less is never more.

This is my favorite shot of the day. When this photo is seen in color, with the man's orange shirt and cap matching the marigolds and the color of the tomb, it's just about perfect.

Someone in last week's *Atención* suggested that since there usually are no flowers on the graves in the gringo part of the cemetery, it might be nice to buy some on the way in and decorate those graves, also. Well, people took that to heart, and, while nowhere as festooned as those on the Mexican side, the gringo graves—even the unmarked ones—were graced with plenty of flowers. I followed suit, and it was quite emotional to read the names and dates on the gravestones, and then to add a flower. One grave featured a bag of M&M's!

How restrained the gringo side looks, but peaceful for sure. I wondered why there was a gringo side, and decided the separation was necessary because most gringos are not Catholic and the Mexican side is a Catholic cemetery. But there may be another reason.

On the gringo side of the **panteón**, *the empty niches await deaths, including mine, as I have signed up with the 24-Hour Association to have my ashes interred here.*

The good folks of Community Church at their table offering sustenance to mourners and visitors alike.

Members of Community Church set up a hospitality table on the gringo side, offering tequila, tamales, and a friendly presence. It's the first year this has been done. I applaud them for it, and I hope it's a custom that the church will continue year after year.

The most poignant thing I saw on the non-Mexican side was what I assumed were former staff of deceased gringos, paying their respects even though that side might have felt alien to them.

If I'm in SMA at this time in another year, I want to go to the cemetery on the night of November 2, as I hear there are thousands of candles burning and just a low murmuring sound as people talk quietly among themselves and perhaps to the deceased.

I do have to wonder who removes the tons of flowers, candles, cans, etc., from the graveyard after the fiesta is over. It must provide plenty of employment for weeks.

On the evening of El Día de los Muertos, I again went to the jardín, where I witnessed a catrina parade, and where a small orchestra played, again, I think, from La Casa de la Cultura. The musical numbers were interspersed with costumed folks reading works about death by famous Mexican poets, such as Octavio Paz.

By reading *Atención* very carefully, as I always do, I found out a significant thing about the "gringo side" in the municipal graveyard. (I'm sure there's a lovelier name for it than that.) Turns out it's privately owned by the 24-Hour Association. Mexican law calls for all dead bodies to be either buried or cremated within 24 hours. Older gringos who live in Mexico may join the nonprofit association for about $500 USD, and fill out innumerable forms, and if they should die in Mexico, the association swings into action, dealing with the deceased's embassy, obtaining death certificates, getting the body buried or cremated according to the prearranged wishes of the deceased, informing next-of-kin, etc. What a valuable service for loved ones who may be in the States, Canada, or elsewhere, may not be familiar with Mexican law, probably don't speak Spanish, may not have a passport, and are, of course, also grieving.

A Trip to La Cañada de la Virgen (Not for the Faint of Heart!)

I had been wanting to visit the ancient pyramids called La Cañada de la Virgen (the "Canadian virgin," as a Canadian friend and wag calls it) since the site opened to the public last February. This Canadian friend went in March, when it was quite hot, and cautioned me to wait until the fall for my visit as it's over four hours of strenuous walking and climbing in unrelenting sun. "Cañada" has nothing to do with the country of Canada (note that it's an *ñ*, not an *n*). It means canyon. The *La Virgen* part comes from a geode that was found on the site with the image of the Virgin, and miracles have been attributed to her.

Two friends from mattress-making and I signed up for a tour beginning at 9 a.m. with Albert Coffee, who is unique among the guides. Albert is an anthropologist and archeologist who worked on the project in excavation, mapping, and the lab. He's also a gringo, so he speaks English. The other guides at the site do not speak English, although I was pleased to see that interpretive signs along the way were in both languages. You cannot visit the pyramids without an official guide.

Albert, driving a van, picked us up, along with four others who were from Montreal and Italy, outside of Starbucks in Centro. I borrowed a wide-brimmed hat from my landlady, bought a bottle of water to supplement the one I always carry, and greased myself up well with sunblock. As we drove the 15 minutes or so to the site, Albert started to fill us in on what we'd be seeing. He told us of the genius of the planting of the "three sisters"—corn, beans, and squash—and how the beans and corn, along with rice, form a complete protein. The beans climb the support provided by the cornstalks, and both of these shade the squash planted below from the intense sun. He said there may be hundreds—perhaps even thousands—of other small pyramids in the area. He pointed out a couple of unexcavated ones on our way. When we passed the *presa* (dam), he said the water level was the lowest he'd seen it in the 11 years he's been in SMA, and it's now only two months since the "rainy season." They simply are not getting the amount of rain that they used to. This year's corn crop is stunted.

One of the reasons I came in the fall was to experience SMA in a different season. I was told that when I came in September, everything would be green, with flowers in abundant bloom. NOT! Everything is dry and brown, as it is when I come in the winter. Albert told us that we do not depend on the presa for our drinking water, but rather on an aquifer, which has only 10 years of life left in it. Somebody told me we were accessing 35,000-year-old water in the aquifer because it's not filling up anymore; we're just pulling from it. Not a cheerful thought for this region.

Although the pyramids are newly opened, there are already 5,000 visitors per month, the second highest of these sites in the country. Located in the central basin of the Laja River, the ceremonial center and elite burial ground are built on a very strategic plateau, since the site is surrounded by canyons and access is not easy. The site was occupied by an elect class of priests and rulers who observed the heavens and their movements as they related to an ancient agricultural/hunting and gathering calendar. It is also the final resting place for those inhabitants. "Given its geographic location, architectural design, and the sanctity of its natural landscape, Cañada de la Virgen was likely the regional center of power, where groups from a variety of cultural backgrounds coexisted," writes Gabriela Zepeda García Moreno in *Cañada de la Virgen: Refugio de los Muertos y los Ancestros* (Cañada de la Virgen: Refuge of the

Dead and the Ancestors). She is the lead archeologist on the project and was the Mexican-speaking guide on site that day.

Before any work could begin, there were five years of negotiations with the very eccentric German owner, Regina Thomas von Bohlen. She would put padlocks on gates across roads to the site that had been paid for with state and municipal funds. She was constantly entering and leaving the country, making setting up meetings with her extremely difficult. Finally, the federal government had had enough and told her she could donate the land or have it seized by eminent domain. She chose the former, and in that way was able to put tons of restrictions on the deed. To this day, she has her own guards watching to see that these restrictions are adhered to.

As we began our walk to the site, a teenager from the group with the Spanish-speaking guide walked off the road, and Albert told us that if one of her guards had seen that, she could shut the whole operation down. The Mexican tour guide yelled at the kid and got him right back up on the road. It is a protected biological site. (As a side note, a front-page headline in this week's *Atención* says, "Cañada de la Virgen Certified as Natural Protected Area," and the article said it was thanks to the initiative and efforts of von Bohlen that it was possible to obtain the certification to support the conservation of this rich natural resource.)

Vehicles are to be parked at the visitor center (also a work in progress, but it did have restrooms), and guests and guides board an official site bus, which drives on cobblestone roads to within about three-quarters of a mile of the pyramids. From there it's almost all uphill walking with no shade. One small *palapa* (shack) was it as far as shade went on the entire visit, and because the guides kept the groups apart and the Mexicans started out ahead of us, they got to it first.

The four architectural complexes were constructed over a period of 500 years, from about A.D. 540 to 1050, in three distinct stages, as evidenced by the different materials used in each stage. Those who studied the pyramids estimate that the site was abandoned sometime between 1050 and 1100, probably because of drought. Coincidentally, this is the same time period in which the Anasazi vanished from the southwestern United States.

You would not believe the list of different specializations of people who worked on the excavation. Some I had never heard of and can barely pronounce: archaeoastronomers and pedologists (soil scientists), for example. The 13-year excavation project cost something approaching $3 million USD.

Our first view of a pyramid.

We saw reconstructed shards in a garden of sorts off to one side. Albert told us that many intact pottery pieces were also found; they're in safe storage awaiting placement in the museum at the visitor center. On the way out, I bought a bilingual book about the pyramids and learned that frequently pottery was "killed" (purposefully shattered as part of a ritual) along with people when human sacrifice was practiced, including of newborns and children. There was also blood-letting, as the inhabitants believed they had to put their own blood into the ground to keep the seasons turning. And then there were mutilation practices for the purpose of ritual cannibalistic communion, practiced only by the high priests and rulers.

Albert told us that you can sum up the lives of the builders of the pyramids in two words: ancestor worship. There are four complexes on the site, only three of which have been excavated. In Complex A, also known as *La Casa de Los Trece Cielos* (The House of the 13 Heavens), a burial site was found of a figure they named *El Jerarca* (the hierarch), so named because he is believed to have been one of the most prominent forefathers of Cañada de la Virgen's ruling caste, due to the antiquity of his bones. Another skeleton, called *La Niña Guerrera* (the girl warrior), was originally thought to be a boy. They are both 1,000 years older than the other burials on the site. It is believed that these bones were kept in a funerary (or sacred) bundle and carried around for all of those years during migration into this region.

A total of 19 burials were unearthed on the site. It is thought that these could have been the collective sacrifice and interment of a defeated family lineage that once embodied the ruling caste. All burials took place along with a dog, usually a chihuahua, as a guide into the darkness of the underworld. When the skeletons were unearthed, a dog's skeleton was always held to the deceased's chest. They also ate chihuahuas.

Complex B, the House of the Longest Night, associated with the winter solstice, had a sweat lodge. Complex D is *La Casa del Viento* (The House of the Wind), and would you believe it, as soon as we neared it, we could feel the winds picking up. Complex C has not yet been excavated, as well as several housing complexes.

According to *Atención*: "All of the complexes are aligned to many important events that occur in the sky over the course of the year. They precisely monitor the movements of the sun, moon, Venus, and Jupiter as they mark seasonal extremes and important dates in the ancient Otomí-Mexica calendar. The structures also imitate the forms of the surrounding hills and mountains, displaying the mind-boggling amount of genius involved in the planning and building of a place that incorporates both the cosmos and the landscape into its architecture."

The most prevalent theory about the sunken patios is that they were flooded with water to allow the people to study the stars without having to look up. Others said the flooding theory couldn't be correct, as the fairly stiff breezes there would create ripples. We were thrilled with those breezes, which blew constantly and made everything much more pleasant. I didn't sweat and I didn't need all of the extra water I had brought.

This tree is being allowed to grow where it is. Excavators found out through bitter experience that the roots of these trees are holding everything together underneath.

The sunken patios were also used as a collection point for rainwater during the rainy season, then channeled by means of a canal system into the nearby pond, Amanalli, which was used as a reservoir. Albert said it provided the people of that time with sufficient water until the next rainy season. The existence of this reservoir was an important factor in the decision to choose this area to build the pre-Hispanic settlement. Interestingly, on the front cover of the book I bought is a magnificent photo of the Amanalli, filled with water reflecting a blue, cloud-filled sky with a pyramid in the background. And many photos inside the book show a green, lush countryside. Those photos must have been taken within the 13-year period of excavation, so not that long ago. Today, there is not a drop of water in the area where that reservoir once was.

Another curious thing is that after all these years of work by dozens of experts, it is not known with certainty who built the pyramids. One theory states that the first settlers of the ceremonial center were of Otomí descent. Others believe there is a link between the inhabitants of Cañada de la Virgen and those of Zapotec villages in Oaxaca. For now, though, research will focus on the Otomí culture.

A few members of our party begin the climb to the top of the pyramid.

We went up many, many steps, narrow and steep. And like almost everywhere else in the San Miguel area, there are no railings or ropes or anything really to hold on to. Most of us went to one side or the other and climbed in a stooped position, clinging to the rocks you see in the photo above. There was one problem, however: On my way down, one of the rocks I held for balance and stability came right off in my hand! Albert said that after the first person falls down the steps, the government will surely cut off stair-climbing access to the top.

Another of the excavated pyramids on the site.

I learned a new word: syncretism, the amalgamation or attempted amalgamation of different religions, cultures, or schools of thought. Catholicism had a relatively easy time taking over or melding with the existing religion, because of the practice of blood-letting (compare to the communion wine being "the blood of Christ"), the cross already existing as a symbol (the substructure of the pyramids was in the shape of a cross and served a public ritual purpose), and processions (which were already an integral part of their rituals).

I was enchanted by this trip and am now eagerly reading more about the site and the people who created it.

Nearing the End

As my days here are now dwindling, I wanted to get in a hike at El Charco del Ingenio, SMA's botanical garden. I went with my sanmiguelense friend of four visits, Chely. The morning was cool when we set out, but soon enough the sun became unbearable and we had to quit.

While I was away from SMA earlier this year, a devastating fire hit El Charco. I had visions of flames licking at the visitor center, but, luckily, it was limited to the far side of the lake. The word around town is that the fire was deliberately set by developers who want that land. The devastation included acres and acres of blackened trees.

We decided to walk on that side for a bit, and came upon a ewe and her lambs, which made us feel much more hopeful. The miracle was that the roots of the hundreds if not thousands of cacti were not affected by the fire, so new growth came out almost overnight. However, some trees, such as mesquite, will take a decade or more to recover.

Last year, at an auction to benefit El Charco, Chely bought a small tree that came from one of the trees in existence when Cortés came here. It is said that after some battles with the Aztecs in which he lost many men, he cried under a particular tree. Cuttings have been taken from that tree and grown over the years. Before we started on our hike, Chely went in to check with the director—a friend of hers—to see where her tree was planted so we could go and see it. Alas, the tree has not been planted because of the lack of water. Her tree needs a fair amount of humidity and it was felt that the growing conditions were not right. She was very disappointed. Who knows when conditions might be suitable.

I went back to Philadelphia soon after that to prepare for the arrival of my family from Finland and the Christmas I would share with them and my daughter and her husband in Philadelphia. The thought of selling my house there and moving to San Miguel was occupying more and more of my thoughts each day, and I welcomed the opportunity to discuss this serious matter with my children.

Some San Miguel Humor

About the lack of availability of men and the transient nature of the population: All the men here are either married, gay, or leaving next Tuesday. The ratio of women to men is 11 to 1, in both the extranjero and

Mexican populations, in the latter case because so many men have gone to El Norte to look for work.

❋ ❋ ❋

My favorite SMA joke about this situation: A woman is sitting in the jardín and spots a man she hasn't seen before, so she goes over and strikes up a conversation.

"I've never seen you here before. Are you new in town?"

The man replies, "Yes, I just got in last night."

"Where are you from?" asks the woman.

"Well, if truth be told, I just got out of jail."

"Oh," says the woman. "What were you in for?"

"I killed my wife."

"Then you're single!" exclaims the woman.

❋ ❋ ❋

Two old gringos meet in the jardín, and one introduces his gorgeous, young wife to the other, who asks him, "How did you get a wife like that?" He replies, "I told her I was 95."

"I think the most interesting parts of human experience might be the sparks
that come from that sort of chipping flint of cultures
rubbing against each other."

Barbara Kingsolver,
author of *The Bean Trees, Flight Behavior,
The Poisonwood Bible*, and many more

And I believe that similar sparks are ignited by the two major cultures
that rub up against one another daily in SMA.
I think we both want desperately to understand the other.
As just one example, I see people
of both nationalities studying long and hard to learn the other's language
and to use it as best they can.

Cynthia Claus

Chapter 6

January 15 – March 31, 2012

Back in SMA for My Fourth Winter

After being back in Philadelphia for six weeks enjoying my family, the holidays, and all that the city has to offer, I left to return to Mexico in mid-January. The temperature that morning was 19 and snow was softly falling. As I told the taxi driver, "It's time for me to leave."

On the flight from Houston to León, I felt as if I were in an updated episode of *I Love Lucy*. The flight attendant was so ditzy that I couldn't believe she made the grade for her job. She knew only about 10 words of Spanish, and half of them she butchered. It seems to me that if you are running a flight from one country to another, it is your duty to have a flight crew that speaks the language of both countries fluently. Indeed, half of the passengers on the flight were Mexican.

I wasn't really expecting to go out and do anything cultural the first day after my arrival, but flipping through *Atención* while eating lunch on the balcony, I noticed that at 3 p.m., there was the second and final screening of a Reel Docs film called *Leave Them Laughing*.

The Reel Docs series is curated by two SMA friends who bring extraordinary documentaries to audiences here, always with a bonus of the producer, the director, or an actor in the film present for a Q&A session afterward. This time we watched a painful, sometimes hysterical, and in the end life-affirming documentary about the devastation of ALS and its effects on a very spunky woman—Carla Zilbersmith, a nationally known performer of ballads, skits, and self-parody who had been compared to Lily Tomlin—and her wise-beyond-his-years teenage son, her supportive and loving father, and a group of wonderful gal pals. Afterward, the associate producer, who was a friend of Zilbersmith's, answered our many questions. Again, a peak experience in San Miguel.

I was in a popular restaurant recently picking up some food for a housebound friend when I spotted a strange juxtaposition on the menu board. The cafe offered chili, gazpacho, mushroom, and chicken soups, and right below, informed all that puppies were for sale here. My advice: Hurry and buy them before they appear on the menu. (Just kidding, of course!)

Just before I left in December, McDonald's had gotten a permit to have one of its restaurants smack-dab in Centro Historico, steps from the jardín and the parroquia. The catch was that the name "McDonald's" appeared nowhere on any of the application forms. Somehow the word got out and the town went nuts. First, an *Obra Suspendida* (work suspended) sticker was affixed to the building, halting work.

Then, the demonstrations against such a restaurant in the historical center began. The first one was the evening before I was to leave. It was fairly small at that point but had about an equal number of gringos and Mexicans, along with guitar accompaniment. We totally blocked the street traffic, and to my complete surprise, the police allowed us to do that, and rerouted the cars. At one point, a police officer came walking toward us, and one of the demonstrators said, "Don't move." I responded that I was leaving the next morning and that if a Mexican police officer asked me to move, I was darned well going to move.

Something surprising on the menu board!

Actually, foreigners are not permitted to participate in any political demonstrations, but I didn't think this matched that criteria. A friend of mine captured the entire demonstration on his iPad, plus some interviews with local activists, and since his ex-sister-in-law worked for Spanish CNN, the cause got good coverage.

An extremely articulate Mexican woman laid out the case against the invasion by McDonald's. There was fear that SMA might lose its designation as a UNESCO World Heritage Site, although that didn't happen with a Starbucks just up the block. Evidently, if the exterior of the building is not compromised, you're OK. There was worry, also, about the obesity issue, as Mexicans are the second-fattest nationality, after those in the USA.

And it's not as if you can't get a Happy Meal anywhere in SMA. On the outskirts of town, in a shopping mall, there is a McDonald's.

A demonstrator against McDonald's in Centro made her case passionately.

In my absence, demonstrations continued every Wednesday evening. The whole thing collapsed (or succeeded, depending on your viewpoint) when the city councilperson who had allowed the permit to go through was forced to resign, and McDonald's quietly slunk away. Hoorah! Power to the people!

I was horrified to read on a daily post I get from *Philadelphia* magazine that "the City of Brotherly Love" (ha!) has been renamed "Kill-a-delphia," since in 2011 it had the highest homicide rate of the 10 largest U.S. cities. And in the first 25 days of January, 31 people were killed. And people worry about me here in Mexico? Now I have some (you'll pardon the unintended pun) "ammunition" when people start up with me on that issue.

CHAPTER 6

TRIP TO CEDESA

The Center for Global Justice here runs frequent trips. You may remember a very informative one I took a few years ago to a successful cooperative organic tomato farm. So when I read in *Atención* of the Center's trip to CEDESA, I signed up. CEDESA is an acronym for Centro de Desarrollo Agropecuario (Center for Agricultural Development), and is about an hour away in Dolores Hidalgo. It is a rural training center that's constantly incorporating new low-cost technologies into its repertoire of ecological, sustainable practices. Not only does it help the surrounding peasant communities with beekeeping and organic agriculture, but it also teaches them how to build and use dry toilets, recycle gray water, catch rainwater, build cisterns, and compost. Many of these technologies focus on saving water, as lack of water has always been a problem in that area.

Father Nemo (a nickname for Guillermo) had been sent to the region in the early 1970s to offer Mass to isolated indigenous communities. He soon realized that the people needed more than just God; in this life they needed land and a way to be self-sufficient, and they shouldn't have to wait until the next life for something better. He taught that the people should be agents of their destiny. Father Nemo taught literacy (the illiteracy rate at that time was 95 percent), opened schools, and preached about human dignity. He was soon joined by several of his women students, who have remained with CEDESA ever since and were key in developing the program.

In 1979, Father Nemo was forced out, but with CEDESA in the hands of the women—many of their men were in the U.S. working—they took care of the land and supported the project without any outside help. From 1980 to 1992 the communities worked together and a decision-making body resulted. In 2000-06, the women taught the construction of backyard gardens with eco-technologies that used the least amount of water.

We were introduced to an oven that uses minimal fuel, a dry toilet, a cistern that collects rainwater from a rooftop, and some ancient gardening ideas brought to life again, like composting and using unglazed pots for drip irrigation.

We learned that in SMA, we get our water from the Independencia Aquifer, which lies under most of the state of Guanajuato. It has been losing several meters of water yearly for the past decade and is not being refilled by current rainfall. Also, tests have shown that water in some pockets of the aquifer contains arsenic and fluoride. These heavy metals are not expelled, dissolved, or made to disappear by traditional purification techniques such as filters. CEDESA and the UNAM researchers have designed a solar water distiller that will eliminate the metals.

The next-to-last thing we were shown was the apiary, with the hives decorated Mexican-style in bright colors. By this time, the sun was very high and hot overhead. I had not eaten in five hours, I'd been standing for about three, and I began to feel a bit woozy. I found a semi-shady place under a tree and drank a lot of my water.

The final item on our tour was a simple water heater, using only the sun, and by now, we were all pretty done-in. I sat far away in deep shade and listened to my stomach growling. A lot of other folks seemed to be in the same condition.

At 1:30 (we'd arrived at 10), we sat down to a home-cooked meal of salad (on our rounds we had seen the lettuce being harvested), spaghetti, chicken, corn tortillas, a very piquante salsa, and an unusual dessert that was a little cube of a fruit substance like extremely firm jam.

On our way out, we visited the store for the community's products. We were all disappointed that there was no honey for sale with the CEDESA label on it, and we were told it wasn't the right season. It had been a good day, I made some new friends, and I learned a lot. (Thanks for some of this information goes to the Center for Global

Justice's article in *Atención* advertising the trip.)

THE WRITERS' CONFERENCE

The seventh annual San Miguel Writers' Conference, during four days in February 2012, really put SMA on the map. The theme was "Creative Crossroads of the Americas," and A-listers from Canada, the U.S., and Mexico delivered the keynote addresses: Margaret Atwood, who needs no introduction; Elena Poniatowska, of whom I'd not heard before but who is one of Mexico's most celebrated, prolific, and beloved writers; and Native American Joy Harjo of the Muscogee (Creek) Nation, who is a poet and musician. Naomi Wolf, activist and writer, spoke on "Writing Riskily: Taking a Stand with Your Prose" as a general session speaker, and later on "Protest 101" after a viewing of the documentary made from her book *The End of America*. (Be afraid. Be very afraid.) The Canadian Embassy in Mexico was so thrilled that homegirl Margaret Atwood was coming to the conference that it covered all of her expenses and sent a car to the Mexico City airport to deliver her to SMA.

Because there is simultaneous translation into Spanish of all the major events at the conference, it bills itself as "the only bilingual and bicultural conference of its kind anywhere in North America." Besides the keynotes, there were daily general session speakers, two time periods each day dedicated to concurrent workshops for both English- and Spanish-speaking writers taught by world-class faculty, author readings, open mic sessions, pitch sessions with literary agents, individual consultations with seasoned experts, book-signing receptions, a "Viva México" reception of enormous proportions, a theater presentation on Dorothy Parker, and a closing party. If anyone had an ounce of stamina left after the four days, and there were those who did—I not among them—there were several two-day intensive writing courses to choose from, and excursions in and around San Miguel.

I had hoped that my attendance at last year's conference would goose me to get going again on my memoirs. I had a truly fantastic time and met many new friends with whom I am still in touch, but I did not get the boost I had hoped for. This year I did. The big thing that had been hanging me up was that I didn't know how to structure my memoir. I had written many individual stories and I had planned to continue on in that way, hoping that a structure would present itself. I came up with a structure that I am thrilled about as the result of a discussion at breakfast with another conference participant that had absolutely nothing to do with structuring a memoir.

And, as the result of one of the workshops I took, I changed the working title, taking the emphasis away from my parents and putting it where it belongs: on me and my life. I now believe that things had been incubating all of that time and could not be rushed.

I had a most unusual encounter with one of the writers. Most of our half-hour breaks were spent standing in line to use the restrooms and then scampering on to the next workshop to get a good seat. In the women's room the first day, I noticed an attractive older woman in a Mexican outfit in a gorgeous shade of purple, not wearing a name badge. She was having difficulty getting the water to come out of the faucet. I demonstrated how to wave a hand in front of the electric eye. Then there was the soap dispenser that required more hand waving, and finally the no-touch paper towel dispenser. After I helped her, she said how she's not good with these modern conveniences. I concurred, saying that all of the gadgets are different and that it was difficult to tell sometimes where to put your hands. She thanked me and we went our separate ways. What a shock when the same woman stood at the microphone later to deliver a keynote address and it was Elena Poniatowska!

I also had an amusing encounter with Naomi Wolf at the fiesta.

I greeted a friend of mine who was standing with a woman I did not know. She introduced herself as "Naomi." Luckily, my brain cells were still working and I said, "As in Wolf?" Yes, indeed, there I was chatting with Naomi Wolf. Well, perhaps chatting is a bit overstated. I was starstruck and tongue-tied. Happily, someone else came along at just that moment and starting really talking to Naomi.

Later on at the fiesta, there were fireworks that spelled out the three keynoters' names: Mgt (spelled just like that), Joy, and Elena. After that, Mexican dancers performed and then took partners from the audience.

I had stopped reading Steve Jobs' biography to read Margaret Atwood's *The Year of the Flood* in preparation for her keynote address, but she barely mentioned it. I'm glad I read it, though. It was humorous and dark, all at the same time. She was extremely witty in her keynote. She has a sort of deadpan presentation with impeccable comic timing.

I took a workshop from Graeme Gibson, Margaret Atwood's partner and also a writer who, among other deeds, founded the Writers' Union of Canada and the Writers' Trust. His class was titled "Non-Fiction: Wrestling with the Gift." I didn't even realize they were a couple until he said something like "Margaret and I hike frequently." He ended his presentation with an incredible story, which I must relate.

He was in Mexico many years ago and two boys approached him with an African green parrot in a burlap sack. The parrot was for sale. As he had always wanted a parrot, he bought it. Somehow he took it home to the U.S., and it lived with him, a former spouse, and their two sons for a year. The parrot learned to say quite a few words. One day, he decided that the parrot was not itself anymore and seemed depressed. He went to the local zoo to see if he could donate it and also to check out the facilities. They were wonderful; the birds could fly around freely and there were many parrots of the same species. He took the parrot to the zoo and stayed around just a short time. As he was leaving, the parrot screamed,

"Daddy! Daddy!" It had never used that word before, but it knew the word, it knew who Daddy was, and it knew in what context to use it. Well, there was not a dry eye in the room.

Someone asked whether he left the parrot or could not bear to part with it. He said he did leave the parrot because he knew that it would eventually be much happier at the zoo. He returned four to five months later and he could not tell his parrot from all of the others of its kind, and his parrot did not come over to him. He said that at the moment the parrot addressed him as "Daddy," he decided to dedicate his life to conservation, particularly of birds. He has served as the joint honorary president, along with Margaret, of BirdLife International's Rare Bird Club, among other conservation roles.

Visit to GAIA

One Saturday, I accompanied seven others in a van to a very special place about a half hour outside of SMA, on a Center for Global Justice-led trip to the nonprofit GAIA. GAIA is an acronym for Grupo Acción Interdisciplinaria Ambiental (Alternativas Sustentables), an interdisciplinary action group for the environment using sustainable alternatives. The "group" turned out to be a lovely, extremely well-educated, and forward-thinking Mexican family who, five years ago, wanting to reduce their footprint on this earth, left their home in Cuernavaca, in the state of Morelos, and after an exhaustive search for land "near jungle and ocean," as they said, bought the land outside of SMA (close to neither!) and began a gutsy experiment in sustainable living.

Each family member is an expert in a different area, such as ecological sanitation, integral water management, education and environmental communication, natural resource management, comprehensive community health, and renewable energy. Whew! When the family bought the land, the locals had been using it for grazing their animals. It was rocky and eroded. The previous owner sold it to pay for his son's wedding. The first thing the new owners had to do was to restore the land.

We started off the tour with the grown son, Atahualpa (an ancient Inca name), nicknamed "Ata," in his late 30s, as our guide. He told us he had studied biology in Mexico, and then went to the U.S. and Canada because there was no career possible then in environmental science in Mexico. He also studied agronomy in Cuba during the oil crisis and learned to do many things without oil.

Ata showed us some sustainable materials and methods of construction of eco-friendly dwellings (in somewhat miniaturized versions). The family is not yet raising all their own food, we were told, although that is their goal as they work toward being self-sufficient. They are totally off the grid, however, as all of their energy needs are met by solar-generated electricity.

Ata's mother in her workshop.

Ata's mother is an extraordinary person. She is 65 and looks far younger. She had the most amazing eyes I've ever seen. I believe they are the eyes of someone totally at peace and filled with contentment. She is a *curandera* (traditional folk healer) and a homeopathist (she showed us her closetful of remedies), and she teaches thanatology (the scientific study of death). She maintains a thriving business in Cuernavaca, as their home there was turned into a clinic. In addition, she is trained and licensed as a psychologist.

When the family first moved into the community, they didn't push themselves onto it in any way. They respected how things were done locally. Soon neighbors started coming over out of curiosity. The newcomers learned that the locals never build with adobe, believing it to be the building material of the poor.

The father of this unique family displaying one of his newest projects.

Then we met the father, an engineer who started studying wind energy 30 years ago. He is 67, and also a handsome, vital, contented-looking person. He demonstrated a miniature version of a solar water heater, which uses cut aluminum soda cans in the solar panel.

A movable toilet was one of my favorite inventions. The toilet is set up in a spot above a one-meter hole. After each use, screened soil and lime go into the hole (preventing odors), and when the hole is full, the toilet is moved to another place. The contents are allowed to sit for a period of time, and when fully decomposed, an ornamental tree (only) can be planted in that space.

Ata points to the enormous cistern that holds rainwater under his parents' patio.

At his parents' gorgeous home—built sustainably, of course—Ata showed us the cistern, which is under the patio. Ata and his sister each have their own homes on the land, also.

During the heat of the day, we sat in their outside living room, snacked, and talked for hours. Several times during the afternoon, a high wind came up unexpectedly, and then died down, and we were told that frequently little tornadoes formed—which to date had not done any harm—but that the family had identified some areas of their buildings that needed a little more battening down.

The family hopes to have a website up soon and to begin an internship program. They also dream of building some cabins and having guests for short periods of time. It was an inspiration to spend the day with a most unusual family.

Concurso (Competition)

I learned of Concurso San Miguel 2012 long before the scheduled early March date for this national final competition of young opera students. It was the fourth year of the competition, returning to SMA after a year in another city. Excitement was running high. As soon as it was announced that tickets were available, I rushed to the Angela Peralta theater only to discover that all of the seats in *la luneta* (orchestra) at 250 pesos (about $20 USD) were sold out. How was that possible? Of course cheaper seats in the nosebleed section were still available, but then again, they're not really seats, but rather long benches that are intolerable for me. I've tried them, and once was enough.

I decided to go early the night of the performance to see if anyone had an extra ticket I could buy. I knew that people get sick or change their minds, their guests don't come, etc.—and I was right. I went to the theater at about 7:15 for an 8 p.m. performance. People were already lined up to get in, as it was open seating within each ticket section. The first person I asked, who had a fistful of tickets in her hand, had an extra, and sold it to me at cost! What superior luck.

The theater is named after an operatic soprano of international fame in the 19th century, Angela Peralta, who came in person to inaugurate the venue way back then. She was called the Mexican Nightingale in Europe, where she sang to acclaim in opera houses before the age of 20. She was also a composer, an accomplished pianist, and a harpist. She died at age 38. Precious few operas had been staged at the eponymous theater since then, so it was with particular relish that this venue was used for the competition.

The concurso was open to opera students throughout Mexico and to Mexican nationals living in the U.S., Canada, and Europe. Some 200 applicants had been winnowed down to the 12 who performed that evening. Special guests were introduced from the stage before the singing began, and the Italian ambassador to Mexico and his wife were seated fairly close to me. This was a big deal!

The plan was this: Each contestant got to sing twice, presumably in an order selected by lottery. In each of the two halves of the program, they sang in a different order and in a different language, and sang arias by composers other than they had in the first.

The prize for the winner was many thousands of pesos and a debut with the Acapulco Opera Company with all expenses paid and an honorarium of 15,000 pesos, a little less than $1,200 USD.

This was the eventual winner of the concurso, and you can see her marvelous dramatic performance during one of her arias.

All of the contestants were nervous, and in my opinion, all improved on their second appearance. Professional opera singers and musicians were the official judges, of course, but the audience members were given ballots to vote for their personal favorites. During the intermission, all of the female contestants changed their gowns, so it was fun to see their new dresses. And all of the male singers, and the extraordinary piano accompanist, whom I'd heard at other musical events around town, wore tuxedos with tails. In San Miguel de Allende! It was something to experience, let me tell you!

While the judges tallied their scores, we were entertained by four opera students (all were only 20 years old) who were not competing. Based on those performances, I'd say opera in Mexico is in very good shape.

All of the contestants returned to the stage to hear the award announcements. The program, though run like a tight ship, was three and a half hours in length, yet it did not seem that long. All announcements had to be made in both Spanish and English, of course, so that took more time. In addition to the audience favorite, there were fourth- through first-place winners, and a special Encouragement Award.

My First SMA Wedding Reception

The actual wedding had been a week earlier and a private affair. (By chance, I met the couple, their two witnesses, and Farley Wheelwright, the 95-year-old retired UU minister who performed the ceremony, at a restaurant right after the service took place.) The marriage was between Betse, a dynamo of an 85-year-old woman, and 70-something Jim. When I arrived by taxi at the private home of a friend of the couple at 1 p.m., I was immediately offered a glass of wine or a margarita; I chose the latter.

Tables with bowls of guacamole, salsa, and tortilla chips were set up everywhere under brightly colored umbrellas. I greeted many friends and then settled down in a shady spot to enjoy the first of the food. Later came barbecued shrimp, small empanadas, stuffed mushrooms, and many more goodies butlered by the Mexican serving staff. More drinks were offered. A mariachi band showed up and played for about an hour as people danced.

Then the hostess invited guests up to a microphone to offer memories, anecdotes, and best wishes to the couple.

Rev. Farley Wheelwright, almost completely blind and deaf, and an amazing human being, offered some humorous comments.

Betse and a partner dancing to a mariachi tune.

Betse herself got up and said, "I'm in the place I really want to be and with the person I really want to be with." Jim said, "Betse was the only woman who didn't bring me a casserole when my late wife died." That brought down the house! Betse had been widowed a long time ago, Jim more recently.

Dessert was a carrot cake served with a champagne toast. Let me tell you, margaritas and champagne in the heat of midday pack quite a

The happy couple, Jim and Betse, during a solemn moment.

wallop! Luckily, I had a couple of hours to get myself together before I had to go teach at 6.

I Have Come to Mexico to Learn Patience

The Toner Cartridge Saga…and the lesson in patience: When I knew I was going to be in SMA for almost six months this year, one of the first things I did in September was to go to Office Depot here and buy an HP laser printer. As usual, the printer was inexpensive ($80 USD), but the replacement toner cartridges cost $100 USD each. Early in March, I began to get messages from my computer that my toner was low. I remembered that a friend here had told me that a computer store on Calle Canal refilled toner cartridges for about $10 USD, so I took the cartridge out of the printer and, following her directions, went to find the store.

It's about four blocks away on a very steep street going down from my apartment. Because of centuries of people walking on the sidewalk, the paving stones are very worn down and slippery, and because the street has quite a downward pitch to it, I walked very, very carefully. Coming up is not as slippery, of course, but it's a workout for the lungs and heart.

The very nice young man in the store confirmed that they could refill my cartridge, but said they would have to order some kind of chip for it to allow my printer to recognize it once they opened it up to refill it. He said it would probably take about a week for the chip to come in. I gave him the cartridge, the model number of my printer, and my name and phone number. Foolishly, I did not get the name of the shop, its phone number, or the salesman's name.

After about 10 days went by and I hadn't heard from him, I walked back down. "Not yet, Señora, maybe mañana." Now, at this point, it's important to review what "mañana" means in Mexico. It does not mean "tomorrow." It only means "not today." So every couple of days, I would walk down since I was thinking that maybe they'd lost my phone number, and every time they'd say, "Perhaps mañana." After 17 days of this, I was beginning to get a little hot under the collar.

By this time I had the shop's name (Galaxy), the phone number, and the salesman's name (Jorge), but phone conversations in Spanish are still a bit of a challenge for me, so every time I would go in person. When I told him that I was leaving Mexico soon and had some stuff I had to print out before I left, he suggested another option: a reconditioned, filled cartridge from the factory. Why didn't he suggest that 17 days earlier? Perhaps because what I said I wanted was to refill my cartridge to save money. Perhaps because the reconditioned one cost about $50 USD, and the refill when the chip came in was going to be much, much less. But $50 is still half of what I'd have to pay at Office Depot, so I took the reconditioned one. Of course, not expecting to be charged 665 pesos for the more expensive option, I didn't have that many pesos with me, so I walked all the way back home and then back down again with sufficient money in hand.

In all, I had probably walked there five or six times, using up much of my time, energy, and good will. When I got home, I popped the cartridge in and behold, it worked. I had been keeping a list of things I needed to print out, and I got to work on them. After about 10 copies, my computer started telling me the old message, "Low toner," and did you hear me screaming all the way from Mexico? That was on Friday. I didn't have time to go during the weekend, and you always have to remember that many Mexican-run stores close for siesta between 2 and 4 p.m.

First thing Monday morning, I walked the reconditioned cartridge down to the store. I totally overshot it by a block, not able to recognize where it was because…it was closed! So on Tuesday, I returned a little later in the day and told Jorge my sad story. He said not to pay any attention to the message, that computers sometimes tell you that with reconditioned cartridges. I suggested that in the future he warn his customers about this before they left the store with the purchased cartridge, but he said it didn't happen with all printers and computers. "Just mine," I said under my breath. Was he telling the truth? Only time will tell. I have surely spent, in time and effort, 10 times the $100 USD I would have spent in Office Depot. I have learned a lesson, too: Just bite the bullet and buy the damned new toner cartridge at Office Depot. The patience lesson: I think I'll have to take a make-up class.

Moving Toward the End of My Visit

We in SMA have probably been in one of the safest places on the planet since the pope came to Mexico in late March. Why? Because he came to Guanajuato, only about an hour away, for four days. The president of Mexico greeted El Papa there, then came to SMA to stay at the new, prestigious Rosewood Hotel for the weekend. There were policía, soldatos, federales, men in suits and sunglasses, and more black Suburbans all in one place than I've ever seen before in my life. It felt as if the town was in lockdown. And Malia Obama was in Oaxaca for spring break with 25 Secret Service agents. Thank goodness the 7.4

earthquake in southern Mexico didn't interfere with any of that.

I was thrilled to be invited for comida at the home of Carlos, my Spanish teacher of three years, and his wife, Claudia, whom I had met a couple of times. We started out with guacamole, chips, and limonada while we chatted in the living room. Their immense German shepherd lay in a shady spot just outside the back screen, and never barked at me, a stranger. Then we moved into the dining room for broccoli soup and my all-time favorite, enchiladas verdes con pollo (enchiladas in green salsa with chicken). Claudia asked how many enchiladas I wanted and I said two. They both laughed at me and I got four on my plate. Since I was already a bit filled up with the appetizers, I really could eat only two, so I got a doggie bag to take the others home. There was carrot cake for dessert.

After more conversation in the living room following the meal, their grown son, Charlie, a freshly minted attorney with a new short-term job for the election coming up in July, came home to eat. I'd been hearing about him from Carlos for all of those years, and it was indeed a pleasure to finally make his acquaintance. I left soon after that, but I'm proud to say that even though everyone in the house spoke English, we spoke Spanish the entire two and a half hours. I wonder who was more exhausted from that exercise.

A friend of mine from Nova Scotia, Karen, whom I had met in SMA several years earlier, had been visiting for a week. I gave a "meet Karen/farewell to SMA" fiesta for 10 friends on the communal terraza of my apartment complex the evening before Karen was to leave. She and I spent the day picking up pre-ordered Lebanese food; buying, disinfecting, and preparing into a dessert lots and lots of wonderful fruits; buying cheeses and crackers at what turned out to be three separate stores; hunting down some elusive items like nice paper plates—called *platos de cartón* (cardboard plates), which is probably more accurate—and choosing wines. Then we figured out on what and in what to serve everything, making creative use of the serving ware on hand, but also repurposing some decorative items in the apartment. It was quite a lot of work, but with Karen's help, it wasn't too bad at all, and we had fun.

We called the party for 5 p.m. because there was an art opening at the home of Toller Cranston from 6 to 10 p.m. that Karen and I wanted to attend, and as it turned out, so did everyone else. *Who is Toller Cranston?* you might ask. If you are Canadian, you know. If you're not, here are some quick facts from Wikipedia:

Toller was born in 1949. As a figure skater, he was the 1971-1976 Canadian national champion, the 1974 World bronze medalist, and the 1976 Olympic bronze medalist.

He wrote three books: *Toller*, a mixture of autobiography, sketches, poems, paintings, humor, and tongue-in-cheek observations; the autobiographical *Zero Tollerance;* and *When Hell Freezes Over: Should I Bring My Skates?*

Wikipedia goes on to say that in 2010 he moved to SMA, where his main artistic outlet is painting, often incorporating skating-related themes. He's also an interior decorator. My landlady hired him to decorate the unit she owns next door, where I've stayed, and there is even a plaque on the entry door testifying to it. He is, to say the very least, a character.

At about 7:45, we all carried the remainders of our feast back down to the apartment and headed off to Cranston's home. He has an immense spread (several acres, which is unheard of in downtown SMA) in a very posh neighborhood just off of Parque Juarez. In addition to his palatial home, he has three or four casitas on the property that he rents out.

Inside the house, there is something in every single square inch. I find that style of decorating exhausting; there is no empty space on which your eyes can rest. I didn't know at the time, of course, but Cranston would die in this home in 2015.

One of Cranston's enormous and magnificent chandeliers.

We left Cranston's home and headed back to mine, but the evening was far from over. As we entered my street, Calle Mesones, throngs of

Bride and groom mojigangas were on hand for photo ops with wedding guests.

people were celebrating a wedding. We saw a custom that was new to me, the launching of small hot air balloons. Several did get up, some quite high, but others burst into flames. We won't even begin to talk about the danger to those around from this practice. Karen and I, plus a bunch of other tenants from my complex, stayed well away on the opposite side of the street.

The owner of the tequila-dispensing burro adjusts its bridle.

A man and his burro were hired to give tequila shots to the guests. The burro had baskets on both sides to hold the bottles, and each guest was given a tiny ceramic mug on a ribbon to put around his or her neck. Frequently the mugs are painted with the name of the couple or the occasion.

The most unusual venue for the concert.

The next afternoon, I attended a music festival about a half hour out of town for the benefit of hospice. A huge white roof covered the seating area, and on a stinking-hot day, we were very comfortable. There was almost always a breeze.

The level of musicianship was extraordinary. I loved the combination of blues, folk, rock, etc. Food and beverages were available for sale by a local restaurant. It was a memorable afternoon.

And thus, another extraordinary time in San Miguel de Allende ends, but certainly not my love affair with the place. Stay tuned.

Addendum

Spring, Summer, Fall 2012

A Whirlwind!

My usual three months in Philadelphia—May, June, and July—were lived at a breakneck pace. First, my neighbor in the row home attached to mine announced that he was putting his house up for sale, and Suji and Geoff hit on the idea of buying it and combining it with mine to make a big house for them with a small apartment for me so that I could continue to go back and forth from San Miguel at will without worrying about home upkeep. After an architect drew up initial plans, Suji and I visited all the neighbors on the block, explaining our plans and asking them to sign a petition agreeing to the necessary zoning change. We were pretty far down this road and quite excited about the possibility when there was a change in the city's property tax law that would have made the tax bill for the combined houses out of reach. The plan was regrettably scrapped.

When Suji called her dear friend Heather to tell her that all bets on the project were off, Heather asked if she could contact me to continue our discussion started the previous summer about them buying my house. Suji said yes, so Heather immediately jumped into action and she, her husband, Dave, and I met at my house for them to take another long, leisurely look around to make sure that this was what they wanted. It was, and I discovered that I was ready to let go of this house I'd been in happily for 13 years, albeit punctuated by long stints in San Miguel accompanied by varying degrees of worry, and to begin my nearly year-round life in San Miguel de Allende.

Soon we had an agreement of sale on the house, which had a stipulation that they had to sell their house in Germantown before they could buy mine. I was fine with that. Their real estate agent said she thought it would take up to a year to sell their house, so I didn't sort through any of my things or pack anything up in what was left of my time in Philadelphia.

Then, just days after I returned to SMA in August 2012, Heather emailed me saying that the second person who saw their house wanted to buy it and that they had to sell it and buy mine before the end of November in order to take advantage of a very favorable mortgage rate. Thus, I had to return to Philadelphia much earlier than I would have for my usual Christmas visit in order to empty my house and prepare it for the sale.

I flew back to Philadelphia on November 1 and began to work like a madwoman. My house was 1,300 square feet and I am not a collector, but I seemed to have a great many things to deal with. I had long since sold my car and joined a car-sharing program, so I used one of those cars to collect more boxes than I could ever imagine I'd need, rented a storage locker beginning later in the month, lined up a moving van to take my boxed belongings to that space, and began to seriously cull, pack, donate, toss, and give away my possessions.

Just days before the moving company was to arrive, and knowing that I was way behind schedule with the packing, I put up a six-foot-long folding table in front of my house and started piling things on it for people to take away for free. (I did put a sign out asking them not to take the table.) A small redbud tree in front of the house had branches low enough to allow me to hang some nice clothes I didn't want or need anymore. My castoffs were in good condition and the items fairly flew off the table and tree. I thanked my lucky stars that it was not raining.

Not knowing what my next abode might look like in Philadelphia, or even if there was going to be one, I packed some of my clothes and kitchenware, and on November 29, a van carried my boxes and the furniture that I was keeping to a storage locker four floors below ground level in a space that had been excavated years ago for a never-completed project, a completely creepy place with no cellphone service.

The following day, Dave, Heather, and I settled on the house on Swain Street amid tears on both sides. I had rented a VRBO house in the same neighborhood from November 30 until early January 2013, where I could unwind after the crazy month of packing and accommodate my son and his family from Helsinki for the Christmas holiday season.

A new, exciting chapter in my life had begun.

ONLY IN SPANISH

Carlos, my Spanish teacher, thinks now that I am an *estudiante avanzada* (advanced student)—his assessment, not necessarily mine—I should be learning some idioms. Well, my favorite so far is *"echar una cana al aire"* (literally, to throw a gray hair into the air). And it means (drumroll, please) to have a mistress! I don't think I can beat that one in English. I've been racking my brain to think how I might use that phrase in everyday conversation. Another favorite, of the dozens and dozens that use the verb *echar*—to throw—is *echarse un taco de ojo* (literally, to throw a taco of the eye), and it means to observe an attractive person of the opposite sex.

You have to love a place that sells *Pedos de Monjas* (Nuns' Farts), little *galletas* (cookies) covered in chocolate, originally from the nearby town of Querétaro.

Perhaps inappropriate, definitely humorous.

Epilogue

The gestation period of this book was strewn with potholes. My original forecast was that it would be published in the summer of 2019, but this was not to be. The first disaster involved my editor, Dulcie, who lives in Wisconsin and works full time editing for some popular magazines, is the minister of music at her church, frequently accompanies performing singers and string players, and offers her expertise on a freelance basis, in this case to me. She is the poster woman for the old saying, "If you want something done, ask a busy person." Wisconsin being Wisconsin in winter, Dulcie fell on ice in February 2019 and broke her right arm very near her shoulder. It took several days for options to be evaluated, and she finally wound up having the "simplest" of the offered surgeries, which involved her doctor putting in 11 pins and a plate. I cannot even imagine what the less-simple options entailed. She was in a great deal of pain for a long time and could not consider working at her day job, let alone for me. She could not even swipe a touch pad, things were that bad.

Fast forward about six weeks. Dulcie was healing well and was hoping to begin physical therapy soon when she was hit by a severe case of acute pancreatitis. She spent four days in the hospital, recovered, and after another month returned to work full time at her job. She still couldn't work for me, though, as her arm throbbed at the end of each day, she was dog-tired, and she needed to go to frequent physical therapy appointments after work. But soon enough, she returned to editing my book.

At just about that exact moment, in May, it was time for Margot, my cover and book designer who lives mostly in Canada, but who comes to San Miguel for varying amounts of time in the winter into spring each year, to have her long-awaited appointment for the removal of her first cataract. The operation was a roaring success, but of course she couldn't do the kind of fine work required of her job on my book with only one good eye. And the other cataract wasn't coming out for six more weeks. She went to Rome to wait it out.

After the second successful eye surgery and a period of recuperation, we three were ready to get back to work, but it had been such a long time since we last were a well-oiled machine, that it took us a while to re-establish where we had left off, what steps were next, and in whose court the ball had been sitting—awaiting action—for more months than we could remember.

We did finally get going again, though, and were steaming toward the light at the end of that particularly long tunnel when I called a halt to the whole operation: I decided that the book was way too long and needed to be cut by at least one-third. My team took this news in stride, and I put my mind and heart into cutting, cutting, cutting. I found it easy to do, which told me that it really had needed some serious trimming. And we all believed that it would be a better book for it.

After some time, we started in yet again from scratch on the editing and designing, but this time, things moved a bit more quickly as the text was familiar and the design had already been established. And then came…the COVID-19 pandemic. One would think that because we were all isolating at home, things would pick up speed. They did not necessarily. Dulcie had to move her day job to her home, schlepping her outsized monitor from her office after a few difficult days trying to work only on her sleek but petite laptop.

Margot and her partner were planning to be married in Vancouver at the end of July but had to cancel the big event due to the pandemic. The reception has been rescheduled to take place in a year, but, in the meantime, they will be married on the originally planned date, with only a handful of family present, and they will be practicing social distancing.

EPILOGUE

※ ※ ※

This book is the first in a series of two about my adventures first visiting and then living in San Miguel de Allende. Because of the time Margot was able to spend in SMA in early 2020 before she was mandated back to Canada by the prime minister, we had the luxury of working together on most of the photos for the second book, as well as choosing the cover photo. Unfortunately, because she had to leave SMA quickly, we missed out on nine of our regular Monday design meetings and will have to make do by email to finish up the photos we didn't get to review together.

We decided to maintain the interior design used in the first book to save time, energy, and money. We don't expect any of the calamities along the lines of the ones experienced in producing this one, and hope to have it published in about a year. While each book can certainly stand on its own, I believe that reading both of them, and preferably in the order they were lived and then published, will give you a very complete picture of the past 11 years of my life in the city I now call home: San Miguel de Allende, Mexico.

7/6/20

Acknowledgments

I am deeply indebted to these persons ...

Margot Boland, my cover and book designer extraordinaire, first for her book cover design workshop that I took years before the book was anywhere near a reality, and for giving me encouragement to keep going after she read just the Prologue and Chapter 1. And, second, for everything that she did to make this complicated book into an eminently readable treasure of word and image, always going the extra mile with good humor.

Jayne Halle, a friend and incredible photographer, for the memorable hours we spent together on a glorious San Miguel morning, as she expertly took dozens of pictures of me for the cover and inside cover of this book and the one to follow.

The late Molly Baush Hill, first a mother-figure in my childhood and later a beloved friend, for making sure, before she died, that I received all of the slides of my trip to Mexico with her, her mother, and my parents, including some images that appear in the Prologue.

Suji Meswani, my wonderful daughter, for saving and digitizing the slides from my family's trip to Saltillo, Mexico, when I was a young adult. Some of them are also in the Prologue.

Dulcie Shoener, my editor par excellence, who has edited for magazines and newspapers that hold high standards to guard against publishing errors—and isn't that exactly whom you want working on your book? Her encyclopedic knowledge of everything having to do with grammar, usage, and punctuation has taught me to be a far better writer, editor, and proofreader of my own work before I ever hand it over to her for her fact-checking, eagle-eye for errors, and spot-on suggestions for improvement.

About the Author

A Lifetime to Get Here: San Miguel de Allende is Cynthia Claus' third book. Since 2005, Cynthia has blogged about her world travels, and her blog entries about visits to San Miguel de Allende in 2009-2012, before moving there as a *residente permanente,* form the basis of this book. Evocative photos from that time period, as Cynthia's stays in the heartland of Mexico grew longer and longer and touched on all seasons, complement the narrative.

Perhaps because of her travels as a youngster with her family, Cynthia has always had the travel bug. In 1968-69, on a nine-week trip with her Indian husband and two-year-old son to India to present themselves to Suresh's relatives for the first time, Cynthia meticulously kept a travel diary and wrote frequent aerograms to family and friends back home, which they saved for her. Close to the occasion of her son's 50th birthday, these resources, plus photos from that trip, finally saw the light of day and became the material for Cynthia's first book, *An Orchid Sari: The Personal Diary of an American Mom in 1960s India,* published in

2017. Her next book, *Ice Cream & Pretzels and Other Stories: A Memoir*, 17 vignettes and a poem, came out a year later.

In 1965, Cynthia received her B.A. degree in English from Temple University in her hometown of Philadelphia, Pennsylvania. After her two children were safely ensconced in elementary school, Cynthia worked with several nonprofits in Philadelphia, including her neighborhood community organization and an alternative school. She then was employed for 13 years at a seminary, retiring as administrative assistant to the president for publications. For the next 14 years, she taught English as a Second Language (ESL) as a volunteer.

Cynthia's family is somewhat of a United Nations. There is the Indian father of her two children, and her son met his Finnish wife in a Peace Corps-like organization in Denmark, with which they served in Angola and Mozambique. They and their two children now live in Helsinki. Cynthia's daughter and son-in-law reside in Philadelphia and in 2004 founded Skeem Design, with the mission of producing beautiful, useful, often reusable products, eliminating excess packaging. Their frequent trips to exotic world destinations have been the inspiration for many of their products.

A second book in the San Miguel series, highlighting events Cynthia experienced while living there almost full time, 2013 to the present, is in the works and should be available in 2021.

Praise for *An Orchid Sari*

"*Orchid Sari* is an immediate, riveting story. It so gracefully respects the author's adopted family and culture. Her courage in undertaking such long and diverse travel with an infant reflects her adventurist spirit. All involved in this story have benefitted from the author's dedication to family, including us readers."

Judy

"Interesting travelog of a young mother to a totally foreign land and culture, vividly detailing the mainly fascinating, sometimes scary, unique experiences. Good read!"

Barb

"I really liked reading this book! I felt I got to know Cynthia better and I particularly liked the photos of her as a young mother with her toddler son. They added a lot to the narrative."

Rachel

"Cynthia writes with great clarity and honesty about her journey to India as a young white American mother in a relatively new marriage to an Indian man who had moved to the States. While her language is down to earth as she uses her words and memories from letters written home, there is poetry and much emotion in the story she tells. Anyone interested in cross-cultural marriage will learn from Cynthia's recollections and revelations. As a psychologist I found this to be a wonderful tale, not only about travel with a toddler and its ups and downs, but a lesson about marital compromise and tolerance."

George

"A rich and highly personal account of a cross-cultural marriage. Sometimes touching, sometimes hilarious, the author takes us along on her eye-opening journey as East meets West in the 1960s."

Catherine

Praise for *Ice Cream & Pretzels*

"This is a WOW story about the effects parents have on each other and their children. In this gripping personal narrative, we see the good, the bad, and the ugly… As we are taken back a couple of generations, we see how a pattern perpetuates itself. Cynthia not only broke the pattern for her children but allows others to benefit from a different and better way of parenting through the example she endured as a child and adult."

Felisa

"Your writing is so wonderful (as usual)—I feel as though I know your family. So many of your vignettes touched my heart and I admire your resilience after a highly restricted life during your growing-up years. Amazing tales by an amazing woman."

Ann

"The author has succeeded in creating an intimate portrait of her childhood, marriages, and philosophy of life. Many will be able to relate to her stories. Cynthia reveals, in a refreshingly honest way, not only the facts but her feelings about her youth and the people most influential in her life. Her revelations are honest, wishful, but not bitter."

Sher

"Cynthia Claus has written a very personal but universal memoir. It's a story that is sad, happy, grateful, and regretful, something with which so many of us who were brought up in the '50s and '60s can identify. Thank you, Cynthia, for reminding us of the ways we felt about life when we were younger, of how our parents were flawed but basically well-meaning and loved us in spite of everything, for reminding us of girlfriends and boyfriends who played significant roles in our lives, and reminding us of the ways we felt about life when we were younger."

H. Miller

"As in real life, Cynthia's strong character comes through in an unassuming way. This very personal and revealing collection of stories that could have easily been written as a 'tell-all' tabloid was instead crafted into a compelling coming-of-age story."

Karen

Made in the USA
Coppell, TX
22 May 2021